Girish Karnad's Plays

Archetypal and Aestheical Presentations

Girish Karnad's Plays

Archetypal and Aestheical Presentations

Bhagabat Nayak

AUTHORSPRESS

Publishers of Scholarly Books

Worldwide Circulation through Authorspress Global Network
First Published 2011
by
Authorspress
E-35/103, Jawahar Park
Laxmi Nagar, Delhi-110 092
e-mail: authorspress@yahoo.com

Girish Karnad's Plays : Archetypal and Aestheical Presentations
ISBN 978-81-7273-566-1

Printed in India at Tarun Offset, Delhi.

Preface

The firmament of post-independence Indian English literature is studded with the names of many writers of national and international repute. While in general Indian English literature has drawn high appreciation for its success, Indian English drama in particular is not on par with its sister genres—poetry, fiction and prose—since its beginning from Krishna Mohan Banerji's *The Persecuted* or *Dramatic Scenes Illustrative of the Present State of Hindoo Society in Calcutta* (1831). The origin, growth and evolution of Indian English drama is based on the tradition of Sanskrit drama in the pre-Vedic era, with its dexterous struggle in the Mughal era and stylised technique of the Western drama in India's colonial past and post-colonial present. In recent times the plays of a few Indian English drmatists forecast its glorious future. Girish Karnad, one of the most leading Indian dramatists in English, has achieved a commendable success in the recent times. In the words of Neelam Mansingh Choudhury,"Girish Karnad is one of the most influential playwrights of our time, and his plays have become a byword for imagination, innovation and craftmanship." In post-independence Indian English literature Karnad has proved that Indian English drama is meagre in quantity but it is of high quality.

Karnad's plays have a tradition both in continuity and innovation. His plays are read as dramatic literature and performing art. With the myth intoxicated mind, folklore fascinated psyche and hypotheticated history his plays are philosophically charged, culturally embedded, politically dysfunctional, and technologically articulated in the stagecraft. With the identity of a 'regional' author he writes his plays in Kannada and transcreates them for wider visibility. In the re-invention and reinterpretation of past and representation of present he aims at dramatising cultural, philosophical, religious and socio-political values and traditions in India's past. Drama, theatre and play writing are synonymous critical faculties in Karnad's creative art. Although he is fluent in Konkani, Marathi and Kannada, English is his adult language in which he writes his plays for (inter)national visibility. In his dramatic manoeuvre he instrumentalises India's myths, folklores and history to propagate India's cultural heritage, philosophical beliefs, religious thinking, political understanding, social values and customs among the people of the West. In the archetypes of myths, folktales, history and contemporary reality he dramatises human emotions, feelings and whims with the assertion of their rights and privileges, desires and despairs, motives and malignity, which explore new meanings and opportunities for his audience and readers. In the dramatic craftmanship and stagecraft he projects the private emotional zones of the individuals with a reflection on their elemental passions and pungent and stinging core of his characters. His plays open up immense dramatic possibilities for human life.

During my research on Indian drama in general and on Karnad's plays in particular I have some findings that is latent in Indian English drama. The book is an exhaustive critique of his eleven plays out of his 13 plays that comprehends his dramatic archetypes and the aesthetics in stagecraft. The book comprises six chapters with discussions, speculations, and estimation of themes. Chapter 1,"The Importance of Being Girish Karnad", gives a salient feature on the status of Kannada drama and theatre during his early life, his self as a dramatist in embryo, growth and evolution, academic achievements, various occupations, excellence in playwriting, and an analysis of his performative art. Chapter 2,"Archetypes of Ancient Myths", examines his existentialist vision in myths in his plays like *Yayati, The Fire and the Rain*, and *Bali: The Sacrifice*. Chapter 3, "Traditional World of Folktales", is a comprehensive analysis of both the national and regional folk myths. In *Hayavadana, Naga-mandala* and *Flowers: A Dramatic Monologue* he examines India's socio-cultural values, tradition and talent, human predicament and individuals' existential dilemma. Chapter 4 is concentrated on medieval and modern Indian history with reference to individual historical personages and events. His *Tughlaq, Tale-danda* and *The Dreams of Tipu Sultan* are based on history with the analysis of our contemporary socio-political praxis. Chapter 5,

"Contemporaneity in Girish Karnad's Plays", facilitates the understanding of contemporary angsts and amnesia of urban middle classes in the process of globalisation and reterritorialisation. Chapter 6, "Conclusion", presents some observations, hypotheses, and references with convincing digressions in themes, meanings and significance. His plays propagate India's cultural heritage, philosophical stasis, religious belief, political understanding, social values and customs. "Bibliography" includes all the tasted, trusted and treasured works on Indian drama and Karnad's plays which I have gone through during the preparation of this book. I have not included two of his plays, *Ma Nishada* and *Anju Mallige,* for the reasons that they are not available in English. However, I have come through the references on both the plays and am impressed that they do not significantly carve out a distinctive niche for him with respect to subject matter, dramatic style, authorial identity, sufficient literary and performatice tradition.

I express my honest sincerity to acknowledge my indebtedness and gratitude to my direct teacher and ideal figure, Professor M.Q. Khan, former Vice-Chancellor of Berhampur University, Orissa, whose blessings, affection, and inspiration have helped me to explore many things through my academic and rescarch pursuits. I feel it my utmost duty to express my gratitude to my teacher Dr. Sudhakar Mohapatra, retired Reader in History, a 'teacher saint', for his constant inspiration in my academic and research activities.

I express my deep sense of gratitude to Professor B.K. Das, Department of English, Burdwan University, West Bengal who oriented me in many ways for research works. I am obliged to Professor and Emeritus Fellow Jasbir Jain, University of Rajasthan, for sharing her valuable opinions and insightful thoughts during my meetings with her at different seminars and conferences. I am grateful enough to Professor Gurucharan Behera, Department of English, Banaras Hindu University, Varanasi for his constant inspiration in my research activities.

My obligations are due to Professor Anand Lal, Department of English, Jadavpur University, Kolkata, and Professor Somdatta Mandal, Department of English and other Modern European Languages, Visva Bharati, Santiniketan, for their pedagogical technique in teaching drama, and cinematic presentation of Karnad's plays during my attending the refresher courses in 2004 and 2005.

In 2006 I had some fruitful interactions with Mahesh Dattani, an eminent Indian English dramatist of our time, and M.K. Naik, one of the doyens of Indian English literature and criticism, at Kolhapur, Maharashtra. I am highly thankful to Girish Karnad for sharing his views over telephone and to Dr. Ramesh Chandra Panigrahi, my teacher and eminent Oriya dramatist, for sharing his valuable opinions on Karnad's plays. During my preparation of this book I have come in contact with the professors and scholars of different regions who have helped me in several ways.

I am grateful to my father whose indepth knowledge and insightful analysis of Puranic texts made me careful in this research endeavour.

My wife, Smita's wholehearted cooperation in spite of her professional and domestic burden to go through the manuscripts, deserve a special mention here. I thank and express my affectionate feelings to my two daughters, Saurya and Shreeya, for sharing my negligence and unattendance without complaints during my preparation of this book.

I am thankful to the librarians and staff of National Library, Kolkata; Parija Library, Utkal University, Bhubaneswar; Kanika Library, Ravenshaw University, Cuttack; National School of Drama; Sahitya Akademi; Sangeet Natak Akademi; and to the Director, National Institute for Research in Indian English Literature (NIRIEL), Gulbarga, Karnataka.

Bhagabat Nayak

Contents

1 The Importance of Being Girish Karnad

Girish Karand, a bi-lingual dramatist of post-independence India, occupies a very prominent place in Indian English Literature. He is one of the most influential playwrights of our time who begins his plays where other playwhights generally end. His importance of being a dramatist is based on his evocative imagination, innovation of ideas and craftmanship. He invests his well researched theme-oriented dramatic manouvres in the matrix of the past and moulds them anew in the contemporany relevance. He has his dramatic evolution in the ancient Indian dramatic tradition that had begun in the pre-Vedic era with Bharata's *Natyashastra,* matured in the hands of great Sanskrit dramatists like Bhasa, Kalidas, Bhababhuti, Visakhadatta and others, and culminated in the hands of Sri Aurobindo, Rabindranath Tagore, A.S. Panchapakesa Ayyar, Thyagaraja Paramasiva Kailasam, Bharati Sarabhai and Joseph Mathias Lobo-Prabhu. In the post-independence period while Indian drama was in the experimental form in the hands of Asif Currimbhoy, Pratap Sharma, Badal Sircar, Vijay Tendulkar, Nissim Ezekiel, Gurucharan Das, Manjula Padmanavan, Mahesh Dattani and many others Girish Karnad has his dramatic enterprises on well researched areas of myths, folklores and history. Karnad's new orientations of his source materials is combined with the Indian dramatic tradition and Western dramatic canon.

Girish Karnad was born on May 19 1938 in Matheran near Bombay. His father was a doctor in the Bombay Medical Service. He spent his childhood in different parts of Maharashtra. His mother tongue was Konkani but had his fluency in Marathi. With his growing in years he was attracted to Marathi literature that influenced him much in later life. But during the Second World War his father retired and got an extension in service with his posting at Sirsi, a malaria-infested area in Karnataka. Sirsi is a small town in Karwar region, one with the other three Kannada–speaking regions of Karnataka, like Dharwad, Bijapur and Belgaum. As his father had given his consent and preference for Karwar region he with his parents moved to Sirsi and got settled there. His father set up practice there. While his father was concentrating his mind in his profession his mother was taking every possible care for Girish's schooling at Sirsi. The new settlement of Karnad's family at Sirsi provided him an opportunity to learn Kannada. His father was an Arya Samajist, very broad in outlook and free from conservatism. Karnad had his schooling and college education there. By this time Sirsi had a college and electricity facility but there was no professional theatre. The small town was geographically facilitated to nurture a theatre culture. Since Sirsi was the trading route to Karwar region many Marathi natak companies and touring Kannada theatre troupes were visiting the town. after the harvest. The traditional Kannada theatre groups like Yakshagana and Bayalata were performing lowbrow entertainment on the stage which comprised a platform with a canopy, and erected black curtain in the open air with the light of the torches. Secondly, the visiting natak mandalis were performing their plays in semi-permanent structures on proscenium stages with the systems of wings and drop curtains. Remembering those days Karnad writes:

> It may have something to do with the fact that in the small town of Sirsi, where I grew up, strolling groups of players, called Natak Mandalis or Natak companies, would come, set up a stage, present a few plays over a couple of months and moved on. My parents were addicted to these plays. That was in the late 1940s. By the 1950s, films had more or less finished off this kind of theatre, though some Mandalis still survive in North Karnataka in a very degenerate state. But in those days they were good or at least I was young and thought so I loved going to see them and the magic has stayed with me (*New Theatre Quarterly* 360).

In his reaction to these two types of theatres he writes:

> In my childhood, in a small town in Karnataka, I was exposed to two theatre forms that seemed to represent irreconcilably different worlds. Father took the entire family to see plays staged by troupes of professional actors called

> natak companies which toured the countryside throughout the year. The plays were staged in semipermanent structures on proscenium stages, with wings and drop curtains, and were illuminated by petromax lamps (*Three Plays* 1.)

Karnad had marked the class hierarchy in the spectatorship of these two types of performances. However his adult eyes were fascinated with the performances of natak companies. As many of the actors were struck with malaria during their Sirsi days they were visiting his father for treatment. This added a privilege to his family to get free passes from the natak companies, like the police and goverment officials. This provided him ample opportunities to see a lot of theatres.

Karnad had his early ambition to be a poet and novelist in English of international repute. But his Srisi days turned him out to be a dramatist. The interest of his family in theatre and their deeply involved discussion about the scenes and actors inspired the future dramatist in embryo. When he came to Dharwad in 1958 to do his graduation in Mathematics and then to the University of Bombay to do his M.A. in Statistics he won the Rhodes Scholarlship to study at Oxford University. By this time he was preparing the manuscript for his first play *Yayati* (1961). While his family was in anxiety in their middle class status to send Karnad to England and were worried that he might decide to settle abroad Karnad was struggling between his destiny and choice. Suspending his family anxiety of his settling abroad he was reworking the myth of Yayati. In an interview to Tutun Mukherjee he says:

> I had never fancied myself a dramatist. In fact, I had tried my hand at writing poetry. When I was at Dharwad, which was the cultural capital of Karnataka, having produced writers like Bendre, Gokak and so on, I would very often pass by the famous Kannada publishing house Manohara Granthamala and wonder if my work would ever be published by them ! During the weeks of preparation for my departure to England—which were as I said quite successful for various reasons—I found myself writing a play (30)

During his university days in Bombay he visited Prithvi Theatre to see Strindberg's *Miss Julie* which was staged with the direction of Ebrahim Alkazi. This had a lot of impact on Karnad. By and by he saw the plays of Shaw, Anouilh, Sartre and theatres of every kind at Bombay theatres. The plays of the Western playwrights left an indelible impact on him. Steadily he learnt the verbal, visual and light impact of these plays which were completely new to him. He also learnt that the technology of lights was helping to study the crucial situations in a play. But during his stay at Magdalen College of Oxford University he felt immensely interested in art and culture. He saw there many brilliant productions of Shakespeare's plays. He also saw there the plays of Shaw, Brecht, Rattigan, Osborne, Wesker, Grotowski, Anouilh and Beckett. With an adult impression on Western drama and British theatre he returned to India with a mind to become a dramatist. His reading a lot about Existentialism, a modern Western philosophy, in the plays of Anouilh, Brecht, Beckett, Sartre and Camus later helped him to frame brilliantly the corpus of his plays.

Karnad has written 13 plays till now. His dramatic archetypes are shaped on the Yakshagana Bayalata conventions from regional sources, forms of *Natyashastra* and *Dasarupaka* from traditional sources, and the theme from "the labrinth of vast multicultural sub-continent of India and the dense thicket of Indian psychology, sociology and anthropolgy" (Dhanavel 97). He presents the Indianness of his imagination in his plays. His first play *Yayati* was written during his preparation for his departure to England. He was inspired by professor K.D. Kurtkoti, the renowned Kannada critic to publish it. It was published by G.B. Joshi in Kannada language after some revision. The play was translated into English by Priya Adarker and published in *Enact*. But with the suggestion and comments from the veteran theatre personalities, like Satyadev Dubey, Dr Shreeram Lagoo and C.R. Simha, and with the persuasion of the theatre artists like Sunita Pradhan and Arundhati Raja Karnad reworked it in English with forceful psychoanalytic reinterpretation of the myth, with great intensity and immense sensibility. Like *Yayati* most of his plays are first written and produced in Kannada and then reworked and staged in English for wider audience and (inter)national visibility.

As a connoisseur of Indian theatre, an icon of Indian English drama and a renovator of traditional proscenium Karnad had enjoyed the "smell of the soil" (Srinivasaraju 140). His mother tongue is Konkani but he writes in Kannada and renders them into

English. All his major plays are reworked in English by him with rich and vibrant contemporary milieu. Karnad is a 'dramatic author' and 'literary playwright' like his contemporary Indian playwrights, Mohan Rakesh, Badal Sircar, Vijay Tendulkar, Dharamvir Bharatri, G.P. Deshpande, Habib Tanvir and Mahesh Elkunchwar. He expresses his ideas and thoughts with objective assessment of incidents and facts with his dramatic genius. He draws his sources from myths, legends, folktales, history and his contemporary reality. While he reworks with them in marvellous characterisation for a serious audience he makes them almost alive and true. Yet his plays have Indian settings and potential thematic values based on Indian philosophy, sociology, religious beliefs, psychology, historical developments, myths, legends and folklores. Karnad attempts his best to project Indian milieu with allegiance to Indian sensibility in all shades and shapes of his plays whether geographical, racial, linguistic, stylistic, thematic, behaviouristic and particularistic. In the construction of plot of his plays it seems that Karnad is influenced by the Western dramatic tradition which he has consciously resisted in his artistic attempt.

In terms of theme and content of his plays Karnad implants his roots in the Indian soil and stretches his dramatic imagination engendering different realities at a junction point where "dream is simultaneously reality, where invisible coincides with the visible, where the object is both itself and the revelation of something not itself" (Coe 213 -14). In the subjective presentation of myth, folklore history and contemporaneity he inscribes the socio-cultural philosophical, political, and empirical specificities. With the presentation of Indian tradition and culture he combines the worlds of reality, fantasy and universality of human knowledge. He always draws the wealth of his dramatic knowledge from the past, weaves them in the present, and makes them desirable for the future. In theoretical approach and thematic exploration his plays have performative potential, effective and cognitive learning possibilities, and widespead awareness. His dramatic imagination is highly charged with humanistic thought, secularist ideology, nationalist commitment, cosmopolitan spirit, traditionalist approach and modernist hypothesis. Tutun Mukherjee rightly remarks, "One could still propose that the activity of 'application'/interpretation could constitute the performance itself—of encountering the audience/ readership whose response would identify and establish the 'text for contemporary times'" (16). He is philosophically an iconoclast, politically prolific, culturally colossus, traditionally tremendous and radically pure in thought. Karnad has the association of sensibility with the indispensable past, immediate present and impending future. In his modernist approach, he makes them his repertoire in contemporary discourse.

Karnad is an innovator of modern and contemporary theatre. While his contemporaries have theoretical and polemical arguments about form, style, purpose, language and influence in a rhetorical genres he offers a fully developed often antithetical theories of dramatic representation and reception of culture in the presentation of his theatre. In his dramaturgical presentation Karnad exemplifies the transformative practices of his generation and carves out a distinctive niche for himself with respect to the subject matter, dramatic style and authorial identity. All his plays are meaningful texts which have important qualities in varying degrees, approaches, serious literary activity and complex verbal art in theatrical practices. With the presentation and performances of his plays one finds th serious commentaries on life and society. His plays can be interpreted outside the boundaries of performance in commercialized entertainment and for topical analysis. In the text, performance, image and word his plays express his commitment to Indian drama. Karnad expresses his range of rhetorical genres in varying degrees, complex verbal art, theoretical activity and serious literary activitiy. In an objective analysis of his dramatic genius one finds his encompassing of philosophical and religious beliefs, historical developments in Indian sociological setting, and its cultural transformation. Karnad's creative imagination is originally Indian. His creative evolution as an Indian dramatist is based on the rich and varied Indian traditions and with the use of the rich plethora of Indian myths, folk elements and historical facts. All his plays have Indian themes with sensibility, style and 'feel'. In the dramatisation of facts in fiction he establishes theoretical and polemical arguments opening up the 'new world of magical possibilities'.

The greatness of a dramatist depends on her / his strategies of 'adaptation and 'application' of his own tradition and talent. A dramatist can take the both in a tact, strategy and with a creative energy. In the textual application of the two he masters, manipulates, and mends them with his own objectivity. Karnad rewrites myths, legends, folklores and history as the rich and suitable subject matter of his plays. Karnad reads the books on them to find a plot, reworks on them in a research, and reflects them with his own logic, hypothesis, philosophy and relevance to contemporary situation. In an objective analysis of his plays one finds that his themes are taken from classical, traditional and historical sources and he presents them with modern touch. He is microscopic to the values and morals in the myths, favourable to the folklores for their relevance, and holistic about the historical hassles. Reworking with the myths he reveals the human mind when it was unable to distinguish between the fact and fiction, virtues and vices, and asuric and humane nature of individuals; and warns the future mankind to remain cautious and careful in human relationship, personal whims and temperament, earning and application of knowledge and wisdom, and obsession and ambition. Like myths, folklores are a constant creative source for Karnad. Reworking with the folklores he discovers the dream world in his constant touch with the world of reality. Hypothesing the Western hermeneutics and harmonising it with the Indian dramatics he enumerates the existential premise in his plays. The touch of Heideggerian and Kierkegaardian existential philosophy serves as the nerve centres to his plays while he consciously anatomises it in Indian myths, folklores and history. From 2000 to 2003, while he was working at Nehru Centre, London, he was privileged to see and understand more Greek plays, with the plays of Shakespeare, Shaw, O'Neill, Anouilh, Beckett, Sartre, Camus, Brecht, Rattigan, Wesker and Grotowski. His thought of Western realism in Indian ethos served as the epicentre of action of his plays. But in terms of his imagination of Indian homes he has tried his best to present them as romantic interludes for a social change. For the presentation of history in dramatics, "He read the history of Kannada literature by Kirtinath Kurtkoti and learnt from him that Indian history has not been handled by any Indian writer the way it has been done by Shakespeare and Brecht" (Dhawan 15). He read history in objective analysis and surmised it in his own logic, hypothesis and philosophy. Karnad never writes his historical plays in the self of a historian rather makes it relevant to his readers reminding them to judge the whims, temperament, eccentricities and follies of the past leaders in the contemporary context.

Karnad is esentially Indian in thought and imagination but quintessentially Western in modernisation and orientation of his ideas. His plays are the thesis plays based on the archetypes of myths, folklores and history. His plays are the signposts of Indian imagination and project the socio-political transformation encompassing the philosophical and religious beliefs of ancient and modern India. The setting of his plays with myths, legends, folklores, history, beliefs, caste and community are the internal aspects of India integral to his imagination. In assessment of these aspects in Indian milieu Karnad is very much polemical. Therefore his study of mathematics and statistics as disciplines maintain a complete balance to structure his plays. He says:

> Mathematics trains the mind to think logically. It imparts a sense of equilibrium very useful for a creative writer. Writing a play is like building a house. What happens to each unit affects the rest of the structure. I was fascinated to find that changing one half of an equation brings about a change in the other half too (Mukherjee 29).

Karnad's education on the one hand, and preoccupation and passion on the other, are binary forces in his creative self but he employs the former to exploit the latter while developing the plot, character and dramatic form and technique. In the portrayal of characters, exploration of plot and drawing of Individual's stressful situation, anxieties, doubts, values, guilt consciousness and social realism he shades them with Indian colour. The Indianness of his imagination is marked with cultural awareness, thought, logic, philosophy and ideology which cogently form the Indian tradition. He is conscious in his belief that "An Indian, then, is a person who owns up the entire Indian heritage and not merely a portion of it. This integral cultural awareness is an indispensable feature of Indianness" (Gokak 24).

Language is the medium, and medium conveys the message in Karnad's dramatic practice. Going beyond the boundaries of his known language he dares to understand the remote territory of Sanskrit the classical language of India. For him Sanskrit is the language of artistic expression and aesthetic perception. Sanskrit sources often provide him inspiration to continue philosophical discourses in his plays. He believes that "Sanskrit drama assumed a specific setting, a steady, well-ordered universe in which everyone from the gods to the meanest mortals was in his or her allotted slot" (*Three Plays* 11). He knows that Sanskrit theatre was once a popular form in Indian society. Although it was not spoken in every home it was the vehicle of artistic expression, language of courtly, literary and philosophical discourses to appeal the mood of the audience. The aesthetics of Sanskrit drama, its presentation of cultural contexts and social setting still appeal to the Indian minds. But with the change of time Kalidas appears too remote, too classical and too perfect now. While the Western influence seriously affects the creative process of his predecessors like T.P. Kailasam, Adya Rangacharya, Aurobindo Ghose and Rabindranath Tagore he consciously resists this in the setting of his plays. While he depends more on classical dramatic tradition in dealing with myths and folklores in his plays Parsi natak stagecraft becomes a deliberate choice for his historical plays. In this context the natak companies in his early days had influenced him much. In the presentation of natak companies he had marked how they were preoccupied with the construct of a Hindu deity or a Muslim legendary hero. Karnad's contemporaries were preoccupied with Indian tradition and had their cultural moorings through myths and legends. Parsi theatre had professed values but it was not creating any effect in ordinary life as the language was spoken by the community limited to Bombay. The audience of Parsi theatre were Muslims. They were only patronising it and professing values in ordinary life. The enterprises in Parsi theatre were financed by Parsis who generally spoke Gujarati. Secularism was the spirit of Parsi theatre in the ethnic heterogeneity of his new entrepreneurial class. Chiefly in 1960s Indian playwrights had their preoccupation with the traditional theatre forms and variety of themes.

Taming a language in regional culture adds credit to a creative artist. Karnad liked two Sanskrit masterpieces, *Shakuntala* and *Mrcchakatika* which were performed successfully on the stage with the touch of Marathi tradition and culture. Although Ratan Thiyam, K.N. Panicker, and Vijaya Mehta have brought Sanskrit plays alive again for today's audience Karnad believes that his contemporary playwrighs write about social life, caste dimensions as well as the position of women in the family beyond the living rooms as mirrored by their Western counterparts. He believes the plays of Tagore to be recontextualised. He believes that the contemporary dramatists present the interior of the house, kitchen room, room of the gods, and living room as the locations of dramatic action. In the rich variety of regional theatres and theatrical devices he finds the Indian social imports, ethos, stage setting and living room set ups in Vijay Tendulkar's *Silence! The Court is in Session*, Chandrasekhar Kambar's *Jokumaraswamy*, Badal Sircar's *Evam Indrajit* and Habib Tanvir's *Charandas Chor*. But Karnad has always tried to create naturalistic theatre in his connectedness and communication to Indian tradition and modernity in response. He thinks that all Indian art forms including highly stylised classical forms are presented by the contemporary playwrights with traditional roots and Western imports. With the influence of Bollywood movies and television new generation youngsters are averse towards certain things in Indian theatre. But this will not make the realistic theatre to disappear. With independence we have decolonised our stage, develoved our style and technique in theatre, removed the regional and language barriers, and have tried it in a common bond of nationality inspite of our cultural plurality.

As an actor, director and scriptwriter Karnad is very much artistic to weave Indian tradition, culture and social settings in his plays. In dramatisation of mythical, folklorish and, historical elements he projects man-woman relationship and India's cultural plurality with modern sensibilities. Karnad takes myth as a faithbuilder for individual's spiritual evolution. He uses folklore to connect the magic and reality, and history for a symbolic socio-political struggle in contemporary reality. He takes history as a positive concept to analyse life and society, brilliant individual characters and their policies, political strategies, secular ideologies and biggest failures. The past is not always dead for Karnad. In his fascination for the fossilised facts and fiction of the past he has made a treasuretrove in his dramatic pursuits.

As a translator of his own plays and others' plays he has served his role as a facilitator of Indian belief, tradition and culture. He has translated Badal Sircar's *Evam Indrajit* (1974) in English and Mahesh Elkunchwar's *Wasansi Jeernani* and *Dharmaputra* (2004) into Kannada. He has also written the script for the film *Samskara* based on U.R. Anantha Murthy's novel which was produced in 1969. During his Stint with Oxford University Press at Madras he was previleged to translate and participate in acting and directing. In *Samskara* he has performed the role of Praneshacharya with the direction of Pattabhi Ram Reddy in 1970 that won the national award for best film in 1971. B.V. Karanth, his lifelong friend and collaborator of the film, had inspired him enough to play his role in it. He had directed, co-directed and acted in the films like *Vamsha Vriksha* (1971), *Godhuli* (Hindi), and *Tabbaliyu Ninade Magane* (Kannada in 1977). He has directed the films like *Kaadu* (1973), *Ondanandu Kaladalli* (1978) and *Chomanadudi* in Kannada; *Utsav* (1984) and *Cheluvi* (1992) in Hindi. *Manthan* (1976), *Swami* (1978) and *Kanaka-Purandara* are his best art cinemas in Hindi.

At the age of 37 Karnad moved into cinema and film acting when his wife, Saras, reminded him about their, economic necessities. Secondly, this might possibly be due to his passion for acting in order to satisfy the living audience. He and Karanth became involved in films and did their best. Karnad became the Director of FTII and Karanth the Director of NSD. Although both were involved in theatre and films Karanth remained with theatre and Karnad decided to stay with films. Film industry was good for him as it had provided him a comfortable life but after 1980 he steadily gave up film acting. For some time he appeared in several TV serials including R.K. Narayan's *Malgudi Days*. He continued to turn up on the TV for weekly "Turning Point". During his association with a Madras amateur group of role players from 1963 to 1970 he worked as an actor, director, and translator for seven years. He actively participated in staging many plays of Pinter, Williams, Shaw, Beckett and translated the plays of Sartre, Pirandello and Chekhov. From 1964 to 1970 he worked with others in staging the plays like *Evam Indrajit, Ashad Ka Ek Din, Six Characters in Search of an Author, Uncle Vanya, The Caretaker, The Crucible, A View from the Bridge* in English. This was an excellent training period to work with the translated plays and learn how language needs to be used on the stage with linguistic and dialectical nuances in translation of source language and the basic interactibility in the target language. He also acted and directed the plays staged by Delhi theatre group, 'Aviyan,' for sometime. In 1972 he acted in Karanth's three Kannada plays, *Jokumaraswamy, Sankranti,* and *Oedipus Rex*. While *Jokumaraswamy* is based on a phallic deity worshipped in the form of a snake gourd and then consumed by those desire to bear children, his acting as Gowda in *Sankranti,* and Oedipus in *Oedipus Rex* during his working with Lankesh and Karanth for Ravindra Kalakshetra in 1971 is highly psychological.

From 1972 to 1987 Karnad enjoyed his busiest years in film and television to improve his status. This helped him to pursue his first love for drama as he had the first love for theatre after visiting the natak mandalis in his boyhood days at Sirsi. But he knew that one can't earn a comfortable living even from a successful play. He says, "Take *Tughlaq*. As you know, it's been enormously successfully as well as in performance. Playwrights in the West have been able to retire on such success—or at least, to devote themselves to that activity entirely. I can't" (*New Theatre Quarterly* 362). In 1999 for his contribution to art and literature he was awarded Kalidasa Samman and Bharatiya Jnanpith that enabled him to improve his financial condition and 'retire' from film. In an actor's private self and sentiment he disliked acting perhaps for his distinction of talent, ability and literary flair in film making. Among all his activities playwriting gives him utmost satisfaction. But he cannot keep himself away from other activities as he knows that the only royalties from writing plays cannot help him for his sustenance. His acting in these plays were very sensational and relevant to the contemporary mind. Even in his recent play *A Heap of Broken Images* he has worked along with K.M. Chaitanya with the brilliant use of technology.

Karnad's life and career as a playwright, poet, actor in film, television and theatre, director, translator, critic and ambassador of culture is marked with his multifaceted brilliance. The lovers of drama and theatre and critics find him a dramatist of exceptional brilliance. Artistically and intellectually Karnad writes brilliant plays for the stage and serious audience. His dramatic genius, acting, filmmaking and activities in theatre and on television carry weight for their regional and national importance. He is lucky enough to come in contact with extraordinary dramatic genius and gifted directors like B.V. Karanth, Alyque Padmasee, Ebrahim Alkazi, Satyadev Dubey, Om Shivpuri, Kumar Roy, Rajinder Nath, Prasanna, Amal Allana, Neelam Mansingh Choudhry and Shyamanand Jhalan. His march from Sirsi to London via Dharwad and Bombay is a giant step in his evolution as a dramatist. The opportunities he availed in Bombay opened up his adolescent eyes. In an interview with

Tutun Mukherjee he says:

> I saw as many plays as I could and for two years filled myself with theatre of every kind : Shaw, Strindberg, Anouilh, Sartre.... It wasn't as though I wasn't acquainted with western playwrights.... Most of all, I was impressed by the way lights were used to determine the visual impact. I was used to our home being lit by lanterns and in the city we knew only how to switch on or off the lights. That lights could be used to manipulate story telling, with the focus and the fade out adding dimensions to the dramatic experience, was completely new knowledge for me (29).

In Bombay he experienced and realised the development of modern drama where the addition of the technology of lights was accompanied by new psychology. When he grew up as a dramatist the interpreters of his plays like B.V. Karanth, C.Basavalingaiah and C.R. Jambe practically improved the qualities and merit of his plays with their advice. Karnad is conscious of his creative self and the discipline of translation that makes his plays to reach a wider audience.

Karnad is happy in the translation of his plays by others but he remains satisfied when he partly rewrites and transcreates them in English without too many changes. He makes his plays more enjoyable and rewarding for his translatorial skill with the use of appropriate rhythm and pace of the original language in its theatrical presentation. While translating his plays Karnad enjoys the great advantage and freedom as a translator. He remains faithful to the text without diluting the fairness of the context. He believes that translating from Kannada to English requires a great deal of rewriting—a kind of transcreation which must therefore, be seen as approximation to the original. While translating from Kannada to other regional languages and vice versa he feels it easy but while translating Kannada to English he faces the problems in searching the appropriate cultural equivalent. All the plays of Karnad are critical, scholarly and performance related in post-independence theatre. The contexts of his major plays can be divided into three aspects of his fascination and choice for myth, folklore and history. His writing of plays, working in theatre and film, and translation project him as an engaged intellectual to cohere and coordinate the volatile

Indian public in a multi-cultural, multi-lingual and multi-religious society. He has contributed to the field of art, culture, literature for the last five decades. All his English plays show his originality in language composition performance and dissemination of multidimensional social-cultural aspects in multiple locations, interpretation of texts and performance.

In search of new theatre Karnad enriches the Indian literary scene by his contribution to art, culture, theatre and drama. He follows a golden means of thought and action when he launches a new play. Kannad is an innovator of modern and contemporary Indian theatre. He tranlates, comments and directs his own plays on the stage with great sensitivity and interest. He projects broader trajectories of traditonal, modern and contemporary Indian life. For several decades his plays have been dealing with several issues of general significance in medias of visibility. Modernity is a link term between tradition and post-colonial experience in India's political autonomy. In his idea of new nation the audience is neither able to reject the continuation of past nor able to suspend the radical connections with the postcolonial present in India.

In chronological composition his plays are distinctly constituted in four categories for their theme, approach and literary appeal. Karnad reworks with the ancient Indian myths like the *Mahabharata* and the *Ramayana* and from some regional sources like *Yashodhara Charite*. Presenting the traditional world of folktales he rewrites the 'folk myths' from *Kathasaritasagar* and regional sources. But while working with the regional and national history of medieval and modern India he has presented the tragic rehearsals of caste, class and community in post independence India. Dramatising the middle class family life in urban areas Karnad presents the loss of values, effect of tecnology, inpact of globalisation and international accessibility of the Indians in employment and empowerment.

Karnad dramatises ancient myths in *Yayati* (1961), *Ma Nishada* (1964), *Agni Mattu Male* (as *The Fire and the Rain,* (1995), *Anju Mallige* as *Driven Snow,* and *Hittina Hunja* (1980) rewritten as *Bali: The Sacrifice* (2004). The playwright highlights the myth of Yayati in the "Adi Parva" of the *Mahabharata,* and his existential suffering for his conflict of choice and assertion between paternal authority and son's obedience. In the projection of Yayati's stressful life, anxieties and uncertainties he presents rivalry between caste and race, reinforcement of the counter-Oedipal logic in filial relations, and dialectical discourses on parent-child relationship. *Ma Nishada,* a short radio play for Ramanavami broadcast is based on Valmiki's *Ramayana* in which Karnad reinterprets Valmiki's mind in his politically concious mind and existentialist philosophy in the dramatisation of Sita's banishment by Rama. The political implication of the washerman's damaging remark on Sita that leads to his virtual boycot by the people, his wife and his beloved donkey and his virtual repentence before rishi Valmiki in the ashram and seeking forgiveness are the central actions of the play. *The Fire and the Rain* is his brilliant production of the myth in the 'Vana Parva' of the *Mahabharata.* "Yagnya" is the central metaphor in ancient Indian society and Hindu psyche. The plot appears like an enormous research on the myth and is shaped like a triology. While the first two parts present the climatic and dramatic moment with human frailty of the lead character's returning home after tapasya the third part is prepared as a debate on human frailty and divine grace with the climatic and dramatic moment of the play.

Anju Mallige, meaning 'Sacred Jasmine' in Kannada published as *Driven Snow,* is based on India's mythological past. It is all set in non-India location in Englad. The play is distinct for not dealing with a mythological past nor a slice of history but the myth of regeneration—death and rebirth—and in the cotemporary scenario blends well to produce a conglomeration of perceptions into the postcolonial consciousness. The play is Karnad's daring attempt to fuse the theme of incest and nation inextricably and to bring out the sinister and frightening process in the perceptions of a man's relationship with woman.

Bali: The Sacrifice is based on the thirteenth-century Kannada epic, *Yashodhara Charite.* The play depicts the myth of the Cock of Dough and define intergenerational tensions and class conflicts that undergird the play's meaning. In the novelty and strength of the play Karnad elaborates his mature philoshophical exploration of love, jealousy, desire, betrayal, and violence between men and women. It presents ties of blood and marriage, intimate personal acts and seriousness of the characters in their religious belief and practice, and the promise of motherhood beyond boundaries of marriage as a motivating force.

Karnad projects the traditional world of folktales and folk elements as aesthetic device in his *Hayavadana* (1971), *Naga-Mandala* (1988), and *Flowers: A Dramatic Monologue* (2004). He presents the timelessness of the folktales with cotemporary touch. In the folktales he enumerates oral tradition in interpretive and performative possiblities. *Hayavadana,* is one of his best plays based on folk tradition and presents the possibilities of indentity in a complex psychological entity and ethical archetype. It resolves the body and mind riddle in a supralogical way. *Naga-Mandala* is in many respects a 'sequel', a companion piece to *Hayavadana* rather than a work of striking originality. Karnad projects his concept of fertility rite that starts from *Jokumaraswamy* (the Phallic deity) in a psychological construct with a willing suspension of disbelief syndrome about the concept of virility and nature of fertility rite in the two oral tales which he had heard from A.K.Ramanujan. In the weaving of two stories Karnad "Continues the turn from the public to the private and the personal that the earlier play had begun, and takes a more elemental approach to the complication and subversion of conjugality" (*Collected Plays*. Vol.II: xviii). *Flowers* is a dramatic monologue that presents a priest's sexual awakening beyond his marital status, and sanctity of his body and mind. Purity and profanity form the psychological dimension in the play. In the portrayal of Priest's 'Whore-Madonna Syndrome', endearing innocence, and honesty he projects the ethical laxity and philosophical height of the play. In all the folk plays Karnad maintains the performative tradition and convention of Yakshagana and Bayalata.

History is an important aspect of Karnad's histrionics. In dramatisation of history he makes it a living subject relevant to his contemporary time. Karnad's interest in history is projected in the recontextualising of events and persons which provide analogues for contemporary time. History is presented in theory and political ideologies with performative energy and carnivalesque to correct the present. With the imagination and 'marvellous' discovery of the fourteenth century Sultan Muhammad bin Tughlaq's dysfunctional politics he minutely projects his observation of post-independence Nehruvian policy and disillusionment of his generation in socio-political realities in *Tughlaq* (1964). He makes the play a political critique and projects the mysterious innner chambers of power politics and the open, public areas of those affected by it. *Tale-danda* (1990) is the reconfiguration of Indian politics in the post-Indira Gandhi years when the National Front Coalition Government was at the centre under the primeministership of V.P. Singh and his implementation of Mandal Commission Report in 1989. With the reservation of 27 per cent posts for the members of backward castes the nation had experienced the sanguine carricature in majority–minority relations. Against the backdrop of fundamentalist caste politics of the 1980s the playwright projects the theme of religious intolerance and perversion of religion in the Virasaiva movement in twelfth century Kalyan of Karnataka. *The Dreams of Tipu Sultan* (1997), his most recent play on history, presents the 'end of history' of the Vijaynagar empire in South India and the rise of th British power in India. In Tipu's power shifts with the Marathas, negotiating with the Nizam of Hyderabad, daring the British and dallying with the French Karnad presents his evolution as an emperor and nation builder. In contrast to these as the irritants to his rise in power Karnad literally presents the British power, British purpose and British ambition which may be historically inaccurate but politically expedient. Apart from the politicial and diplomatic aspects of Tipu's career and life he lilterally presents Tipu's artistic and civilisational taste in giving the architectural designs to the city of Mysore. Presenting Tipu's political perceptiveness as a tragic figure in India's modern history Karnad deals with some aspect of the then Indo-British relation, fervent nationalism, reformative intention, fascinating and vulnerable sides, ironic dimensions as a traditionalist and nationalist of southern Indian.

Contemporaneity in Karnad's plays is focused in past and present contexts. While contemporaneity is a time and incident factor in history it is a philosophical hypothesis of tradition and culture in myths and folklores. But contemporaneity in Karnad's *A Heap of Broken Images* (2004) and *Wedding Album* (2009) is treated with twenty-first century reality. While the former presents the politics of language in Indian literary culture, dishonesty, desperation and cowardice nature in an author's plagiarist self in the latter Karnad slowly peels off the middle class pride and glory revealing the emotional and sexual zones in funny and unnerving way. The distinct feature of both the plays is their dramaturgical presentation through tech media and television which reveal the emotional zones of the human characters and expose their volatile public and private spheres.

The importance of being Girish Karnad lies in his activities like writing drama, staging theatre, writing scripts and performance which are related to his conceptual thinking. He interlinks them in search of essence, values and rules in the performing art, 'scripted text' and 'theatre'. Drama is a tight, verbal narrative that allows little improvisations. It exists as a code independent of any individual transmiter and can be transported in time and space unaffected by the people who carry it. Theatre comprises a specific visible / sonic gesture, it is the visible aspect of the script, and the exterior topography of the interior map. Script is the interior map of a particular production by the writer, director and master which can be either tight or loose or developed through the performance. Performance encompasses the whole event and includes the receptors, performers and technicians, who are dominant of this process. But all they exist in a play, a literary written text which is interpreted or performed and all the above aspects "enclose one another, overlap, interpenetrate, simultaneously and redundantly arousing and using to every channel of communication" (Schechner 94).

Performance is an essential part of our lives but it is not an easy concept to define. Although it is difficult to write about performance in simplistic terms it is an activity by an individual or a group enacted in the presence of another individual or a group. Performance theorists like Erving Goffman, Victor Turner, Ray Birdwhistell, D.W.Winnicott, Richard Schechner, Rebecca Schineider, Clifford Geertz, James Clifford and George Marcus insist to involve the activities like games, sports, dance, and music in preformance which are primeval and present in all cultures. While drama, theatre and script frame the archetype of a play, performance adds aesthetics to it.

In Indian theatre there is both performatic and cultural essence that continues from enactment to enactment through centuries despite individual variations and interpretations. Indian theatre traces its beginnings to the Fifth Veda as revealed and propounded to Bharatmuni by the Creator, Brahma himself to celebrate ancient rituals and seasonal festivals of the country. But the growth of Christian drama is linked with the scriptural enactments in the nave of the church through the Middle Ages and the Renaissance. However in the Eastern and Western performative tradition a 'play' as a literary written text is governed by certain rules integral to its structure and form. A 'drama' as a classified genre in literature and the 'theatre' as a stage peformance present the activities in our everyday life. In totality theatrical performance has some holistic approach and social impact. In action and understanding, "Theatre leads to the rejection of the usual limitations of man and man's powers, and infinitely extends the frontiers of what is called reality" (Artaud 13). The mutual development of each domain play and drama find fulfilment in theatre through apprecitaion. The textual world of play, the literary world of drama, and performative world of theatre have a mutual development both meaningfully and successfully in audience's leisurely imagination, successive learning capability, and participation in social function.

As a whole the textual, literary and performative structure of a play have verisimilitudes in the notion of theatricality, visual embodiment of ideas and unique system of intelligibility. In the thematic exploration of Karnad's plays there are performative potential, theatrical strategies, widespread awareness and literay approach. There are effective and cognitive learning possibilities for the readers, researchers and audience. Karnad believes that theatrical function, texture of the dramatic texts, thematic shape and performance may change in social contexts but for the differences in reception there lies a collective consciousness in their central reality.

Karnad's plays are widely performed in Europe and America and have received international recognition. Apart from Indian languages some of his plays have been translated into foreign languages like Hungarian and German. Karnad never writes his plays in first impression. Rather he nurtures his impression on a particular theme for long, makes research on it and recapitulates it in a new shape, thought and philosophy. His *Yayati* is a play of juvenilia that involves his potential sensibility, intensity of thought and psychological reinterpretation. *Ma Nishada* involves his creative attempt to explore the dilemma of the washerman with his guilt consciousness. *Tughlaq* is a thesis play on Nehruvian dysfunctional politics. *Hayavadana* is a complex psychological and supralogical play on the problems and possibilities of identity.

The play presents his motive and human spirit in understanding human nature and body chemical. *Anju Mallige* is a philosophical play on death and rebirth. *Hittina Hunja* reworked as *Bali: The Sacrifice* is a philosophically debatable play on violence and non-violence in religious faiths. *Naga-Mandala* expresses his owing allegiance to the philosophies of folk culture on the question of personal ethics and social responsibility. *Tale-danda* is a play on history in past perfect and present continuous. *Agni Mattu Male* rewritten as *The Fire and The Rain*, his well researched and one the the most brilliant plays in Indian English drama philosophises knowledge and wisdom, human fraility and quest for divinity in the myth of Yavakri. It presents the story of partricide and fatricide, selfishness and sensuousness. *The Dreams of Tipu Sultan* is the dramatisation of the glory of the history of southern India and the rise of British as a power in Indian subcontinent. *A Heap of Broken Images* presents the complex position of Indian bilingual authors and the glorification of pseudo-authorial self in our contemporary literary sphere. *Flowers: A Dramatic Monologue* is the dramatisation of spiritual, aesthetic, sensual and divine intentions in the personal and private world of a priest with his love and attachment to a linga, the phallic representation of Lord Shiva. *Wedding Album,* his recent play presents the pride and prejudice of a middle class Saraswat South Indian family where the young members in their exposure to materialism, globalism, fascination for progressivism, and with the effect of neo-colonilism are uprooted from their culture.

Karnad's recognition as an amateur dramatist for the Indian stage is extablished as a multifaceted personality. He writes about himself, "I have been fairly lucky in having a multi-pronged career..... I've been an actor, a publisher, a film-maker. But in none of these fields have I felt quite as much at home as in playwriting " (*New Theatre Quarterly* 362). His *Tughlaq* is translated into Hungarian and German, broadcast by the BBC, London in 1979 and performed in London by the National School of Drama Repertory Company with the direction of Ebrahim Alkazi at the Festival of India in 1982. His *Hayavadana* was presented at the Berlin Festival of Drama and Music in Germany in 1985 with the direction of Vijay Mehta, broadcast by the BBC, and presented at the Ark Ensemble in New York in 1993. *Naga-Mandala* was presented in German by the Leipziger Schauspielhous at Leipzig and Berlin for the festival of India in Germanny in 1992 with the direction of Vijay Mehta. It was also performed at the University Theatre at Chicago and prestigious Guthrie Theatre in Minneapolis USA in 1993. He was also commissioned by the Guthrie Theatre to end his 37 years of struggle with the myth of Yavakri in the *Mahabharata* and complete his *The Fire and the Rain*. He was commissioned by the BBC to write *The Dreams of Tipu Sultan* to commemorate the fiftieth anniversary of Indian Independence. The play *Bali: The Sacrifice* was broadcast by the BBC and presented by the Haymarket Theatre, Leicester, UK.

Karnad's importance as a dramatist is marked with his academic excellence and dramatic achievements. He received the Rhodes Scholarship and went to England. On his return to India in 1963, he joined the Oxford University Press, Madras as the assistant manager and then as the manager, He received the important assignment as the Director of the Film and Television Institute of India, Pune in 1974. In 1987 he went to the USA on Fulbright Scholar-in-Residence to work in the Department of South Asian Languages and Civilisations, University of Chicago. He served as the Chairman of the Sangeet Natak Academi (National Akademi for the Performing Arts) and Children's Film Society, New Delhi from 1988 to 1993. He has won the Homi Bhaba Fellowship to work on the folk forms of northern Karnataka. In 1994 he was awarded the Doctor of Letters degree by the Karnataka University, Dharwad.

Apart from his academic excellence he has received many honours and awards. He got Mysore State Award for *Yayati* in 1962; Komaldevi Award of the Bharatiya Natya Sangh for the Best Indian Play for his *Hayavadana* in 1972. He received a number of awards like the B.H. Sridhar Award in 1992, the Karnataka Natya Akademi Award for the best play of 1990-91 in 1992 and the Karnataka Sahitya Akademi Award in 1993 and central Sahitya Akademi award in 1994 for his *Tale-danda*. He was awarded by the *Granthaloka*, the Journal of Book Trade for the play. He received the Karnataka Sahitya Akademi Award for his *Naga-Mandala* in 1989. He has also received the Government of Mysore Rajyotsava Award in 1970, the Sangeet Natak Akademi Award for playwriting in 1972, the Karnataka Natak Akademi Award in 1984 and the Nandikar Award of Calcutta for playwriting in 1989. He received the Bestsellers' and Publishers'Association of South

India Award in 1992. He received the Gubbi Veeranna award from the Government of Karnataka in 1997. Apart from this he has received Padmashree in 1974, Padma Bhusan in 1992 and Jnanpith, the highest literary award, in 1999 for enriching Indian literary scene and for his contribution to art, cultute, theatre and drama.

Karnad's multifaceted personality and his contribution to Indian English literature and culture is marked with his education, fluency in Marathi, involvement in Marathi and Kannada literatures, devotion to Sanskrit and influence of Western drama. His evolution as a dramatist, involvement as an artist and profession as a script writer and director of films is realised by every Indian lover of performing art.

Works Cited

Dhanavel, P. *The Indian Imagination of Girish Karnad*. New Delhi: Prestige Books, 2000.

Karnad, Girish (In an inteview with Aparna Bhargava Dharwadkar). "Performance, Meaning and Materials of Modern Indian Theatre". *New Theatre Quarterly*. 11:44 (November). 1995, 355-70.

______________ . "In His Own Voice: A Conversation with Girish Karnad". *Girish Karnad's Plays: Performance and Critical Perspectives*. Ed. Tutun Mukherjee. New Delhi: Pencraft International, 2008.

Dhawan, R.K. "Girish Karnad: The Man and the Writer". *The Plays of Girish Karnad*. Ed. Jaydipsinh Dodiya. New Delhi: Prestige Books, 1999.

Gokak, V.K. "The Concept of Indianness with Reference to Indian writing to English". *Indian Writing in English*. Ed. Ramesh Mohan. Madras: Orient Longman, 1978.

Panikkar, Kavalam Narayana. "Panikkar's Drama Magic". *The Times of India* (21st Oct.) 2003:10.

Schechner, Richard. *Performance Theory*. London & New York: Routledge, 2004. rpt. (First published in 1997).

Mukherjee, Tutun. "Of Text and Performance: Girish Karnad's Plays". *Girish Karnad's Plays : Performance and Critical Perspective*. Ed. Tutun Mukherjee. New Delhi: Pencraft International, 2008.

Artaud, Antonin. *The Theatre and its Double*. Trans.Mary Caroline Richards. New York: Grove Press, 1958.

Coe, Richard N. *The Vision of Jean Genet: A Study of his Poems, Plays and Novels*. New York: Grove Press, 1968.

Murthy, U.R. Anantha, Prasanna and Girish Karnad. "Girish Karnad, the Playwright: A Discussion". Trans. Sukanya Chandrasekara. *Indian Literature* 38:5 (Sept-October). 1995.

Karnad, Girish. "Author's Introduction". *Three Plays*. New Delhi: OUP, 1995.

2 Archetypes of Ancient Myths

Myth is one of the principal roots of drama. The origin of myth is as old as that of the human civilisation. It embodies knowledge in the form of image that is more potent than statement. It is aptly described as the language of the primitive. Myths are specific accounts of gods or superhuman beings involved in extraordinary events or circumstances in a time that is unspecified but understood as existing. In general discourse myth stands for something false, fictitious and far removed from reality and history. It is prehistoric and preliterary. It is a traditional legendary story usually concerned with deities or demi-gods and the creation of the world and its inhabitants. It deals with the problems of cosmogony.

Myths play a very significant role in human psychology and society from its beginning as primitive religious narrative to its recent adaptation as an aid in the exploration of the unconscious mind. They are the stories which explain the mysteries of the creation of the universe and its destruction, of how people and animals first came to be, of the characters of the gods and goddesses they worship. They demonstrate culture, tradition, fantastic events with no proof or with no factual basic. They enhance spiritual insight and spirituality helps to clean away negativity in human mind. Further, spirituality means converting negative thoughts to postivie ones and helps us release our emotional suffering by building a positive attitude buffering our self-esteem, and by inspiring the individuals to explore and use their abilities to the fullest.

Myth is a great literary forte of the great writers, like Valmiki, Vyasa, Homer and Virgil who in their scriptural texts present the heroic exploits of their protagonists. Through the ages writers have dealt with the stories of myths for the ethical and spiritual progress of people. They present the achievements of divine incarnations in fictional way and the mystery of divine existence and the spiritual destiny of man. Myth symbolises an incessant conflict between the forces of good and evil. In myths however the evil is big and powerful is bound to lose at the hands of good. The most obvious function of myth is the exploration of facts, whether natural or cultural in its art forms like painting, sculpture and literature or in religious traditions and cultic celebrations. As myth is both true and false at the same time one must always be prepared to accept the truth contained in it with all his worldly wisdom, strength, power and courage he can never be able to behave like the hero of a myth or can not brave dangers, and accomplishes heroic exploits and adventures. The plot and theme of the myth not only presents this but defines the limits of individual life for which one fails to reach his expectations. Myth is neither history of a civilisation nor history can become the myth of a civilization in its literary tradition. While history presents a higher form of truth with authenticity myths contain a symbolical truth with higher degree of reality. Myths are taken for moral guidance and they act as social archetypes. The study of myths make people deeply inclined to philosophy, idealism and universalism. Myths are always pro-social; they enforce morality, discourage immorality and falsehood, and promote peace and prosperity in life.

In the Indian context myth is an integral part of human ethos and consciousness. The Indians, particularly the Hindus believe, in myths and they have myth making qualities. In India myths are called *Puranas* in Sanskrit which means 'Pura api navam' (though old, ever new) or 'Pura navam bhavati iti' (old becomes new).The *Puranas* are the ancient narratives about the supreme and sacred souls and deal with the matters related to old world stories and legends. The *Puranas* deal with kings and their subjects, astronomy, superstitions, omens, portents, unfavourable planets, dynasty of monarchs, coronation and duties of kings, their politics, science of war, use of arms, dancing, agriculture, gardening, construction of images of deities, description of the doctrines of knowledge, devotion, theological and philosophical doctrines; values of tolerance, adaptability of worthy social system; and nobler ideas on social, political, economic and religious problems. For the Indians mythical protagonists in the *Ramayana* and the *Mahabharata* remain always as ideal figures in their collective consciousness. Myths not only make the Indians bound to their family, linguistic community, faith community and ethnic community but connect them to the past for moral values, and emotional and social security from it. They become the examples for the common people and directly influence them in their everyday decision-making actions. Contextualising myth as a serious subject in his plays Girish Karnad dramatises a few mythical stories of his choice with contemporary relevance. He recreates them with universal overtones and operates them in almost all spheres of life. In the dramatisation of myths he purposefully initiates virtues in life. Through myths he visions the welfare of the human beings and harmony in the society.

Karnad uses myths as archetypes in his plays to express meaning for the contemporary life. He believes that the significance of myth never dies. For him myths are the part of the collective consciousness of the people. In the archetypal myths he shows modern man's predicament. In an age of postmodernism and globalisation he observes people's craze for materialism and their crude imitation of Western civilisation. He thinks that this nature of men makes them suffer from a lamentable spectacle of cultural amnesia. As a conscious dramatist he valorises myths, parables, legends and folktales in his plays. He rewrites them in his plays as they provide immense scope for living. While he uses mythical episodes in his plays he significantly aims at using them for social, religions and philosophical purposes. He presents certain episodes of myths from the *Mahabharata* and contextualises them in contemporary human situations. It is observed that his plays on myths are rooted in the ancient Indian dramatic tradition as set in Bharata's *Natyashastra* and Abhinavagupta's concept, that the highest goal of drama is to realise the *purusharthas,* –namely *dharma* (relating to the spiritual sphere), *artha* (political and economic power), *kama* (sexual or aesthetic gratification) and *moksha* (release or final liberation from human bondage). In the mythic imagination of his plays he revives this ancient dramatic tradition in the celebration of the human and humane. Presenting myths in human condition he links the present with the eternal, and the contemporary with the archetypal. D. Maya rightly remarks:

> Karnad links the past and the present, the archetype and the real. Issues of the present world find their parallels in the

> myths and fables of the past which lend new meanings and insights through analogy, reinforcing the theme. By transcending the limits of time and space, myths provide flashes of insight into life and its mystery. They form an integral part of the culture consciousness of the land, with their associative layers of meaning, their timelessness and relevance to contemporary issues (68).

Karnad deals with mythical episodes in his plays and interprets them in contemporary reality. Linking the ancient and modern dramatic traditions in his plays he links the natural and supernatural phenomena in human conditions. Thus, following the Sanskrit dramatic tradition established by Bharatha and Kalidas, and the folk theatre of Karnataka on the one hand, and sophisticated Western dramatic tradition established by Bretcht, Shaw, Strindberg, Anouilh, Sartre and Beckett on the other hand he combines the Eastern and Western dramatic traditions with continuous parallel between contemporaneity and antiquity.

Karnad does not take the myths in their entirity. He takes only parts of them that are useful to him and the rest he supplements with his imagination to make his plot clear. He takes refuge in Indian myths and makes them a vehicle for new vision. In the use of myths he presents the absurdity of life with all its elemental passions, conflicts and individual's eternal struggle to achieve perfection. While dealing with ancient myths he aims at plunging us into the sentiment of devotion because he believes that the sole reason of our suffering in this world is that we have forsaken our faith in gods. In terms of form and content his plays focus on new discourses on Indian myths. Investing bits of myth Karnad introduces us with India's ancinet tradition and culture which provide us hope and consolation.

Some major minor regional classical elements are found in his plays on folktales which are often called as "folk myths or folk *Puranas*". Karnad does not incorporate any definite myth in them from the epics. While his plays on myths present the themes with universal appeal, his folk *puranas* have only regional implications. Although *Hayavadana*, *Naga-Mandala* and *Flowers* are based on folk *puranas* or folklores of Karnataka they are different from the plays based on the episodes of the *Mahabharata*. Therefore, an attempt has been made in the project to analyse only his mythical plays – *Yayati, The Fire and the Rain,* and *Bali*: *The Sacrifice.*

Yayati (1961) is Girish Karnad's landmark contribution to Indian drama significant for its artistic maturity and a high consciousness of purpose. It is his first play written with an impulsive enthusiasm on the context of the persuasive philosophy of Existetialism. Incorporating the myth of Yayati from the *Mahabharata* he has projected the conflicting philosophies, physical, emotional and psychological repercussions of his characters in an attempt to integrate his creative enterprise on duty and responsibility, existence and essence, and ethics and aesthetics. He had written the play with his juvenile enthusiasm while he was moving to England to study at Oxford University after winning the Rhodes Scholarship. But he did not know that the play would earn him such credibility and identity as a dramatist in future. He says in an interview:

> I had never fancied myself a dramatist. In fact, I had tried my hand at writing poetry... During the weeks of preparation for my departure to England – Which were as I said quite successful for various reasons – I found myself writing a play. This was *Yayati*. Though I had trained myself to write in English, I found myself writing the play in Kannada. The story of King Yayati is from the "Adiparva" of *Mahabharata*. At the prime of his life, the King is cursed with senility because of a moral transgression. Concerned only with himself, he pleads with his sons to exchange their youth with him and only the youngest son Puru agrees. Puru takes upon himself the curse of the father and becomes old, older than his father (Mukherjee 30).

Narrating his state of condition in England as a forced / imposed– preferred alienation Karnad tells about his impression on the story of the play:

> I saw it as a way to escape the stressful situation. But when I recall the time, I'm amazed how closely the myth reflected my anxieties and uncertainties, and my resentment at all who seemed to demand that I sacrifice my future. But it did serve me as an outlet for my doubts and provide me with a set of values (31).

The play is fascinting for mysteries in it, interesting incidents of love and romance, instantaneous exchange of youth and old age, and a sensuous father's robbing of his son's youth. It appears that,

"*Yayati*, emerged out of his sublimated protest against his being suffocated by the responsibilities thrust on him by his parents" (Babu 69). The play demonstrates 'the theme of responsibility' and issues related to it. Karnad presents an unusual myth about a parent's aggression against his offspring. Yayati's attempt to circumvent the catastrophe for his sexual misdemeanour by demanding his son's youth is presented as moral insensitivity in philosophical and psychological dimensions.

The play is an "exploration of Yayati's and Pooru's inner conflicts". The play resonates the original myth of Yayati but in dramatisation Karnad rejects the traditional glorification of Pooru's self-sacrifice in the dictum of *pitru devo bhava* (Father is God). He presents the psychological cannibalism of Yayati. He writes in the 'Afterword' to his play *Yayati*:

> The story of King Yayati that I used occurs in the *Mahabharata*. The King, for a moral transgression he has committed, is cursed to old age in the prime of life. Distraught at losing his youth, he approaches his son, pleading with him to lend him his youth in exchange for old age. The son accepts the exchange and the curse and thus becomes old.... But the old age brings no knowledge, no self-realization, only the senselessness of a punishment meted out for an act in which he had not even participated. The father is left to face the consequences of shirking responsibility for his own actions (73).

The play is based on the backdrop of lust, jealousy and racial tensions which foreground the tragic intensity of the play. Among all Karnad is interested more in Yayati's sensual pleasures and craving for immortality. He presents how Yayati's desires generate his inner struggle. In an interview with Rajinder Paul he says:

> I was excited by the story of Yayati, this exchange of ages between the father and the son, which seemed to me terribly powerful and terribly modern. At the same time, I was reading a lot of Sartre and the Existentialists. This consistent harping on responsibility which the Existentialists indulge in suddenly seemed to link up with the story of Yayati (*Enact*).

During his stay in England he saw brilliant productions of Shakespeare. He also saw many productions of Shaw, Brecht,

Rattigan, Osborne, Wesker and Grotowki. Significantly French and English plays had impressed him very much. After seeing these plays he had drawn the impression that Western drama had nothing much to give us. The only thing he realised that European theatre was more inspirational, Western society was very individualistic, and the European playwrights only valorised individualism in their plays. While presenting realism in their plays the Western playwrights chiefly concentrated their themes on individualism and existentialism. Karnad incorporated those ideas in the structure of the play while dealing with kinship, class, caste and so on. Looking back to ancient Indian dramatic tradition he found Kalidas too remote, too classical and too perfect. While reworking with the manuscripts of the play he had cultivated the tension for Indian theme, tradition and culture; and Western form and technique. He had avidly studied Anouilh, Sartre, O'Neill and the Greeks. This helped him to present Yayati's existential suffering for his extreme selfishness. He presents Yayati's anxieties and uncertainties due to his old age and decrepitude in youth. Reading of Western canons and intriguing elements of Existentialism he has presented them in many dimensions of his characters in the play.

Karnad was very much impressed with the predictive behaviour of Yayati. For presenting Yayati's alienated self and stressful situation he has reworked myth with the Existentialist philosophy of Beckett, Sartre and Camus. He says in an interview:

> It is true that Existentialism was the persuasive philosophy of the time. My attempt was to emphasise the calm acceptance of grief and anguish. Puru's old age is a sudden transformation and not the eventuality of life. It brings no wisdom and no self realization. It is a senseless punishment for an act he has not committed. I was also intrigued by the idea that if Puru had a wife, how would she react? So I introduced Chitralekha. Every character in the play tries to evade the consequences to their actions, except Sharmistha and Chitralekha (Mukherjee 31).

The projection of tragic force in the play is very much similar to the Greek tragedies. At a very early age when he focused this in mythical framework he showed the manuscript to G.B. Joshi of

Manohara Granthamala before his leaving for England. But during his days in England Kirtinath Kurtkoti wrote to him asking for the manuscript and it was published first in Kannada by G.B. Joshi after polishing the language. However, in the play Karnad has presented individualistic and existentialist approaches to his characters. He was also influenced by the nativist Marathi novelist, V.S. Khandekar's novel, *Yayati* (1959) that had earned the State Sahitya Akademi Award in 1960 and the Jnanpith Award in 1964 for his fictional presentation of Yayati's craving for materialism. At the same time the philosophy of cosmopolitan existentialist philosophers like Heidegger, Kafka, Sartre, Camus and Kierkegaard in the Western world had influenced him much for the success of the play.

The play established Karnad's reputation as a dramatist in Kannada. It helped him to launch a celebrated career in the Indian theatre. Although the play is translated in many Indian languages, the excellent translation in English was produced by Priya Adarker and it was published in *Enact* in the midsixties. But for some reason Karnad was not comfortable with the work Secondly, for its non-availability in English he decided to translate it into English. The text was originally written in Kannada when he was 22 but when he got tempted to translate it at the age of 69 he rewrote it entirely. He writes about it in the 'Preface' of the play:

> Confronting the play again, the temptation to tinker with it has been irresistible. But it would be not just silly but disastrous to tackle at the age of sixty nine a play I had written at twenty-two. I would have to write it entirely. On the other hand, when I wrote it, I had no experience of theatre, and over the years I have been fortunate to have received comments from the professionals who have actually staged it.... It would have been unfair not to incorporate their insights into the text before making it available to a new public. But these suggested revisions, small as they were, were scattered through the play. So... I decided to translate the revised text myself (vii-viii).

Incorporating the traditional *Puranic* theme Karnad gives a fresh interpretation to the play. While interpreting the myth he has concentrated more on Yayati's craving for a sensual life and traditional glorification of Pooru's self-sacrifice. Dealing with these two central characters he has stressed on existential philosophy in individual's personal responsibility and his relation to the universe. Old age and youth, sensual and psychological, mortality and immortality, existence and essence in life occupy the centrestage of the play. Aparna Bhargava Dharwadker rightly remarks:

> *Yayati* establishes at the outset of Karnad's career that myth is not merely a narrative to be bent to present pusposes but a structure of meanings worth exploring in itself because it offers opportunities for philosophical reflection without the constraints of realism or the necessity of contemporary setting (*Collected Plays,* Vol. I: xvii).

In the original myth Yayati is the tenth in the line of Brahma's family. In Indian mythology Brahma is the first ancestor. From Brahma came Daksha, from Daksha came Aditi, from Aditi came Surya, from Surya came Manu, from Manu came Ilanamni Kanya, from Ila came Pururava, from Pururava came Aayu, from Aayu came Nahusha and from Nahusha came Yayati. While selecting the traditional story of mythological King Yayati for the play he has given some new interpretation to old age, youth and immortality. Delineating Yayati's longing for eternal youth he explores the complexities of life in King's struggle for bearing responsibilities and fulfilling his expectations. In the play Karnad dramatises Yayati's personal dilemma, inner conflicts,moral insensibility, desire for sensual pleasure and responsibility to his kingdom and family.

In the *Mahabharata,* Yayati, one of the six sons of King Nahusha, rules the whole Aryavarta. In one of the episodes of the epic he is presented as one of the most intriguing and fascinating characters. In Vyasa's narration Yayati was a great scholar and one of the noblest rulers of olden times. He followed the *Shastras* and was devoted to the welfare of his subjects. Even the king of gods, Indra, held him in high esteem. Married to seductively beautiful Devayani, in love with her maid, Sharmishtha, and father of five sons from the two women, yet Yayati unabashedly declares, "My lust for pleasure is unsatisfied..." (from the 'blurb' of V.S. Khandekar's novel *Yayati*).

He is the young prince, highy sensuous, angry, energetic, and ambitious. He has the ambition to enjoy youth eternally and desires to rule his kingdom with all privileges and pleasures. In the storyline Yayati marries Devayani, the beautiful daughter of Shukracharya, the guru and preceptor of *asuras,* in an unexpected situation. Before her marriage Devayani had fallen in love with her father's disciple, Kacha, the son of Brihaspati who in course of time rejected her. When Devayani cursed Kacha, he in return cursed her to marry a kshatriya being a brahmin daughter, and went to heaven with Sanjeevani power from her father. After this Devayani became very close to Sharmishtha, the daughter of Vrishparva, the king of *asuras*. One day after their bath they were drying their undergarments under the sun. But god Vayu exchanged them. When they discovered that they had worn each other's undergarments they had a quarrel. But Sharmishtha was under the impression that Devayani had done this deliberately. She told Devayani accusingly that a brahmin could not be a kshyatriya by wearing her dresses. The ego conflict in the then classridden society is revealed from the quarrel of the daughters of two elite classes. In anger and jealousy Sharmishtha not only insulted Devayani but also slapped her and pushed her into a dry well where she started crying for help. Meanwhile, King Yayati who was passing by that way heard Devayani's cry and stretched his hand to lift her up. Of course for this Sharmishtha was punished by her father and she was ordered to serve Devayani as her *dasi* (maidservant) for ever. After this incident Devayani's unrequited love for Kacha had a shift for King Yayati. As per the prevailing custom of the time a kshatriya was unable to marry a brahmin girl. The consent of Shukracharya was sought for the marriage of Devayani and Yayati. Yayati also agreed to this *pratiloma* (inter-caste / inter-class) marriage in the hope of achieving immortality as a blessing from Shukracharya for his knowledge of 'Sanjeevani' vidya. As per the tradition after their marriage Sharmishtha was sent with Devayani with her other maidservants as dowry to her in-law's house.

In course of time Devayani had two sons—Yadu and Turvasu. But due to Yayati's clandestine affair with Sharmishtha she had three sons from him—Druhya, Anu and Pooru. When the two friends—one as mistress and other as maidservant—soon enjoyed their status as queens they had serious misunderstandings. Devayani could not see the Yayati-Sharmishta relationship as a healthy sign for her future. She left the palace and went to her father to complain against Yayati. In anger and fury Shukracharya cursed Yayati to become old. When Yayati implored him for a respite Shukracharya wished him that he could exchange his old age with other's youth. Yayati requested his subjects, soldiers and sons to exchange their youth with him. All the first four sons–Yadu, Turvasu, Druhya and Anu—refused to accept their father's decrepitude. Yadu responds without hesitation that old age involves many inconveniences to drinking and eating, and is accompanied by white hair, melancholy, flaccid muscles, wrinkles all over the body, deformities, weakness, emaciation, incapacity to work, and inspires aversion. Turvasu who is more sober but no less peremptory says, old age prohibits pleasures, destroys strength, beauty, intelligence, memory and finally life itself. Druhya remarks, an old man can no longer benefit from elephants, horses, or women, and that he stammers when speaking. Anu also declares his dislike for old age as people eat like infants, soil themselves constantly, and can no longer even make liberation on the fire altar at the proper times. When nobody came forward Pooru, the youngst son of Sharmishtha agreed to fulfil his father's wish and accepted the burden of his father's old age. When Pooru's wife Chitralekha committed suicide for her husband's untime old age Yayati surrendered his youth to Pooru and went into the forest for penance.

In Karnad's version of the myth Pooru is not the son of Sharmishtha. He has also introduced Chitralekha as Pooru's wife to philosophise her existentiality. Both Yayati and Chitralekha crave for youth. But while Yayati aspires to live long in order to enjoy youth, Chitralekha takes her husband's sacrifice, a curse when Pooru shares his youth to his father. In the original myth Yayati implores Shukracharya to mitigate the effect of his curse but in Karnad's play Yayati sends Pooru to implore Shukracharya to redeem the effect of his curse. The theme of Yayati's attachment to life and pleasure-seeking nature lead him finally to renunciation. While reworking with the myth Karnad presents Yayati's nature, desire and renunciation that comes through the horrors of life. Yayati's sensuality and quest for immortality have many symbolic encounters. While portraying the existential condition of Yayati, his inner and outer conflicts, moral morbidity and ethical numbness the playwright makes an attempt to subvert the male world. In his presentation the great King appears less cerebral but more institutional.

Articulating myth in dramatic framework Karnad analyses some minor issues. Parents are generally the well wishers of their children but they become predators when they develop their cannibalistic nature. Portraying the characters he has investigated the inner recesses of human psyche. In Yayati's life he has analysed his ideas of glorifying ideology in the performance of duty and acceptance of responsibility. Yayati is the victim of his existentialism and unhappy consciousness. He acts according to Sartrean dictum, 'existence precedes essence'. Yayati's fear for death and quest for immortality isolate him. His fear invites all sufferings. All existnetialists believe that man's nature is infinitiely variable and this is why individual is responsible for making his own destiny. In the play Yayati has a nobler intention to rule his kingdom by enjoying immortality but behind this motive he has a craving for sensuality. He is completely drenched in sexsual pleasures. As a self-conscious existentialist he is torn between the dilemma of responsibility and essence in life. In other characters Karnad invests epic force in their existential condition. Their motives, desires and frustrations in epic dimensions are the reminiscences of the characters in great Greek tragedies. Exchange of youth for sensual satisfaction is an unusual subject matter in the myth. But Karnad has dramatised this myth with Pooru's 'self-sacrifice' for his father's long life. Pooru accepts his father's old age and commits a great sacrifice in the history of mankind. Pooru sacrifices his youth to his father out of loyality, devotion and obligation but Yayati sacrifices his son to bear the responsibility of his state for its peace and prosperity. If Yayati commits a great injustice to Pooru, Pooru commits the same to Chitraleka. He takes such a risky step without consulting her in which she has every word to say because Pooru's youth is related to her feminine finitude. Pooru's decision makes her life miserable and her future dark.

Necessity is generated out of eventuality in life. The exstentialists think of duty and responsibility to meet the eventualities in life. In the play Yayati's marriage with Devayani and his clandestine affair with Sharmishtha are his self-conscious acts but Shukracharya's curse of old age is an eventuality. Eventuality is not destiny. While eventuality is consciously earned by a person due to his action or decision, destiny is unconsciously thrushed opon one by his fortune. Yayati has the desire for fulfilment in life. He has desire for enjoyment of life, long living and power which are although transitory he attempts to make them eternal. Man's fight against the eternal is a crime. Death is an eternal truth. But Yayati's fight against this eternity invites his son's old age and daughter-in-law's death. His craving for immortality may be the primary desire of his life but through it when he aims at enjoying sensual pleasures and taking the institutional responsibilities it becomes disastrous. The primary and secondary desires do not complement each other for which Yayati takes his moral responsibility to renounce everything and go into the forest for penance.

Karnad's interpretation of a familiar myth on the exchange of youth with old age between a father and a son baffles the modern readers. Pooru's sacrifice of youth to his father is rare and exemplary in history, but this is a great injustice on the part of Yayati who commits a crime by exploiting the ethics and loyalty of his son. Youth has become the source of contention for all the characters. Those who crave for it are crushed in the course of time. Yayati is anxious to live with Pooru's youth. But without Pooru's youth Chitralekha prefers to die. Pooru considers youth negligible before his duty. Both Devayani and Sharmishtha are in warring nature for Yayati's youth. To enjoy the pleasures of youth the characters are in psychological conflicts and each one enjoys his/her position in existential dilemma. Karnad presents how "Each one exists only through the other. They mutually develop one another and find through one another clarity and reality" (Kierkegaard 225). Except Pooru for others existence is more important than essence in life. It appears:

> Either that existence is inherently meaningless so that individuals have, by the exercise of the will to create their own values. Or that, for each individual, there is a hidden meaning embedded in existence which, by the exercise of total personal resources, the individual has to discover and to live by (Childs and Fowler 79).

The characters are presented in the dynamics of their filial relationship, conflicting psychology and moral insensitivity. But for their existential dimension A. Shankar rightly remarks, "The characters are titans, and their desires, motives, fulfilments and frustration too are of epic dimensions" (*Bharat Jyoti*).

The *sutradhara* (the stage manager) introduces us about Yayati's existentiality. His son, Pooru returns after many years of absence. He has completed his education in the hermitage under renowned gurus. Yayati is happy that the future king of Aryvarta is not only made worthy by successfully completing his education but also has brought a bride, Chitralekha, the princess of Anga. The king has promoted it to an auspicious occasion. The whole city is jubilant enough with the expectation to welcome them. The people from every corner of the kingdom have rushed to the city to welcome the royal couple. They are expecting that the royal couple will make it a magic kingdom of love, ambition and power. The *sutradhara* tells us about the play:

> Our play has no gods. And it deals with death. A key element in its plot is the 'Sanjeevani' vidya – the art of reviving the dead, which promises release from the limitations of the fleeting life this self is trapped in. The gods and the rakshasas have been killing each other from the beginning of time for the possession of this art. Humans have been struggling to master it. Sadly, we aspire to become immortal but cannot achieve the lucidity necessary to understand eternity. Death eludes definition. Time coils into a loop, reversing the order the youth and old age. Our certainties crumble in front of the stark demands of the hearts (6).

The audience listen to the talk of Devayani and her maid, Swarnalata, from the inner chamber of King Yayati's palace where they express their grievances against Sharmishtha. Although Sharmishtha is sent as a dowry with Devayani to serve her as her mistress, she becomes a nuisance for others in the palace. Sharmishtha always teases Devayani and Swarnalata. They think as if her words are the 'dirty insinuations', and she is in satanic temperament. Both Devayani and Swarnalata call her with all spiteful words. Even Swarna calls her a 'rakshasi' and a 'whore'. She tells Devayani, "Why don't you send back to her tribe?"(7). Devayani knows Sharmishtha's nature and temperament for long but she cannot send her because she has become a necessary evil for her due to the incident in her life. On the other hand, Sharmishtha is destined to serve her friend for her quarrelsome and warring nature. Her crime is that she had pushed Devayani into a well. For this she is cursed by her father with the responsibility to serve Devayani for ever. Although their quarrelling was due to an existential situation in their life they fell victims to it – when Devayani was pushed into the well and Sharmishtha is destined to serve her friend as a maidservant. In the palace of Yayati Sharmishtha enjoys the royal privileges but regrets her relegated status as a maid. She has made a great sacrifice for the community because she had gone through the ordeal of being a maid to Devayani, who hates her. In anger and jealousy against Devayani, Sharmishtha behaves "like a cheap harridan"(17). She complains that only for Devayani the atmosphere in Yayati's palace has turned her into a domesticated animal and her "will to act is destryoyed"(17). She repents because she has no way to escape from this hell. She says, "I am a rakshasa woman"(17), "I am a princess by birth" (18), but due to her misfortune she is sent to a "kshatriya palace, ruled over by a brahmin queen!"(9).

To become a queen of Arya race was the expectation of every princess of the time. When eventuality favoured Devayani to become the queen of Yayati this enrages Sharmishtha. She serves Devayani as her maid but never leaves her in peace. She taunts Devayani, "he (Yayati) is not lusting for you, you poor darling, he lusts for immortality. Your father's art of 'Sanjeevani'" (11). She presents her best psychoanalysis of Yayati and Devayani in the following words:

> Yayati, the scion of the Bharata dynasty. He is not short of women, is she? Women of his own kind. Sensuous kshatriya maidens. Virgins reared for him. But he chooses you. Why? You know the answer. You, only You, could lead him to the ultimate goal: a sanctuary beyond the reach of death (11).

She reminds Devayani that it is no magic of her youth that impressed him but the magic of her father's 'Sanjeevani' vidya that drugged Yayati for his ambition to immortality. 'Sanjeevani' is the supreme previlege in Shukracharya's hand to win a favour for his daughter whatever the worth she deserves or not. It is Yayati, the King of Bharat dynasty who has the world in his palm only fears mortality. He is ultimately trapped in Devayani's love to relish the nectar of immortality. Yayati's love for Devayani is marked with his selfish desire. Sharmishtha tells Devayani not to feel proud of her foolish estimation of love for Yayati and as the queen of Arya race. She reminds her sarcastically:

> Don't you remember?... When I closed my eyes, I was the princess of the rakshasas. You were the offspring of a destitute brahmin, dependent upon my father. I had everything. Beauty, education, wealth. Everything except birth – an Arya pedigree. What was your worth? That your father knew the 'Sanjeevani' spell. That is all. Yet I worshipped you. No, I loved you. To me, the most wondrous power I possessed seemed to be my ability to shower gifts upon you – things you hadn't asked for but which you so gratefully accepted (10).

Chastising Yayati's love for Devayani she says that the king married her only for his urge to conquer death.

The quarrel between Devayani and Sharmishtha brings misfortune for both. But while it brings good fortune for Devayani for a short time for Sharmishtha it is a life-long servitude. Devayani falls in the well. She is rescued by Yayati and marries him. But her happiness does not last long as her happy love with Yayati is snatched away by Sharmishtha. In her servitude she wins the heart of Yayati for her virility and intelligence. Devayani's love at first sight does not last long because Sharmishtha becomes a serious contender to her love. Devayani tells Sharmishtha that after her affairs with Kacha and his betrayal to her she was despises men. But she breaks her oath because she says:

> I was in the well, crying out for help. Frightened, distraught. And I heard someone call. A face peered into the well. An arm stretched out and pulled me up. I recognised him instantly. I had seen him from far – dreamt of him – and now I was there in a flesh and blood. I shared, spell-bound (12).

She tells Sharmishtha how she was honest to plead before Yayati, "Sir, I am a maiden. And you have held me by my right hand". That's it. Only two sentences. Fourteen words, " ... could actually so completely change a life"(13). But Sharmishtha does not take it easily rather remarks sarcastically. "Even with prostitutes picked off the street, the first thing a man does is ask her name.... So while he was locked in your embrace, you quickly told him you were Devayani, daughter of et cetera et cetera"(13). The presumptions show that Devayani married to Yayati in the presence of the sacrificial fire and before the brahmins. But their marriage does not connote the union of two hearts because perhaps her love for yayati was not so intense as it was for her first and ardent lover Kacha. Secondly, she desired to marry Yayati out of her ambition. Thirdly, "It follows that Sharmishtha must have brought Yayati something which Devayani was unable to give. He must have found happiness beyond sex and lust from Sharmishtha" (Khandekar 6).

Devayani feels sick of Sharmishtha's presence in the palace. Although she is the daughter of a brahmin teacher all her knowledge fail to defend herself from Sharmishtha. Sharmishtha's nuisance makes her existence unbearable. When Yayati proposes Devayani to send her back to her home Sharmishtha says, "Home is just a blank spot, sir, erased from my life. This is the dowry my father gave me when I left home" (21). Defending her position in the place she says assertively, "My father has given her father his word that I shall be her slave"(17). She says that she is deprived of the natural privilege of living at home and destined to live in chaos. She asserts that she has every reason to be a barbarian and act savagely. She says to Yayati in contempt and arrogance, "I did not mean to trap you in my words. I know I have no life but of a slave. But please, Sir. I cannot go on living, floundering around in this hell hole" (21). When Yayati asks her, "Is pushing a friend into a well an act of worthy of a princess?" she replies that *rakshasas* can not be lucid and rational like Aryas. She reacts that it is Devayani who came into her life and behaved in a savage manner.

Yayati dislikes Sharmishtha's nature of illtreating, assulting and misbehaving to Devayani. In the myth it is presented as a conflict between two friends over love but in the play Karnad projects it as a ego conflict between races and classes. Yayati dislikes Sharmishtha's arrogance and asuric kshatriya tendencies but he appreciates her intelligence. Even being a kshatriya king of Arya race he visualises the grand design of life through her. As a kshatriya king he has loved many women but has never met such an intelligent woman like Sharmishtha. He knows that she is an "evil beyond redemption"(28) but he loves her very much and declares, "I am making you my queen"(26). Devayani is shocked with the Sharmishtha-Yayati affair and to her misery finds her life unbearable. Yayati consoles her that Sharmishtha will be his queen but her (Devayani's) position as a royal consort will remain undisturbed. In the play Karnad translates a queen's mind with realistic touch when her *dasi,* a subordinate, becomes her equal in status. In her opinion, a slave can be a concubine but she cannot approve of Sharmishtha's status as a queen in the palace. When Sharmishtha taunts her, "I got him (Yayati) into bed with me. That was my revenge on you"(29), Devayani implores Yayati, "Please take as many wives as you want. I don't care. But not this reptile. Not her." She says earnestly, "I have never asked any favour of you... I implore you now. I too can bare my fangs. I too can draw blood. Don't provoke me on account of this woman"(30). Yayati is in perfect accord with Devayani but he is bewitched and entranced by Sharmishtha's sorcery of beauty and intelligence. He thinks, "Not to marry her (Sharmishtha) is to lose her"(30). He assures Devayani, "you don't need to worry, devi. Your position will not be touched. You will remain the senior Queen. You will share my throne. You will be at my side in all public celebrations... She can never be a threat to your position, You know that because of her : race"(29). He tells her that Sharmishtha would be lodged in a separate residence.

The myth is contemporanised in the play. When there is an attempt to cohere and compromise the racial and caste consciouness there it becomes dangerous and tragic. While the two queens, Devayani and Sharmishtha, are in conflict for their racial and caste consciousness King Yayati attempts his best to compromise their egoes in his secular spirit. When the two are in conflicting philosophies he rationalises his love and duty for the both. Devayani feels deprived of her due, Sharmishtha feels subordinated in her restricted status, and Yayati is confused in his existential dilemma between duty and responsibility. In anger Devayani leaves the palace to inform her father about Yayati's sexsual misdemeanour with Sharmishtha. Yayati is anguished by his standing between Scylla and Charybdis. With Devayani's departure Sharmishtha senses a terrible mess. She is neither able to tame Devayani nor capable of averting the tragedy. In her existential dilemma she thinks of coming back to her father for the peace and prosperity of the kingdom but she fails to do this because she knows that her father will not accept her for severing his commitment. They struggle their best for existence but keep the essence optional.

On the other hand, with Devayani's complaint "Shukrachaya is so incensed he has cursed His Majesty"(41). He is angry because

Sharmishtha has humiliated Devayani. He curses Yayati to old age. With the falling of his curses Yayati loses his youth and becomes a decrepit by nightfall. He persuades Pooru to save the situation by convincing Shukracharya. He feels the reality but fails to imagine the transfer of his youth to old age. He stands as "a dessicated fool". He expresses his despair before Sharmishtha, "Old age! Decrepitude! By night fall! And then? Then what?... you she-devil! You are the cause of all this. You are responsible. You trapped me with your wiles"(42). He is terrified with the claustrophobic imagination of old age. In anguish, grief and nightmarish thought he reacts to Sharmishtha's advice to have patience. He tells her, "Patience of a man falling into a bottomless pit. Patience? The deafening rush of emptiness. What can be more terrible than that?"(42). Yayati cannot bear his solitude in old age. The very thought of old age makes him repulsive. He desires to live long and enjoy the pleasures of youth. But when it is lost he searches for it like a blind man searches for an object. He tries to recapture his youth. When Sharmishtha tells him, "No one can escape old age. You have just hastened its arrival. Let us accept it"(42), he accuses he. an outsider of his anguish. Recollecting the rarest moments of his youth he says how he has slaughtered enemies, razed hostile cities to the ground, made his queens writhe in pain and demanded their love in gratitude. In anguish he tells Sharmishtha:

> You can only watch. With such care, with such pride, I had gathered the rarest moments of my life in my palm like precious stones. So I could play with them. Relieve them. Juggle them. And suddenly, they explode, each moment hurtling through my muscle and bones like a meteorite (42-43).

He becomes outraged for a moment and says: "I shall go and catch that wizened old fool (Shukracharya) by his beared and demand"(42) to withdraw his curse. Again waiting for Pooru's return he says, "Here I am on a bed of burning coals"(44). He becomes unable to realise that man is a slave to cirmustances and "What man needs is to find himself again and realise that nothing can save him from himself not even a valid proof of the existence of God" (Sartre 56). With the approach of old age he feels the hollowness within and thinks seriously how to save him from this perennial isolation.

Pooru becomes partially successful to convince Shukracharya for redeeming the effect of curse on his father. He conveys to Yayati about Shukracharya's wish that the "curse will not have its effect on you if a young man agrees to take it upon himself and offers his youth to you in exchange"(45). Shukracharya relents to withdraw the curse of instant decrepitude before nightfall. He agrees to mitigate the effect of old age with somebody's youth. Yayati is alluded with the impression that many will come forward to exchange their youth with him out of love, respect and gratitude. But soon he realises that people hesistate to step forward for this "holy martyrdom"(46). Their reverence neither implies their starving for his old age, nor their for commitment for a great sacrifice nor their denial an insolence. They are neither fools nor yogis to sacrifice their youth for Yayati's enjoyment of life. In their subjecthood they pay taxes and tributes, and remain loyal to the king. They do not like to come over the natural bond of relationship between the ruler and the ruled. He is of the impression that his soldiers are trained to lay down their lives for him. When all refuse to exchange their youth Yayati tells Pooru to convince them that:

> Their kith and kin will be looked after. They will live like the royalty. Not just riches, Pooru. Let them think of the glory and the fame. The world will look up to them with reverence (47).

Pooru conveys his inability to convince others to accept his father's senility. He expresses other's impression that all big words of truth, glory and sacrifice, loyalty and commitment are meaningless before old age. For everybody old age is inevitable and one can not avoid this simply calling it a wretched fate. Realising this greater truth in life Yayati says, "I am not trying to shun old age, Pooru. I am not that foolish. I know it is inevitable. Let me have my normal term of youth. I shall take back the curse and whatever comes it after a few years"(47).

Yayati becomes cynical of human life and human nature. He feels as if he is deserted in the oblivion of his misery. The support and good wishes of Sharmishtha and Pooru do not make him sufficient to live. The palace appears a noxious pit and a stuffy place for him. Pooru comes forward to accept his father's old age and decrepitude. He is ready to do this grand sacrifice. His decision, "I want to root myself back in my family" provides Yayati the "spasms of imminent birth"(50). One may call his decision an utter stupidity and his desire for self-sacrifice a rank perversion. Pooru accepts his father's old age for the reputation that adds a halo to the glory of Bharata dynasty. But his decision for this reputation invites sheer injustice for Chitralekha. Chitralekha's *arati* lamp drops on the ground and she makes a scream when she discovers the effect of curse on Pooru. She tells Pooru, "Please don't come near me... Don't touch me..."(58), "I was a fool, blind to your greatness. I don't realize my good fortune"(57). Being panic striken she says, "I will not let my husband step back into my bedroom unless he returns a young man"(61). She becomes confused, traumatic and uncertain about her future. In faith and despair she says, "I did not know prince Pooru when I married him. I married him for his youth. For his potential to plant the seed of the Bharatas in my womb. He has lost that potency now"(65). Pooru's warmth, considerate and loving nature without any kshatriya arrogance are no more the attractions for Chitralekha now.

Yayati presents his logic of transferring old age to Pooru. But soon after this exchange he is disillusioned with youth. He feels defedant to reply to the questions of Chitralekha. Yayati tries his best to convince her about life, love, old age and immortality for the betterment of his subjects and kingdom. He reminds her about the duties of a wife. He tells her, "Do you remember the vow you took not so long ago – with the gods as your witnesses, in the presence of the holy fire? That you would walk in the path marked by his foot-prints: whether home or into the wilderness..."(62). She knows that she has taken the oath even to enter into her husband's funeral pyre. Pooru's decision has delivered uncertainty on her future. Yayati explains to her, "Pooru took it on of his own free will. Without a word from me. Without saying a word to me"(63). He tries to exploit the situation emotionally with the words, "You are an educated woman, versed in the arts, trained in warfare. You could have displayed more self-control. Now act in a manner worthy of an Anga princess and Bharata queen. Act so that generations to come may sing your glory and Pooru's"(61). But Chitralekha views that his old age may be a challenge but his fear to face it is an act of cowardiceness. Yayati craves for existence in youth than essence in life but he advises

Chitralekha that essence should be the aim and purpose of life. While he prefers existence that precedes essence he encourages Chitralekha to prefer essence that follows existence. He tries to convince her that Pooru lacks enough experience to rule the kingdom. But through his "grand sacrifice"(68) he desires to rule his kingdom for long and make it prosperous. He believes that his responsibility to the kingdom and Pooru's transfer of his youth to him are the necessities of the hour. He cannot avoid the situation because he says:

> Unfortunately, recently, unexpected troubles have started brewing in the corners of my realm. Enemies on the border, rebellious forest tribes, the prospect of a famine, the danger of rakshasa depredation. I tried discussing these problems with him. But he is not interested. That is where I need your help (63).

Individual idealogy cannot be a general philosophy always. And any attempt to impose this can be devasting and tragic. Yayati's ideology and philosophy may be heuristic to solve the problems in his practical life but his solipsistic attitude does not solve the problematics of his existentialism. For him the burden of youth in old age is more than the burden of old age in youth. His quest for immortality makes Chitralekha cynical. When she married Pooru, the next sovereign of the land of Aryas, she had the dream to become the Empress of Aryavarta. But now due to her father-in-law's ambition and selfishness, she has her inner turmoil. When Yayati needs time to think, time to recover, time to heal, Chitralekha thinks, to have patience for her future will earn uncertainly in its entirity.

Pooru's acceptance of his father's old age adds despair to Chitralekha's life. She realises that Pooru has no more the qualities to be her husband. She thinks it foolish on her part to have patience and brood over his youth. In her existential suffering, despair, and shattered dream she still tries to hold the centre of Bharata dynasty. She invites Yayati for fornication and encourages him to rise above all trivialities. She says, "You have taken over your son's youth. It follows that you should accept everything that comes attached to it." Adding further she says, "I know. It is part of the sacrifice we all have to make"(66). For Chitralekha's spurious thoughts and filthy words Yayati calls her a beast. But in defiance and defection to the royal tradition she takes a lethal poison and commit suicide. Suicide is the Sartrean device to escape from the frustration and exhaustion of her life. She commits suicide when she thinks her youth is slaughtered, ambition is amputated and aspiration for motherhood has ended before its beginning.

Yayati struggles between life's predicament and finitude. He is drunk with immortality and dreams to build his glorious future in it. When Sharmishtha reminds him that the foundation of his glorious kingdom is based on the death bed of Chitralekha and old age of Pooru he thinks of his inhumanness. He is torn between the thoughts of his 'glorious vision' and 'grand sacrifice' of Pooru. He says, "I thought there were two options – life and death. No, it is living and dying. We have to choose between"(68). When Sharmishtha reminds him that "A woman (Chitralekha) is dead, another (she herself) gone mad, and a third (Swarnalata) in danger of her life," Yayati thinks that he is not living but existing in the meaninglessness of life. In crushing exhaustion he speaks in a soliloquy:

> ... I see myself, my animal body frozen in youth, decaying, deliquescing, turning rancid. You are lying on your pyre, child, burning for life, while I sink slowly in this quagmire, my body wrinkleless and grasping but unable to grasp anything (68).

Chitralekha, "the first martyr to His Majesty's glorious vision"(69), changes his mind. Yayati returns from his imagination to reality. He requests Pooru, "Take back your youth. Let me turn my decrepitude into a beginning. Let me go and face my destiny in the wilds"(69). On his realisation Seema Suneel rightly remarks, "Everything is at wit's end to make Yayati accept the responsibility for his action. Puru also asks Yayati to accept his old age and go to the forest" (Dodiya 109-110).

Yayati renounces the material world of pleasure and sensuality and moves into the forest in search of spirituality. He realises that his senses were blighted with selfish desires which earned evils and adversities in life. The playwright projects Yayati, a turned altruist at last. In the dynamics of youth, immortality, old age and death Karnad presents Yayati's struggle for *dharma, karma* and *moksha*. In the presentation of Yayati's existential situation he analyses common man's rationalisation of life thourgh youth, Pooru's philosophising of life through his 'grand sacrifice', and Chitralekha's idealisation of life through death.

Redrawing the myth in his play Karnad presents Yayati's tale, a subsidiary part of the *Mahabharata*. His Yayati is a symbolic portrayal of the common man who craves for momentary happiness, enjoyment and animal pleasure with a mistaken concept to make his happiness eternal and gropes like Yayati in the twilight of a world in which the old spiritual values have been swept away and new spiritual ones have yet to be discovered. In the myth of Yayati he presents that the idea of pleasure is not always limited with sensuality and if this becomes the sole aim of a man it will lead one to degeneration. He portrays Yayati's scholarship, valour and his lust for pleasure; Devayani's egoistic, ambitious, and spiteful nature and her lust for power; Sharmishtha's romantic interests; Kacha's selfish attitude; and Pooru's estimation of values as the philosophy of life. Had Devayani become successful to marry Kacha the play would have two heroes like two heroines and the theme of man's pursuit for knowledge in love, romance and ambition would have ended in man's sensual pleasures. The conflict between Sharmistha and Devayani, Yayati and Pooru, Yayati and Chitralekha are the products of social hierarchies. While the play operates upon the binary oppositions of brahmin Devayani and rakshasi Sharmishtha; kshatriya king Yayati and his unkshatriya son Pooru the myth presents that the tenure of youth is necessary but old age and death are indispensable to enjoy the finitude of life. When Yayati realises this truth he goes into the forest to wash his sins.

The Fire and the Rain (1995) is intellectually an ambitious play of Girish Karnad. It is one of his best plays and one of the best of the plays based on myth in Indian English drama for its consummate craftmanship, displaying of powerful emotion and exhibition of the sublimal and volatile passions of men. Karnad in his creative pursuit and artistic licence likes to demolish the monolithic structure of patriarchy and casteism in the version of the myth. In the play he "constructs a story of passion, loss and sacrifice in the contexts of the Vedic ritual, spiritual discipline (tapasya), social and ethical differences between human agents..."(*Collected Plays*. Vol. II : xvi-ii). In an elaboration of myth in the play he presents the conflict between brahmin versus shudra, ascetic versus actor-performer, god versus demon, *yajna* versus *natya* and so on. But in celebration of cultic rituals he forges closer connections between his principal characters, gives them rounded personalities and inserts an unambiguous intentionality into their actions. The play presents the celebration of fire with Vedic rituals for the appeasement of the divine, and peace and happiness of the mankind. But just behind the screen of the art he associates the aesthetics of brahminism with the mind-games of egocentrism.

The play is the transcreation of his Kannada version of the play, *Agni Mattu Male*. Although the theme of the play is an approximation to the original myth it appears mindboggling as well as mindblowing when it is cinematised as *Agnivarsha* with the direction of Arjun Sajnani. Defining the title in the 'Notes' of the play Karnad counterpoints two physical elements which are normally seen antithetical. He writes in 'Notes':

> 'Agni' is the Sanskrit word for fire. And being a Sankrit word, it carries, even when used in Kannada, connotations of holiness, of ritual status, of ceremony, which the Kannada word for fire (*benki*) does not possess. 'Agni' is what burns in sacrificial altars, acts as a witness at weddings and is lit at cremations. It is also the name of the god of fire...
>
> 'Male' is a Kannada word. It means rain, pure and simple. It has none of the aura of romance, mystery and grandeur that surrounds Sanskrit words of rain when used in Kannada. 'Mattu' means 'and'. It is usually left out in spoken Kannada. 'Mattu' means 'and'. It is usually left out in spoken Kannada (63).

In the Vedic age fire was worshipped as Agnideva, the destroyer of sins, destroyer of treacherous foe, dispeller of night, discoverer of prosperity and nourishment. In Vedic tradtion Agni, the interlocutor between the human and the divine, has always been held to be sacred and it conveys human aspirations to the higher power through *yajna*. In Hindu religious belief Agni is symbolically used. The outer fire is the spiritual flame that burns in our heart. The inner fire is the blazing one that gives a spiritual spark and provides divine realisation. But in the lower dimension fire expresses insatiable desire for worldly possessions or negative aspects such as emotionally disturbing manifestations of anger and revenge. In the play Karnad deals with the higher as well as the lower dimensions of fire.

The *Vedas* define the fivefold *path:yajna* (performance of agnihotra for purification of the atmosphere), *daan* (practice of cultivating non-attachment), *tapa* (practice for fruition of aspirations), *karma* (practice for self-purification) and *swadhyaya* (practice for liberation) for a happy and peaceful living. *Yajna* is the first principle and practice ordained by the Supreme Father for the purification of atmosphere. By offering specific substances like raw rice and cow's ghee into the fire with the accompaniment of chanting *mantra* and nurturing the feeling of total surrender to the will of Almighty one removes his selfishness. *Yajna* bestows abundance and balances the cycle of nature. The performance of *yajna* creates pure, clean and medicinal atmosphere. During some *yajnas* the juice of the medicinal herb *soma* is offered to the fire which has tremendous purifying and healing effect on the atmosphere. The performance of *yajna* creates pure, clean and medicinal atmosphere. *Yajna* is the Kamadhenu, the infinite giver, worshipped with devotion using body, mind and speech. The great seer Patanjali states that *yajna* cleanses the negative effects of pollution on *prana* and relaxes the mind by unburdening if from all stress and strain. The practice of *yajna* is regarded as an alternative to the practice of *yoga* and all other disciplines aimed at liberation. Regular practice of *yajna* activates a healing cycle in nature making the plants and animals happy and peaceful. In the Vedic period 'Yajna' the fire sacrifice was organised by a king or wealthy man in order to obtain benefits like sons, cattle, postpone old age, avoid death, rain and shine in glory. The duration of the fire sacrifice could stretch over years and in the intervals only some rituals were performed. J.L. Brockington rightly remarks:

> The sacrifice (Yajna) is performed on behalf of an individual householder, technically called the sacrificer, accompanied by his wife, but all the ritual acts are performed by priests, varying in number from one to sixteen.... A special area is consecreted for each performance of ritual and the sacrificer undergoes a consecration setting him apart from the profane world. In essence, the sacrifice can be regarded as periodic ritual by which the universe is recreated, with the sacrificer like his prototype Prajapati incorporating the universe (34).

Further, M. Hiriyanna says:

> What prompted the performance of sacrifices was no longer thought of prevailing upon the gods to bestow some favour or to ward off some danger; it was rather to compel or coerce them to do what the sacrificer wanted to be done. This change of spirit is explained by many among modern scholars as importing of the magical element into Vedic religion and... as a sign of the transfer of power from the gods to the priests (16).

In the play fire sacrifice is taken as a central metaphor to underline any activity like academic study, love-making, reading of epics, marriage, etc. Fire in Indian mythology is a deity, and all Hindu rituals and rites are performed in the presence of this deity. Karnad chooses the words 'fire and rain' deliberately in the context of the myth which suggest. "the elevated and mundane" and "the sacred and the secular" (63)

Fire sacrifice is the central theme of the play. In the celebration of it the playwright presents the myth to delineate its finer issues in human actions as rewarding and regreting. He narrates his intention of incorporating myth in the play. He writes in the 'Preface' to the play:

> The myth of Yavakri (or Yavakrita) occurs in Chapters 135-38 of the Vana Parva (Forest Canto) of the *Mahabharata*. It is narrated by the ascetic Lomasha to the Pandavas as they wander across the land during their exile. I have met Sanskrit scholars who were unaware of the existence of the myth : it is easy to lose track of a short narrative like this in the tangled undergrowth that covers the floor of that epic.
>
> I first came across the story of Yavakri and Paravasu, while still in college, in C. Rajagopalachari's abridgement of the *Mahabharata*. That Rajaji was confronted with the stupendous task of abridging the world's longest epic to about four hundred pages, should not have discarded this seemingly peripheral tale is a tribute to his sensitivity and judgement.
>
> It was fortunate for me that Rajaji did not do so, for the moment I read the tale, I knew it had to be turned into a play. For the next thirty-seven years, I struggled with it, trying to fit all the ramificatious of the myth within some sort of a manageable shape (ix).

While incorporating the myth of Yavakri in the play Karnad converges the myth of Indra, the custodian of rain with it and digresses from centre to periphery to narrate the virtues and vices of life in existential human condition. Presenting the myth of Yavakri he delves deep into the Greek myth of Aeschylus's *Oresteia*. He derives the joyous genius in presenting the human frailty, divine grace, and supernatural agency that avenges.

'The myth of Yavakri' is a myth of the cosmic sacrifice of *purusha*. The myth expresses the fear of brother destroying brother and betrayals in fraternal bonding. In his creative manoeuvre Karnad turns it into "a play about sacrifice, about an overwhelming sense of loss" (*Sunday Times of India*, 14). He uses rituals as a method of self-discovery in the play. The 'Prologue' defines the background and setting of the play. It presents how ten years' rainlessness has caused ravaging draught for which the king has organised a *yajna* to propitiate Indra. The King hosts the chief priest and other priests who are engaged for the celebration of this fire sacrifice for seven years. Karnad develops the story of the play from the original myth with some digression. He presents society's age-old attitude to women, actors, lovers and low castes. In the mythical frame work of the play he reconstructs the story in three acts. He presents the two sages, Bharadwaja and Raibhya (as two friends in the *Mahabharata*), the two brothers are very learned in their respective fields of ascetic practice and learing. While Bharadwaja concentrates on his ascetic practices, Raibhya as a learned man lives with his two sons–Paravasu and Arvasu (spelt Aravasu in the *Mahabharata*). In the field of learning and ascetic practice conflict arises between Bharadwaja's son, Yavakri, and Raibhya's sons, Paravasu and Arvasu. For his learning Raibhya is respected and honoured in the society. His elder son Paravasu is invited to preside as the chief priest of the *Yajna* by the king. The respect and recognition of Raibhya and his elder son burns the heart of Yavakri who thinks that his father and he himself are deprived and neglected by the society. In anger and jealousy Yavakri nurses his grievances against his uncle. He tells about it to Vishakha:

> I cried at the humiliations piled on my father. He was one of the most learned men in the land. Probably the most brilliant mind. But he was scorned while this unscrupulous brother of his grabbed all the honours.

Reacting much to his grievances he says to her:

> What matters is that I hate your husband's family. My father deserved to be invited as the Chief Priest of the sacrifice. But that too went to Paravasu, your husband. But in the midst of my austerities I wept when I heard the news (22).

Yavakri goes off to the forest and does his 'tapasya' (penance) in order to obtain the knowledge of the *Vedas* directly from the gods. He spends ten years in the jungle and does rigorous *tapasya* for "Universal Knowledge"(9) from Indra. In order to oblige Lord Indra he practise rigorous austerities in the forest and chanted hymns. It was found:

> Yavakri stood in the middle of a circle of fire and started offering his limbs to the fire – first his fingers, then his eyes, then his entrails, his tongue and at last his heart – that's when the god appeared to him restored him limbs, and granted him the boon (9).

In order to gain spiritual powers Lord Indra persuades him to cut short his austerities and gain knowledge by diligent study and from human gurus. It is because a guru keeps the disciple is absorbed in the love of God and helps him to flourish with knowledge and diminish his sorrows. A human *guru* is a mediator who brings man and God together. A *guru* removes ignorance from one's own potentiality and can make his disciple competent and qualified to gain wisdom. Indra's advice to Yavakri to gain wisdom is marked with a purpose to light his *atman*. But Yavakri is so adamant that he likes to receive knowledge from the gods and thought that learning from human gurus is a small matter. Indra relents in his attitude and lets him have his wish which he uses to fulfil his desire instead of using it for the benefit of the public.

Bharadwaja cautionsYavakri not do run after the delusions of omnipotence. The caution of the father becomes a concern for others when Yavakri applies his Faustusian knowledge to fulfil his own motives. He is granted with the Universal Knowledge to win some "grandiose prize" (13) but he applies this to take revenge on Raibhya's family. Since women become the targets, to victimise the enemy Yavakri targets first Vishakha to penalise Raibhya and Paravasu. He thinks of his past love for Vishakha, presently Paravasu's wife and abandoned by him for seven years to act as the chief priest of the fire sacrifice. A.B. Dharwadker rightly remarks: "Her marriage itself appears to be an arid contract: after a frenzy of sensual gratification Paravasu has abandoned Vishakha to Raibhya's care and the relationship between the three are startling in their lovelessness and malevolence" (*Collected Plays* Vol.II: vii). For his bitterness with Paravasu he wants to take revenge on Vishakha by reviving her past love for him. One day he approaches Vishakha in her loneliness and stubbornly reminds her about his love for her:

> Ten years ago I had come to your house to bid you goodbye. And you led me quickly to the jack-fruit grove behind your house. You opened the knot of your blouse, pressed my face to your breasts, then turned and fled... Ten years later I opened my eyes and I knew I was hungry for that moment (14).

Ten years of rigorous penance has not changed his teenage fantasies. Vishakha objects to his desire and says that she is the wife of his elder brother now. Her husband has been acting as the chief priest of the fire sacrifice for seven years. This has deromanticised her emotion. In between time and space her "breasts hang loose now" (14) and her life has become painful. Accusing Paravasu she says that for his happiness "He used my body and his own body, like an experimenter, and explorer" (16). In her feminist assertion she criticises Yavakri's idea that "a woman is only a pair of half-formed breasts"(16).

Vishakha is left like a drought-hit land dried up without a drop of love. In her deprivation of Paravasu's love and in Yavakri's renewed access she develops her adulterous nature. Yavakri's narration of his penance for Indra's grace kindles her love and sympathy for him. She as impressed with the horror and hallucination in which Yavakri has been practising his penance with all austerities. She is surprised when Yavakri narrates before her how "One night in the jungle Indra came to me and said: 'You are ready now to receive knowledge. But knowledge involves control of passions, serenity, objectivity.' And I shouted back: 'No, that's not the knowledge I want. That's not knowledge. That's suicide! This obsession. This hatred. This venom. All this is me.

I'll not deny anything of myself. I want knowledge so I can be vicious, destructive!'"(23). He tells her again:

> ... I think Indra came to me several times, I was never certain. The first time he appeared he said, "No, Yavakri, you can't master knowledge through austerities. It must come with experience. Knowledge is time. It is space. You must move through these dimensions. I said, 'No, I must have it. Grant me all knowledge' (13).

Yavakri is anxious to sit and talk with her. Soon Vishakha becomes hungry for words. To him she says, "You are hungry for words. And so am I. So let's talk. Sit down." When Yavakri tells her that he was avoiding women for ten years because of her and Indra, the presiding deity of his life, Vishakha reveals her mind, "I live in this hermitage, parched and wordless, like a she-devil. And words are like water–precious. I was afraid to bathe. Now I want to drown. Listen to me. You went away. I was married off...."(15-16). Disclosing her mind about her husband she says:

> I was married off to Paravasu. I didn't want to, but that didn't matter. The night of the wedding my husband said to me: 'I know you didn't want to marry me. But don't worry. I'll make you happy for a year.' And he did. Exactly for one year. He plunged me into a kind of bliss. I didn't know existed. It was heaven – here and now – at the tip of all my senses. Then on the first day of the second year of our marriage... He used my body, and his own body, like an experimenter, an explorer. As instruments in a search... he did his own. I had a sense he was leading me to something. Mystical? Spiritual? We never talked. Only the sense pervaded the air.... Then one day he received the invitation from the King. To be the Chief Priest of the fire sacrifice. And he left. The site of the fire sacrifice is only a couple of hours away from here. But in all these seven years he hasn't come back.... Alone, I have become dry like tinder. Ready to burst into flames at a breath. To burn things arround me down at the slightest chance – (16).

As they fail to resist their temptation they go behind the Champak tree on the bank of the river. They do not know that they are followed by Nittilai, the tribal girl and her lover Arvasu, the younger brother of Paravasu. While following them Arvasu and

Nittilai discover Vishakha's water pot left on the ground. Peeping out of the bushes and from behind a Champak tree Arvasu and Nittilai discover the torn clothes of Vishakha and her mud–covered back. Arvasu also sees how Yavakri pickes up his *kamandalu* and goes away undisturbingly after his affair with his sister-in-law.

Vishakha's uneasy homecoming makes her miserable when she reaches her hermitage. Her father-in-law, Raibhya, sees her condition and finds Arvasu carrying the water pot on his shoulder. He mistakenly thinks that Vishakha and Arvasu have developed their relatiohship as her husband has been away for seven years. Raibhya, the thin and emaciated old man, though physically active is infuriated in their supposed honour killing act and grabbing Vishakha's hair starts beating her mercilessly. Raibhya is mad with anger. As Arvasu comes to her rescue he says. "I want the truth and I'll kill her if necessary" (20). When Vishakha reveals the truth, he loses his Brahmanic patience and curses her and Yavakri for their misdemeanour:

> You whore – you roving whore! I could reduce you to ashes – turn you into a fistful of dust – with a simple curse. But let that husband of yours handle you. Paravasu, Chief Priest of the sacrifice! Let him clean up his own shit! Yavakri – So this is what ten years of austerities amount to! So be it. So Yavakri, now it's between you and me (20).

Vishakha's feminine soft-heartedness, love for Yavakri and fear for violence make her weak. She says: "No, please! don't do anything to him. It's my fault... I'm willing to face the consequences – punish me. Not him. Please" (20). Without thinking wisely about the consequence Raibhya starts his meditation and opening his eyes he says:

> Vishakha, go and tell your lover I accept his challenge. I shall invoke the 'Kritya' and send a Brahma Rakshasa, a demon soul after him.Let Yavakri save himself. He need only to and hide in his father's hermitage. I loved my brother and will not desecrate his altar. Let Yavakri cower in there like a dog. If he steps out, he will be dead. Tell him this, too – that if he can manage to stay alive for another twenty-four hours, I, Raibhya, shall accept defeat and enter fire (20).

With Raibhya's invocation 'Kritya' appears. Kritya, the Brahma Rakshasa, is a cursed brahmin soul caught in the emptiness between death and rebirth. His feet never touches the ground, only flies in smoke and disappears in flames. It appears from one strand of Raibhya's hair and from the other strand appears a woman exactly like his daughter-in-law. The Brahma Rakshasa appears almost naked, thin, and holding a trident run in the direction of Yavakri to destroy him. But Yavakri has preserved the consecrated water in his *kamandalu* for his safety as this would neutralise the Brahma Rakshasa and make him powerless. When Vishakha informs him through Arvasu of the consequence, he says, "I'm not here to run away—I've triumphed over Indra, the lord of Gods"(24). But to his misfortune the woman in the form of Vishakha enters Yavakri's hermitage and seductively pours the consecrated water from his *kamandalu*. With this Yavakri becomes more vulnerable to danger. As soon as the Brahma Rakshasa appears he discovers to his misery that the *kamandalu* has become empty. He starts running towards a lake in search of water but it dries up. When he approaches his father's hermitage and tries to enter it the guard Andhaka, a blind man of shudra caste, prevents his entry. In the meantime, Brahma Rakshasa kills him.

The death news of Yavakri is conveyed to Bharadwaja by Andhaka. The old father breaks down in distress. Although he knows that his son is to blame for molesting Raibhya's daughter-in-law he cannot check his anger against Raibhya's sending of Brahma Rakshasa to kill his son. In anguish and pain he curses Raibhya to die at the hands of his elder son. But, later, he realises that he has cursed his brother and in shock he immolates himself and ends his life.

In another part of the myth Raibhya's elder son, Paravasu, is conducting the fire sacrifice for rain. One night Paravasu returns home despising the austerities at the *yajna* site. When his father asks him about the cause of his return before one month of the end of the fire sarifice he explains to him that it was only for his blessing. Raibhya warns him that it is not the ethics of the chief priest to come back home before the completion of the *yajna*. He tells him that it is a deliberate denying of gods.

Raibhya apprehends that Paravasu's sneaking out at night from the *yajna* site would not only displease gods but also help them to retaliate for any loss. He is very much disturbed for

Paravasu's violation of *yajna* rules. He suspects that Paravasu is either thrown out of priesthood or he is disturbed by his wife's reputation. He does not like Paravasu's seeking of his permission to talk with Vishakha. He thinks it might be due to Vishakha's fornication with Yavakri or for his emotional acrobatics in a moment's imagination.

Paravasu knows that he has been invited and offered the job of the chief priest for his knowledge and for his father's old age. The king knows that this job for Raibhya would be difficult for its lengthy time. Seven years is a long time for Paravasu and Vishakha. The time and space between them test their life. Paravasu comes back from the *yajna* site affecting the greater cause for his personal cause. Similarly, after his ten years of penance Yavakri comes back with Universal Knowledge but with little wisdom. He goes to Vishakha with an oblique motive to avenge on his father's enemies. Vishakha is forced under certain conditions to come closer to Yavakri. As Arvasu is often remaining out and she has to stay with her father-in-law alone, she narrates her agony to Paravasu:

> Something died inside your father the day the King invited you to be the Chief Priest. He's been drying up like a dead tree since then. No sap runs in him (pause). On the other hand, there's his sense of being humiliated by you. On the other, there's lust. It consumes him. An old man's curdled lust. And there's no one else here to take his rage out on but me. (pause). At least Yavakri was warm, gentle. For a few minutes he made me forget the wizened body, the scratchy claws, and the blood, cold as ice. And he paid for it with his life (32-33).

This reveals Vishakha's mind as a devoted wife and dallying beloved. D. Maya rightly remarks, "Vishakha's willing surrender to Yavakri is more an involuntary submission to the demands of the body than act of love (71-72). If marriage for a woman is mandatory, motherhood is a dream, and a forced celebacy compels her to be a living corpse. Vishakha knows that her expectations are in a morbid state. She looks back to her past for at least a streak of happiness in life with Yavakri.

Vishakha prays to Paravasu to liberate her from such hellish life by making her a sacrifice for the *yajna*. Paravasu realises that both Yavakri and his father are led on the same blind fury by the forces of jealousy. He feels suffocated, loses his patience and shoots an arrow in the darkness which killes his father instantly. Bringing an end to Vishakha's humiliation he says to her, "He deserved to die. He killed Yavakri to disturb me in the last stages of the sacrifice. Not to punish Yavakri, but to be even with me"(33). But to Arvasu he explains, "In the dark, I-9 mistook him for a wild animal–"(34) and advises him that "There's no time to howl and wail now. I have to get back before I'm missed. If anyone gets wind of what's happened here, the fire sacrifice is ruined"(34-5). He consoles him not to brood like a child but to arrange for the cremation of their father. He says,

> We must atone for Father's death. I know I should perform the rites of penitence. But I have to return. Immediately. So there's only one person who can do that. You. As his son, it's your prerogative and your duty (35).

As the elder son of his father Paravasu has to perform his cremation and penitential rites. But he leaves everything for Arvasu. While he is walking away through the jungle the Brahma Rakshasa appears before him and requests for his liberation and new birth to "human life" (36). The Brahma Rakshasa identifies himself as his father's brother and seeks his liberation with these words:

> ... after my death I was not reborn, as any ordinary mortal would do. I became a Brahma Rakshasa. A soul locked in nothingness like a foetus stitched up inside its mother's sac. You can't imagine the horror of that existence. Nothing to look forward to : no birth, no death, nothingness stretching endlessly. Your father plucked me out and put me back in time, in order to kill Yavakri. I didn't want to, but I obeyed. And as a result, now I have something new. Hope. Of release – release from this state – (36).

He requests Paravasu, "Free me from this pain. Liberate me. I want to fade away"(36). His prayer for *moksha* reveals that the *asuric* spirit seeks liberation in the hope of getting satisfaction in human life but in contrast to this in the human world men with knowledge and power like Bharadwaja, Raibhya, Yavakri and Paravasu become asuric for their jealousy, anger, lust, gender and caste biases, and ignorance. Ironically, when the human world craves for immortality (that invites suffering), the Brahma

Rakshasa's *asuric* spirit seeks death and finale release for mortality that provides happiness in life.

In the finale part of the myth Karnad analyses the Hindu concept of the origin of *varnas* and jealousy in brotherhood. Arvasu returns to the fire sarifice after performing his father's penitential rites. But as soon as he reaches there his brother's attitude surprises him. He is surprised that the man who has "been a mother, father, brother, nurse, teacher – everything rolled into one"(8) can be so cruel and harsh to him. Paravasu accuses him before all, a stranger, a criminal of patricide and called him a demon who desecrates the sanctified precincts. Apprehending some danger for *yajna* the king orders his servants to throw Arvasu out of the sacrificial enclosures. Arvasu's protesting shouts of his innocence is heard by none.

Betrayal in brotherly relationship is common in the divine world as well as in the human world. Karnad writes in 'Notes' about this in the myth of Indra:

> In the *Rigveda,* Vritra, 'the shoulderless one' (a serpent) swallows rivers and hides the waters inside him. Indra, by killing him, releases the waters and 'like lowing cows, the rivers flow out'. The importance of this deed to the Vedic culture is borne out by the epithet, 'Vritrahan' or the slayer of Vritra, by which Indra is repeatedly hailed.
>
> In the later version of the myth, Indra is anxious that Vishwarupa (also called Trishiras, the three-headed one), son of Tvastri, may dislodge him from his throne. He therefore destroys Vishwarupa treacherously. Tvastri then gives birth to another son, Vritra, by a female demon, and tells him: 'Kill Indra'. Indra unable to overcome the new enemy, again has to resort to ignominious trickery to survive. Having killed Vritra, he suffers from the guilt of Brahminicide (68).

Digressing from this original story of the myth of Indra-Vritra Karnad incorporates the myth of Yavakri with his two cousins – Paravasu and Arvasu. He writes in 'Notes' about the variation of the original myth :

> The tale of Arvasu and Paravasu fascinated me as an unusual variant of this Indian obsession with fratricide and

> it seemed logical too that Yavakri should be their cousin, though the *Mahabharata* does not explicitly say so.

Being fascinated with this myth he writes about his self-reflexivity:

> A myth seems complete in itself and yet when examined in detail, contains subconscious signals which lead you on to another myth which in turn will act as a conduit to a third one while illuminating the one you started with (69).

Converging the Indra-Vritra legend in the central episode of Paravasu-Arvasu Karnad makes the play a complex framework. He deals elaborately with the plot of Arvasu's betrayal by his brother Paravasu. D. Maya rightly remarks on the betrayal of Paravasu:

> Myth becomes ritual and performance and performance doubly reinforces the myth as Karnad casts the betrayed brother Arvasu in the role of Vritra, the betrayed brother of Indra, in the play within a play. Arvasu, who had always worshipped his brother as a father figure for his superior intellect and great scholarship, is shattered by his brother's rude condemnation in public when he goes to the sacrificial site after performing the penitential rites for patricide on behalf of Paravasu. Paravasu, the worshipped, infallible brother, thrusts the heinous sin of patricide onto his innocent brother's shoulders and asks the others to throw him out as a demon encroaching into the sacred site (70).

In the play the horrors of myth is softened with the final result of *yajna* when Lord Indra is pleased to bring "an end this long draught which ravages our land" but the priests of the fire sacrifice say, "a sacrifice doesn't have to be so dreary" (2) and "A play has to be performed along with it. If we offer him (Indra) entertainment in addition to the oblations, the god may grant us the rains we're praying for"(3).

As the archetypal myth echoes the brothers' self-annihilation through overweening arrogance Karnad introduces the real motive of myth that provides values, morals, happiness and peace. In the Arvasu-Nittilai episode he provides lessons to the caste-ridden societies where Brahminism in its superior caste consciousness dominate over the low-castes. It seems that Karnad blasts at the Vedic concept of brahminic superiority for their birth from Brahma's mouth and for the origin of Shudras from his feet. Transgressing these disparities Karnad presents Arvasu-Nittilai relationship which faces obstacles from two sides. Arvasu seeks his brother's permission who prevents him to do so for his caste superiority. Similarly, the elders of the tribal community prefer Nittilai's marriage to be done according to their custom. As per the tribal custom "The elders will gather under a big banyan tree and ask few questions" (5) which Arvasu has to answer and declare before the public, "I want to take her as my wife. I am potent. I can satisfy all her needs..." (5). Nittilai's father was very conscious about the high caste male psyche who seeks pleasure by sleeping with their low-caste women but refuse tc marry. Like every father of a marriageable daughter he called the village council immediately. Nand Kumar rightly remarks, "This conviction of a mythical father closely resembles the thinking of the father of a low-caste beautiful girl of the so called civilized society of today" (161). Arvasu expressed his love for Nittilai before Paravasu. He said,"I can't give up Nittilai. She is my life. I can't live without her—I would rather be an outcaste..."(8). As Paravasu forbade this kind of marriage Arvasu failed to appear before the village council. This annoyed the village elders and Nittilai's father. Expressing his regrets to Nittilai's brother he says:

> I'm afraid my father was a little hasty. But he was tired of waiting. He felt angry, humiliated. 'This daughter of mine has made me a laughing stock in the eyes of the world,' he said, 'I'm willing to marry her off to anyone who'll take her'. Fortunately, it was a nice young man, one of our relatives, who stepped forward. Nittilai will be happy. Console yourself with that thought (27).

Arvasu is fed up with his caste that invites his frustration. That caste in which he is trapped has taught him anger, jealousy, enemity, knowledge but little wisdom. He likes to shun it as it has taken away all his happiness. He thinks it a great conspirator that has betrayed him. Karnad focuses that in the caste hierarchy individuals have their paradigmatic struggles. Arvasu's relationship with Nittilai poses an antithesis to the performers of Hinduism – Raibhya, Paravasu and Yavakri. He loses Nittilai because of his inability to abandon orthodoxy at a crucial moment of his life's decision making. It is obvious that his relationship with Nittilai splits between nature and culture, humanism and Brahminism, othodoxy and ascetism.

On the closing day of the fire sacrifice many people wait at the outskirts of the city for the concluding feast. Among them are mostly the starving villagers, Nittilai and her husband wait for this. Arvasu also lives in the outskirts of the city after his expulsion from the sacrificial enclosure. Knowing about his presence there Nittilai comes to share her love and sympathy to him. She tells him,"When I heard what'd happened to you... I almost died when I heared they'd thrashed you. I got up and ran all the way here"(41). In replay Arvasu says, "my brother knew I would marry you even if he forbade it" (43) and expresses how his brother is responsible for his failure to marry her. He tells her "I'll avenge myself on him" because "if such an evil man continues as the chief priest of the sacrifice, it'll rain blood at the end" (43). With love, fear and expectation of impending danger on Arvasu's life she tells him:

> Leave that to the gods, Arvasu. Look at your family. Yavakri avenges to his father's shame by attacking your sister-in-law. Your father avenges her by killing Yavakri. Your brother kills your father. And now you in your turn want vengeance—where will it all end? (45)

This shows that in spite of her birth in low caste Nittilai has her worldly wisdom. The ordinary in her appears extraordinary for her understanding of virtues like love, grace and dignity. Her feminine grace and understanding eclipse the halo of high caste's glory and quest for knowledge when she says:

> Arvasu, when I say we should go together—I don't mean we have to live together—like lovers or like husband and wife. I have been vicious enough to my husband. I don't want to disgrace him further. Let's be together—like brother and sister. You marry any girl you like. Only please, Arvasu—spare a corner for me (42).

In the portrayal of mythical Nittilai Karnad demolishes the *varna* system of Hindus which establishes the myth that superior caste means superior knowledge. Karnad "like an iconoclast" (Kumar 172) presents that those who are even created from the feet of the

Creator can think better and act better than those who are born from the mouth of their Universal Father.

After the fire sacrifice and towards the end of the myth Arvasu retires to the jungle and prays to the sun god. When the gods appear before him, he asks them to restore Bharadwaja, Raibhya and Yavakri to life. He prays to the gods to make Paravasu forget his act of betrayal. The gods grant him the boon and reprimand Yavakri on his folly, and ask him to pursue knowledge in the right manner. But in the play, a theatre group is ready to stage a play at the end of the *yajna*. The Actor-Manager has set all the things ready to stage a play, *The Triumph of Lord Indra* before the king, the priests and the people. Karnad has arranged a play within a play in an attempt to contextualise two myths: the myth of Yavakri and the myth of Indra. Transporting us from mythical world to artistic world he forges the two myths in order to make us understand the divine and human qualities.

In the proposed play Arvasu is to perform the role of Vritra with the desire of the Actor-Manager as this character needs to dance more which can only be done by Arvasu. The Actor-Manager will play the role of Indra. When the show begins there is a struggle between Vritra and Indra for which Arvasu has masked his face with Vritra's. In order to keep himself undiscovered from Nittilai's brother and husband he has also camouflaged his body. Although Nittilai hides herself after running away from her husband she does not like to see Arvasu perform the role of Indra. She says:

> He (Indra) is immortal. When someone doesn't die, can't die, what can he know about anything? He can't change himself. He can't—create anything. I like Vritra because even when he's triumphant he chooses death. I always wonder—if the flowers didn't now they were to fade and die, would they have ever blossomed? (51-2).

As the play begins in the 'Epilogue' Arvasu performs a violent dance wearing the mask of Vritra. He gives a wild roar with the sound of the drums and jumps up to the stage. The Actor-Manager dressed up as Indra enters from other side. But Vritra embraces Vishwarupa (the role played by another actor) in the play. It reveals that Indra is the first son of Brahma who has the desire to rule over the three worlds. He establishes his personality to rule over *swarga, martya* and *patala*. But Vishwarupa, Brahma's second son, and Indra's human brother, is born by a human womb. As he draws praises and admirations in the human world Brahma makes him the king there. Seeing this Indra feels threatened for Vishwarupa's rising reputation and thinks that his sovereignty over the three worlds is endangered. Brahma had also mated with a woman from the nether world, a demoness, and had his third son, Vritra. He had made Vritra the king of the nether world and had also advised Vritra to protect his human brother Vishwarupa by risking his life if it would become necessary.

Now, Indra being jealous of Vishwarupa's rising reputation, plans to kill him. In order to materialise his plan he organises a fire sacrifice in honour of his father Brahma. He invites Vishwarupa to the sacrificial enclosure. When Vritra follows his human brother for his protection, Indra says, "No, Vishwarupa, You are most welcome, but Vritra, who is accompanying you, may not enter the sacrificial precincts... he is a demon, a Rakshasa. His mother was a demoness and demon blood flown in his veins"(54). He explains to Vishwarupa about the ritual sanctity, rigidness of the sacrificial precincts and prevents Vritra's entry with the plea that it will desecrate the place. As Viswarupa enters the enclosure believing Indra he instructs Vritra, "You wait here outside the enclosure"(54). But Vritra knows about Indra's nature. He warns Vishwarupa, "Brother, my father gave me life so I could protect you. Let me come in with you. This Indra is treacherous..."(54). Vritra's caution comes true when Indra strikes his thunderbolt on Vishwarupa's back. When Vishwarupa screams Vritra comes to his rescue and says, "I must put an end to this conspiracy"(56). He tells Indra, "You can elude me Indra, but you can't escape me. Even if you fly like a falcon across ninety nine rivers I'll find you. I'll destroy you. I'll raze you befouled sacrifice to the ground"(57). Thus, playing the role of Vritra, Arvasu challengers Indra (the Actor-Manager). He surprises everybody by chasing Indra. The Actor Manager tries to restrain him but Arvasu becomes demonic. The audience believe that the mask has come alive, the human has become demonic and the scene is lost in insanity. It seems, "Arvasu becomes Vritra the demon in search of vengeance. Arvasu's earlier mask of deference and obedience is now replaced with a realistic representation of an actual empirically verifiable reality outside the literary text" (Nair 247). Seeing this Nittilai comes out of her hiding place and rushes to take off Arvasu's mask, and throws it away. When Nittilai's brother and husband step out to bar him on his way he makes an angry declaration: "I am a Brahmin. If you try to stop me. I'll kill myself. And the sin of killing a Brahmin will be on your heads. I am a Rakshasa! and I'll kill anyone who tries to stop me..."(57). This declaration still expresses his male and Brahminic ego. This reveals that Arvasu has learnt less from the follies of his Brahminic trait. Nittilai tells him, "I'm sure your dancing will bring the rains"(52) but she fails to enjoy it as her brother knocks Arvasu down and her husband slashes her throat with a knife. Nittilai dies like a sacrificial animal. In shock and agony Arvasu stares at her. It is felt as if his insanity is over with Nittilai's death. Meanwhile the voice is heard from the skies. Indra says, "Arvasu, son, do not grieve. We are pleased with you. Ask for any boon and it shall be granted"(59).

In grief and sigh of relief Arvasu thinks of asking for the restoration of Nittilai's life. But the Brahma Rakshasa implores him that his father had given him life and he is now to release him from bondage. He reminds Arvasu, "If Nittilai lives again, she'll live a life as tormented as mine—tormented by the knowledge that her resurrection condemned me beyond salvation. And every moment of her life, she'll hear my screams. What you are asking for is not a boon. You are asking Indra to condemn Nittilai to hell-hole much worse than the one I'm in"(61). Arvasu thinks that mercy and love will triumph and prevail at the end. He implores Indra to release the Brahma Rakshasa who vanishes in a flame with a scream. While Arvasu holds Nittilai's corpse in his hands and calls it in delusion it starts raining. The nature and her creatures enjoy the smell of the wet earth in happiness. Arvasu still calls Nittilai sitting by her dead body, "It's raining, Nittilai! It's raining!"(62). The playwright presents Arvsasu's reason to sacrifice the particular for the general that evokes the spirit of humanism. In fact, the Nittilai–Arvasu episode presents that Nittilai loses her life because she can not resist her human impulse for the sake of Arvasu and Arvasu relinquishes Nittilai for the common good. On the other hand, "Arvasu's identity as actor further complicates the treatment of brahminism, because in terms of both origin and practice theatrical performance complements Vedic ritual and has a place within it, although the professing of acting is particular to the shudra caste" (Dharwadker Vol-II: xix).

Karnad uses "myth for the purpose of social change and amelioration of the low-caste people" (Kumar 177). Dramatising the caste structure in the myth he demolishes it in his contemporary perspective. Concentrating on the role of caste in life he contrasts the life of discipline and sacrifice with the life of instinct and emotion. In the portrayal of Vedic society and men of knowledge he presents how caste consciousness causes social instability, jealousy, anger and avenging spirit. He condemns caste and ridicules its proprietors. Making modern approach to myth he analyses its social, religious and philosiphical aspects. Conveying the two myths in the play he presents the fear of brother destroying brother. He writes in the 'Notes' of his play :

> This fear branches out fully and nakedly in the *Mahabharata,* where the bonding of brothers within the Pandava and the Kuru clans is close as the enemity between the cousins is ruthless and unrelenting. In the *Ramayana,* the fraternal bonding in the Raghu family – Rama and his brothers – expresses another facet of the same anxiety, with the betrayals of Sugriva and Vibhishana (Interestingly in the cause of the ethically correct side) marking the counterpoint (68-69).

Karnad analyses power, love, lust and sacrifice in the paradigms of myth. Presenting the suffering of women like Vishakha and Nittilai he castigates gender bias in Hindu society where woman is reduced to sexual exploitation. Rama Nair remarks, "The fire of passion, lust, revenge and betrayal consume both good and evil. The flaming hostility between the two cousins, Paravasu and Yavakri, scorch and lives of all principal characters. The dramatic action moves between of two opposing polarities of Yavakri's vengeance and Arvasu's humanity"(Nair 243). To conclude, it can be said that Karnad in his dramatic possibilities on a little-known myth from the *Mahabharata* has exposed the universal themes of love, lust, power, tension, loneliness, betrayal, murder and seduction with philosophical underpinnings.

Karnad's *Bali: The Sacrifice* (2004) is the translated version of Girish Karnad's Kannada play *Hittina Hunja.* It is an ethical thesis of some philosophical hypotheses that questions the validity of rigvedic practice of animal sacrifice in Hindu rituals. While dramatising this in tragic rehearsals of animal sacrifice he presents

India's conflicting religious and cultural ethos. The play was finalised when Karnad was at Nehru centre, London and was performed at the Hay Market Theatre, UK in 2001. It presents how the individuals often fall prey to the conflict between their private and public selves. In its mythological super structure Karnad projects myth as a support to the dimensions of social life. During the Vedic period animals were slaughtered as offering to gods. This tradition was in vogue for many centuries. Later, when Jainism and Buddhism got separate indentities from Hinduism both the Jains and Buddhists found that slaughtering of animals as offerings to gods as repugnant. In course of time brahmin priests too renounced the practice of animal sacrifice. This steadily promoted individual's belief in non-violence violence which remained as a hidden motif in human psyche. Although the brahmins and Jains renounced blood sacrifice in order to propitiate their deities, miniature figurines made of dough were made as substitutes for live animals and sacrifice for the same purpose. This led to the conflict between two beliefs – violece and non-violence between Hinduism and Jainism.

Selecting an ancient Jain myth of the thirteenth century Kannada epic *Yushodhara Charite* by Janna which refers back to a ninth century Sanskrit epic *Yashastilaka* by Somadeva Suri Karnad offers a fresh perspective on rational, social, moral and religious structure of individual's faith in his private involvements in love, sex and passion for the gratification of his public life. In an interview to Tutun Mukherjee the playwright says:

> *Bali* worried and excited me. It is a discussion play that interrogates the notion of "violence" and is based on a thirteenth century Kannada epic, "Yashodhara Charite", which refers to various other texts dating back to the ninth century. It deals with the idea that violence is pervasive, laying just beneath the surface of our everyday behaviour and is often masked by a conscious effort. It also posits that human thought, intention and action are all interlinked. It debates the jain notion that intended violence is as condemnable as the action itself. The mere thought of bloodshed or brutality can condemn one as much as the deed would. The play debates the conflict of faith (49).

In its social, moral and cultural ramifications the play presents a great philosophical thinking on the Indian tradition and idealogical contents about values, moral conflicts and dilemas.

Dramatising this ritualistic practice of bali he presents human passion for love and perjury, and makes an attempt to wash away the sin in the demonstration of replacing the "actual violence with the violence in intention" (*Bali: The Scrifice* 69). Putting the Hindu and Jain faiths *vis a vis* in a hyphenated and debatable hypothesis he points out that if one resorts violence to purify the soul from moral debauchery in Hindu conviction, the Jain position condemns the actual violence to evade the effect of a sublimal act of moral crime. Karnad has drafted the tale version of the myth with niggling alterations. He presents his debates over the conceptual merits of violence and non-violence in a complex negotiation of ideologies of the characters. On the other hand a discourse on the play reveals the conflicting religious beliefs in Jain and Hindu religious philosophies. It presents the gap between ideal and the moral. Infidelity is forbidden and non-violence is promoted in every religion. The myth presents infidelity at the centre of the plot. But dealing with infidelity the playwright expresses his concern how a religion that promotes violence to preserve the halo of its sanctity and the other favours non-violence at the cost of morality.

The play becomes a site for struggle between personal authority and popular culture of cruelty. There are four characters in the play. They are the King and the Queen, the Queen Mother and the Mahout. In an unbelievable situation Queen Amritamati (literally means one of the life-giving elixirs) is swayed away from her royal self to a relegated one for her sexual gratification. The Queen is under the public pressures to commit the debauchery for her procreation. Her self is divided in an existential dilemma. While surrendering her private self before the public self she deviates from her royal stance for an emotional relief to secure her social position. In her self assertion she seeks freedom from the cultural domination, defamation of barrenness, and suppression of her sophisticated public self in her search for the Mahout, the elephant keeper, a cultural 'other' who provides her psychological, emotional, conceptual and physical happiness at the cost of her ethical elitism. The Mahout, an excellent singer, appears as "ugly as a bendicoot" (75). He was born on the day of lunar eclipse when the beneficial powers of god were weak and his mother was in terror as a snake had crept into the nest of a sparrow and had gobbled up its eggs in their house. Yet he is a bohemian, masochist, good lover and very decent man towards women. In his socio-cultural 'otherness' he never thinks of sneaking into the sophisticated world of the elite class where their elephants don't mind his ugliness but the Queen takes him as the forbidden fruit in her romantic enchantment. Karnad presents him as the most intriguing figure of all for his character and symbolical significance. He says in an interview:

> The mahout is the catalyst who releases the repressions of the different characters in the play, especially the Queen. He is ugly and crude but that does not matter to the Queen. She is seduced by his music and in forgetting all inhibitions and barriers of decorum, commits adultery in thought even before their physical union. Likewise, she is shocked to realise that, not necessary through explicit behaviour, one can be violent in intent or thought. Her violence is aroused when the cock of dough that she had been caressing like baby is snatched from her and the entire edifice of her ideology crumbles (Mukherjee 50).

In Karnad's Biblical motif she loses her royal paradise in her strange imagination,"I was just a women, any woman" (87) and requests the Mahout to call her "Kamalata-Surasundari" (76) to have his sexual favour with a desire to keep the roryal family tree alive. She likes to end her existential struggle in her emotional surrender to the Mahout.

The Queen is sophisticated in her royal glamour, yet primitive in her passion and instinct. She loves her royal identity, but struggles to dispel its vain glory embedded with superstition, orthodox practices and belief in cruelty. She loves the heavenly voice of the Mahout and appreciates it more than his physical beauty which the handsome commander-in-chiefs lack in her army. She knows that the Mahout is a moron but he has a "heavenly voice" (78) and desires to enjoy his company for his voice. She narrates her sorry state of affairs, "I live surrounded by such men and I am sick and tired of them" (77). She has spent her life in the midst of flatterers who always flatter her without love. This is the reason why she is appreciated falsely, in public life and insulted in private life for her miscarriage. Now her "fickle womb" (115) struggles for a liberation from sterility in defiance to her royal position and is drowned in guilt and sin. She translates her mind about the crime before the King very confessionally:

> I was sleeping by your side. His signing woke me up. The song was so—don't know how to describe it. But suddenly the notes caressed me, enveloped me. They carried me away. For a brief moment, nothing mattered. The place. Me. You. Only the song. I felt like a flame burning bright. Pure. When I came to my senses, I was here. By his side. That's all there is to it. It just happened (119).

She knows that her desire for motherhood will remain unfulfilled with the King. Being torn between her existence and essence in life she surrenders herself to the man, a cultural nether. Now she feels fuller, richer and warmer. She is not ashamed of her act as it was not planned by her and it was just a passion. She likes to see no tongues wagging against her in the palace and in the kingdom. She has the desire to see the entire kingdom burst into festivities with the news of her pregnancy. She knows that she was in despair for motherhood, and the Mahout's song mesmerized her superior self and feminine weakness. Mahout's music brought her into the temple of an absent deity. Her attraction for Mahout's song by passed her reasons of royal glory to get involved with this "savage ape", and the "ugly beast" (121). The King realises the Queen's desire for motherhood at the cost of her royal honour and the personal ethics. In an attempt to save her from public humiliation she wilfully involved herself in infidelity.

The King and the Queen have married for 15 years but remain childless. The royal couple are under tremendous psychological pressure for a heir to fulfil their duty to the kingdom. The King is devastated when he discovered his Queen involved with an elephant-keeper. He loves the Queen even after her committing the crime and pleads with her at least to be true; "we are coupled in the eyes of God. We need not be ashamed of anything. We must strip ourselves of any sense of shame. Become naked like our Saviours" (120). The Queen is unaware of the fact that the King has followed her up to the temple after her escape from the palace. The King has followed her and is sitting on a shock stupor at the temple. Ironically he sits alone on the steps and is heaving out painful sighs while the Queen is in love making with the Mahout. She is also unaware of his presence inside the temple when the Mahout deliberately produces sounds of love making to send away all unwelcome strangers. In a dream reality the King narrates his suffering like a common man before the Queen:

> At midnight, he (the Mahout) started singing in a distance. I felt you wake up. I felt you slide out of my bed. You got up. Left. I opened my eyes, saw you press yourself against the window and listen. And then slip away. I followed. Through the biting chill and you didn't even have a shawl on....You went out of the royal garden... into the street. You entered this ruined temple. The singing stopped. Those noises. Those horrible, animal noises from inside. (101-102)

As the Queen keeps her intention secret from the King she keeps her identity secret from the Mahout. Even the Mahout doubts her before their recourse of love and tells her, "such long nails. You are no bazaar woman, I can see that. You are from the upper floors. And you haven't done a day's work. That's for sure. Those nails are for a dainty life" (78). The Queen wants herself to be a nameless woman at least for that night before the Mahout. The aesthetics of Mahout's heavenly voice makes the Queen hysteric. She abandons her personal ethics to get merged with Mahout's aesthetics. She dares the devil reputation with a passionate heart. She praises the Mahout, "Nobody has ever talked to me like you have" (82). She speaks to him what should not be spoken to. She narrates her "beautiful" (119) moment with the Mahout. The Mahout appears to her as the *primordianpurusha* through whom she needs to keep her family tree alive.

The King follows the Queen into the garden and then into the temple. He watches her morbid interest there in a sordid sight. He discovers to his surprise that there is "sin in the inner sanctum" (85) of the temple. As he knocks at the door he discovers the Mahout coming out, touches his feet and pleads with an alibi that he had come to sleep there since a bat had entered into the elephant stables. The situation becomes more difficult for the Queen. She comes out from behind the pedestal. Pushing back the veil from Queen's face the King says in despair, "I'm concerned about you. You about him" (87). In this delicate situation the Queen bribes the Mahout with her jewellery and persuades him to leave the place. The Mahout refuses to avoid further disadvantages. In his existential anguish the king threatens him to establish his own rights of authority. Ironically, the Mahout denounces the King's patronage and says that his pomp and power in social life without him is meaningless. He says, "people mock at Mahouts. 'Call us low born'. But where would all your princes and Kings be without us. I want to know. What would happen to their elephants? No elephants. No army. No pomp and splendour. No processions. No king!"(80). He reminds the King about his elmentary contribution to the royal glory and reputation.

The Queen Mother discovers her son in a distraught state in the garden. She asks him about his condition but the King fails to keep his intention secret. He finally confesses the truth before his mother, "Around midnight, I had a dream. It woke me up.... I saw that the royal swan in our garden had got caught in mud and was flapping its wings" (103). For this he came out of the palace to help the swan as it was caught in the mud and crying out for help. Symbolically the King explained his mind about the loss of sanctity of the royal dynasty when Queen got involved in the muddy affair of adultery with the Mahout for pocreation. He is shocked that the Mahout has clipped the royal swan by abusing its royal majesty. The Queen Mother displays her horror over this degeneration of royal line, and decrees for the sacrifice of hundred fowls in order to satisfy the parched throat of her goddess and effect absolution for the sin committed by the Queen. The Queen Mother believes that the Queen will inflict an evil-impact upon the well-being of her son and the kingdom. The Queen Mother believes that the desecrating of royal dynasty can be purified only by the sacrifice of blood. But for the Queen the horror of the rite of sacrifice is in no way less than the horror of her perjury that affects King's megalomaniac authority. With the King's persuation the Queen Mother agrees to sacrifice an inanimate object (a cock of dough) for the absolution of the family, and propitiation of the evil potent that has besieged the Queen. The Queen Mother appears to be the playwright's personification of the continuing belief in *bali* which is the culmination of all worship, and a means to achieve something in life.

The King as a Jain lacks conviction in the killing of animals in sacrifice to propitiate the divine. He thinks that a religion that promotes *bali,* the bloodshed as a purificatory is bound to leave the lasting impact on the young minds. His mind is obsessed with the belief in the ritual which jainism rejects. But between the two beliefs he is torn fore his love for his wife and allegiance to his mother. The Queen Mother's goddess, a typical Hindu deity, is attired in silk robes, eats chicken, is thirsty for blood and marries as a living being. The King's acceptance of Jainism, his wife's religion for its principle of non-violence, appears debatably doutful for him. It cannot be said that by renouncing Hinduism the King has become a Jain every inch. For example, his decision and action appear conflicting in dual ideologies. When he perceives that the Queen is involved with the Mahout, in an unguarded moment, being a Jain he draws out his sword to kill the Mahout. Again he epresses his helplessness before his mother's decision to organise the sacrifice of hundred fowls. His helplessness doubles when the Queen makes an open declaration to relinquish him and go to the Mahout. In willing suspension of his reasons in Jainism and surrender to his belief in Hinduism he makes a compromise. His existential struggle between traditional practice and ethical essentiality compels him to negotiate between his private and public selves. He can neither bear nor tolerate Queen's acts of infidelity, nor can he accept his mother's ideas of sacrifice for his own mental peace. He is in a quagmire of his existential dilemma whether to support the Queen Mother for her readiness to celebrate a violent practice in order to satisfy her goddess for the prospect of a grandson, or deprive the Queen of her rights for her cardinal sin.

The Queen Mother opposes her son's conversion to another faith and his denial to her worship. She thinks that her son is under the influence of the Queen. She thinks that a mother is the well wisher of her son and has every right to celebrate *bali* and perform the rite to cure her son for a grandson. She likes to see her family tree bloom and glory spread. If the King desires to achieve this blessing through his mother by celebrating the ancient culture, it becomes difficult for him to deal with the nurturing of Jain culture and tradition of his wife that removes his intention of violence. Sacrificing life for the sake of life is unethical in his ethical consciousness. He says "... I am a Jain. My son will be a Jain—a Jain King. I cannot have his birth greeted with infliction of death" (98). With a nauseating feeling towards bloodshed in sacrifice he promises the Queen, "there will be no blood sacrifices in honour of our child" (97). On the other hand the Queen Mother thinks infidelity a kind of epidemic that will affect her generation, and therefore prescribes the offering of bloody sacrifies to suppress the evil and clean the mud from the royal swan. In order to avert the disaster and propitiate her deity she asserts her right, "I shall offer the goddess a hundred fowl in sacrifice" (105).

The personal relationship between mother and son, and husband and wife is greatly affected by their existential dilemmas. They fail to choose between the moral and the essential. Each one has a suffering in his / her belief and decision. The Queen Mother accusess the King of betraying her and his religion for his love for the Queen, which is a common feature in the filial relationship. She accuses him of submerging his kshyatriya antecedents in a self-willed amnesia. His obligation and allegiance to his religion and family tradition are greatly affected by his loyality to his wife and to her religion. But the Queen Mother thinks it a loss of his royal tradition. The King's suffering becomes acute with his mother's accusation:

> You're treating my goddess as though she were a cheap, tribal spirit... you were not born a Jain. You were born my son. But you betrayed me and my faith. In stead of choosing the woman and bringing her to your fruit. Instead of choosing the woman and bringing her to your faith, you choose hers (98).

The King fails to provide justice to his mother and wife in his existential dilemma. On the one hand he thinks of his mother's irrational pleading for sacrifice to propitiate the divine; on the other he cannot imagine his Queen's demonic zeal to drown his family's name and fame like a harlot "lying between someone's thighs" (107). In despair he observes his mother's reaction when she says, "Kill the harlot and her lover. If you won't do it, I'll do it. Let me fetch my sacrificial knife from the temple. I'll..." (107). With the Queen's perjury the King feels as if his puffled royal profile has vanished and private ego is deeply hurt. Even his mother says, "you have lost your manhood" (107). In existential dilemma between wife's quest for sensual pleasure and mother's quest for a strange spiritual satisfaction he fails to conquer the real. In utter helplessness he sighs, "Is there no way to escape this hell?" (106). Through him Karnad projects the rationale of *bali,* If sheep, goats, buffaloes and human beings are sacrificed for sins graded in their intensity, how can the same act of committing a sin evade another sin? It will earn no result for a nation like India where the spirit of religion is often relegated and rituals are highlighted in individual's belief in superstition and personal ego. Karnad has used myth for integrating religious communities, sects and beliefs for nation building.

No religion has place for violence. Hinduism is marked with its superstitious rituals like *bali*. In the later stage of Hinduism brahmin priests conducted animal sacrifice, like the horse, the ox, the sheep and then the goat, and finally the rice-cake as offerings to gods. Even the Jains were repugnant to the practice of *bali*. To the Jains any kind of violence, minor or accidental, forfeits one's moral status as a human being. The Buddhists also joined in this philosophical standpoint. Although violence has been the central topic of the debate in the history of Indian civilisation the Jains propagate non-violence and Gandhi turns it to a political philosophy. It abhors the killing of animals to propitiate the divine. In a multi-cultural and multi-religious country like India it is a hard and vibrant issue to negotiate between violence and non-violence. The King is caught in the crossfire between two religions—one is the root and the other is the shaddy foliage. He stands between the two women—the mother, the nurturer of his life and symbol of past tradition, and the wife, the source of his supraconsciousness, his inspiration for future humanity. Both wield power and that makes him powerless. He can neither support his mother because her only solution is to sacrifice the live animals to evade the evil, nor can he support his Queen for her insisting that the Queen Mother's intention is a direct provocation to her belief.

Every woman desires to achieve motherhood. No woman irrespective of her class consciousness can escape from this cosmic truth. Similarly, in Indian perspective no mother likes to see her son go heirless. Now neither the Queen nor the Queen Mother are free from their philosophical standpoints. The King in his willing suspension of belief accepts his mother's advice and persuades the Queen for the act of *bali*. The Queen in her childlessness is compelled to negotiate with her mother-in-law's religious belief. In this context Sumita Roy writes, "But now she is no longer willing to do this because now she has a powerful tool in the shape of her pregnancy which she will wield in order to negotiate with the King and get rid of her rival" (287). The Queen Mother exonerates the King and he agrees to her mode of sacrifice in a compromise for no bloodshed as "A symbolic gesture" (111) to satisfy the bloodthirsty gods. As the King says, "We're going to have a baby" (94) and "I cannot have his birth greeted with infliction of death" (98) the Queen Mother tries to convince him to make the sacrifice, at least a bloodless one, of a cock of dough as a mark of penitence to blot out the disgrace brought on by the Queen which seems like a "witchcraft" (105). The King as the upholder of justice and believer in the principle of compassion and non-violence declares that "there will be no blood sacrifice in honour of our child" (97). The Queen Mother gloats in her happiness and says, "you have made our family tree bloom. May you beget a son whose glory blinds the eight directions .... I must go to my shrine and celebrate" (94).

The play deals with the Queen's adultery. The King, the Queen Mother, and the Queen are divided in their opinions over the related issues to adultery. The King stands in the middle of the battleground where his wife, a believer in non-violence, and his mother, a compulsive perpetrator of violent sacrifice are confronting each other. The King stands in between as a sacred sacrificial beast with his ideas of tolerance just for effecting a balance between his mother and his wife. As a renouncer of Hinduism and pronouncer of Jainism he maintains the hyphenated position between his distraction and attraction of two divergent ideologies. While negotiating between religious philosophies the dramatist deals with the social, cultural, religious and psychological aspects of the King in which he attempts to achieve his completeness. They are in their existential dilemmas in the Nietzschean sense, and struggle to their best abilty to survive in love, honesty, truthfulness, faithfulness, loyalty and sacrifice. The Queen compromises between her royal past and altruistic present in her hysteric pursuit of a less idealistic love which is necessary for her family free. The Queen Mother compromises between her own tradition and her son's talent of non-violence. The King negotiates between the ethics and ideology, faith and fanaticism, belief and beauty in the aesthetics of religion, tradition and talent, consciousness and supraconsciousness, and humiliation and humility.

One is confined to his socio-cultural parameters. Whatever good or bad, a person never gets ready to accept a faith or philosophy. Often a compromise becomes necessary between the divergent ideologies and faiths for the greater interest of humanity. But Karnad is very skilful to deal with the agony and anguish of his characters in the mythical structure of the story. The marriage of true minds faces the impediments for different religious and cultural practices. One cannot surrender before the other but one can be convinced to merge with the other for the greater interest of the humanity. Merging together of two beliefs is often negotiated. Karnad brings out this truth both in the Indian and in the cosmic perspectives. The King's initiation to Jainism may be a personal gain of the King for his love for the Queen but it is an emotional loss for a mother. It is a great sacrifice of a mother for the cause of the humanity. She spits her anger on the Queen for her adultery. No religious belief permits perjury. It is not her authoritarian attitude but an attempt to preserve her family purity. In anger and despair she tells the King, "feed her to wolves and vultures" (107). She understands her son's mind when he says, "whatever's happened, concerns me, my wife. And I need her (Anguished). I can't let her go" (109). The King and the Queen Mother negotiate over the sin committed by the Queen. All the three are compelled to do this for a successful heir. The King and the Queen accept the unacceptability that even they have the conflict between self and soul, ethics and essentiality, virtues and visions, *dharma* and *karma*. In contemplation they compromise, in confrontation they surrender and in assertion they justify views, vices, ideology, ethics and celebration of blood. The Queen declares, "Ours son will be a Jain. He will have to uphold the principle of compassion for all living beings, of non-violence. Should we allow a blood rite to mark his arrival? It would be wrong. Terribly wrong!" (97). Analysing her philosophy of non-violence Karnad writes in the 'Preface', "if intended violence condemns one as surely as actual violence, that is, if one is morally responsible for merely intending to commit an act one has not actually carried out in real life, is one not shutting oneself up in a solipsistic world, a bleak, guilt-ridden existence with no hope for absolution?" (70).

The Queen is portrayed with her turbulent inner self. She takes the side of the Mahout in his encounter with the King. In spite of fervently believing that the King is a wonderful person, a loving and generous husband she cares him much with her genuine love. She begins to negotiate herself with the issue of fidelity in her marriage and humiliation of childlessness as a frustration that causes her to indulge with the Mahout. Their meeting and ensuing togetherness in illicit encounter raise questions about negotiating the space between private idealisation and public appreciation. As her identity is meaningless without any progeny she negotiates with her ethics. Her ideology must cater to the needs of mankind. She is restricted both at the private and public fronts but fails to revolt and negotiates with Queen Mother's wrath and King's right to become a father. As the Queen Mother comes with "... the ritual materials like flowers, saffron, myrrh and camphor stands a life size replica of a cock with its head raised and beak open, as though it was crowing" (110) the Queen agrees to the sacrifice of the dough cock. Both the King and the Queen agree to the sacrifice of the dough cock. The King and the Queen go forward for the sacrificial ceremony. Now the King persuades her for the ritual involving the killing of the cock of dough, a totem. The King places her hand on the hilt of the sword and they advance for the sacrifice to cleanse their sins through this "Divine Bird" (123). He declares "Let the whole world see. We are coupled in the eyes of God" (120). Karnad makes the myth a magic as the cock begins to crow during their performance of symbolic sacrifice for the well being of their child and kingdom. They are startled at the sound of the cock and wonder in horror what to do and stop plunging the sword into the dough-cock. The dough cock's crow symbolise the rise of a new dawn and suggests that even inanimate objects contain life. The pause helps the Queen to rethink this act of sacrifice which means to damn herself as an adulteress and she "...presses the point of blade on her womb and impales herself on the sword. Collapses into his (King's) arms. The King holds her uncomprehending, listening to the cock's crowing. It's dawn" (124). The Queen punishes her evil womb through her act. But Karnad allows the audience to think this non-violence as the intended violence in the symbol of the dough-cock that begets violence.

The sacrifice of dough cock is considered harmless and is followed through rituals with total conviction. It is not intentionally directed against the Mahout or the Queen. Yet the question which troubles the audience is that if compassion and non-violence go hand in hand for a Jain, can the Queen remain true to her faith in Jainism at the time of King's intense agony? One can argue that the Queen has taken a wrong step by betraying her marriage vows. Karnad has beautifully drafted out the inner self of the Queen. The King is agonised for his Queen's perfidity and his mother's confirmity. He brings his private affairs for public affirmation. The Queen Mother makes fun of Queen's non-violent stance and taunts her that if she is against the shedding of blood, she should have remained a virgin. She thinks her sterility is a divine punishment and chastisement for the Queen's defiance and wickedness. The King also believes that Queen's sterility is due to his mother's wrath and says, "if we had listened to mother we may not have lost our child" (113). The Queen defends her position in self-assertion, "Late in my life, I became pregnant and I have a miscarriage—and you are saying that was a punishment meted out to me for my defiance" (113). However, one observes that the three think differently and they are responsible in different ways for the family's devastation. Karnad impresses upon the audience that "tradition can be given up, or at least changed" (96) in our accepted ideologies and beliefs which is necessarily extended and undesirably restricted to our practices. It is significant that Karnad begins and ends the play with the cult practices in pain, duress, sacrifice and bloodshed which inextricably connect with the process of creation. This truth of cosmic design cannot be negated by those who believe in non-violence.

The play is a thesis of tradition in the devastation of a royal family. One can understand it through a discussion of God, religion and culture. Karnad uses the context of the play with a hint at a positivist and inclusivist possibility of all ideologies and necessary human bonds in human relationship. By way of exploration of philosophies Karnad tinges myth in conjugal life of a royal family with divergent religious beliefs, cultures and historicity of practices. It is about numerous interesting possibilities often refusing the illicit relationship that undergoes terrible ordeals in the form of one's psychological suffering. In this context Shalini Umachandran rightly remarks:

> It's a play about a conflict of beliefs. The Mahout is not merely the reason for the queen's transgression, he symbolizes the belief in a listening, logical God. The queen believes that salvation comes from living a life of compassion, and the queen mother follows a goddess who needs to the satiated with blood to be benign. In between is the king who has forsaken the faith he grew up into embrace Jainism and is now torn between guilt and confusion about the right path (*The Hindu*).

Apart from the cultural and religious implications infertility, miscarriage and violence are the thematic constituents embedded in the myth that dominates the play for the cause of chastisement, curing sterility and wickedness. From the philosophical standpoint the miniature figurines are there as the substitutes for live animals in the continuing practice of non-violence. Even though no animals are slaughtered and no meat is consumed in the play these figurines of dough, the mimicking form of real animals obviously carry the original impulse of violence within them. The Jain faith defends this not as a solution in one's survival strategy. Karnad makes a strange paradox of *bali* which is synonymous with a person's sacrificing of another living being to propitiate the divine and giving up something as a prize which the King does with his religion for his love.

In the successful draft version of the myth Karnad negotiates between the culture and needbased ideology in their functional relevance and philosophical thinking. The play evokes some practical wisdom in Indian tradition, in individuals' existential dilemmas and moral conflicts where truth of irrationality in family life is marked with contextual overtones. The play deals with the validity of crime like infidelity and celebrating *bali* for the atonement of sin as existed and practised in contemporary Indain society. The practice of *bali* in the religious institutions was initiated by the brahmins. Karnad denounces this practice in individual's belief and practice for supplication for and explication of his faith.

Analysing myth at the centre and morality at the periphery Karnad projects the psychological suffering of religious believers in their quest for identity and aspiration for life's plenty. In existential dilemmas they assert their personal reason and practical wisdom of life as if they donot know 'life is a tale told by an idiot signifying nothing'. Karnad believes that non-violence in Jain faith and in Gandhian ideology is necessary for the cultural and political survival of India. As the history of Indian civilisation is overflowing with numerous religious reformations Karnad goes a step forward to propagate in favour of a reformation in conservatism and change in ideological preoccupations. Aparna Dharwadker rightly remarks, "Karnad has shown us how the matter of myth and legend resonates in modern experience, and how the past history of the nation prefigures its present. The intuitive intensity of such a method should be the reason for appreciation, not devaluation" (*Collected Plays*. Vol. I : 87). In his heuristic attempt Karnad dramatises the perpetual battle between religions, ideologies and practices of cults in an individual's consciousness and ignorance. Delineating the sufferings and dilemmas of individuals in their existential realities he resonates the Gandhian ideology that violence cannot earn victory, and no ideology is insular in a multicultural and multi-religious country like India. Thus with his clear understanding of the existentialist and essentialist positions of his characters in the myth Karnad dramatises them with new orientations in the polarised forces of orthodoxy and heterodoxy in the pan-Indian situation.

Summing up myth in Karnad's plays it is observed that *Yayati* is the dramatisation of individual's elemental passions for sensuality and power. Dealing with the theme of love, friendship, sensuality, youth, and old age the playwright glorifies the Existential Philosophy in individual's performance of duty and acceptance of responsibilities. *The Fire and the Rain* highlights the theme of quest for knowledge and its result without wisdom, fraternal jealousy, relevance of patience and tolerance, religious philosophy, caste consciousness, social customs and convictions in the Myth of Yavakri, the Myth of Agni and the myth of Indra. *Bali*: *The Sacrifice* presents religion and culture of a society that safeguard a person from the corroding influences of life. But in the hope of keeping the family tree alive the members of the royal family sacrifice their religious faith and ideologies in their conflict between two religious faiths.

Works Cited

Babu, M. Sarat. "A Psycho-Cultural Study of Karnad's Plays". *The Plays of Girish Karnad*: *Critical Perspectives*. Ed. Jaydipsinh Dodiya. New Delhi: Prestige Books, 1999.

Brockington, J.L. *The Sacred Thread*: *A Short History of Hinduism*. Oxford.: OUP, 1992.

Childs, Peter & Roger Fowler, ed. *The Routledge Dictionary of Literary Terms*. London and New York: Routledge, 2006.

Dharwadker Aparna Bhargava. "Introduction" to Girish Karnad's *Collected Plays* (Vol. II). New Delhi: O.U.P. 2005.

Gopinchand, P. and P.N. Suseela. "Cultural Nuances in Karnad's *Bali*: *The Sacrifice*". http://www.kritya.in/0301/En/name of poetry, html, 20/05/08, 1-4.

Goyanka, Jayadayal ed. *Samkshipta Mahabharat* (Adi Parva). Gorakhpur: Geeta Press, 1986.

Hiriyana, M. *The Essentials of Indian Philosophy*. London: George Allen and Unwin, 1949.

Karnad, Girish. *The Fire and the Rain*. New Delhi: OUP, 1998 (All textual references are made to this edition).

______________ . *The Dreams of Tipu Sultan* and *Bali: The Sacrifice*. New Delhi: OUP, 2004 (All textual references are made to this edition).

______________ . *Collected Plays* (Vol. I). New Delhi: OUP, 2005.

______________ . (Interview) "In his Own Voice: A Conversation with Girish Karnad". *Girish Karnad's Plays: Performances and Critical Perspectives*. Ed. Tutun Mukherjee. New Delhi: Pencraft International, 2006.

______________ . *Yayati*. New Delhi: OUP, 2008 (All textual references are made to this edition).

Khandekar, V.S. "Introduction" to his novel *Yayati*. New Delhi: Orient Paperbacks, 2008.

Kierkegaard, Soren. "That Individual". *Existentialism from Dostoevsky to Sartre*. Ed. Walter Kaufman. N.Y.: New American Library, 1975.

Kumar, Nand. *Indian English Drama*. New Delhi: Sarup and Sons, 2003.

Maya, D. "Karnad's *The Fire and the Rain*: A Return to Indigenous Tradition". *The Literary Criterion*. Vol. 36; 4, 2001.

Murthy, Anantha, Prasanna and Girish Karnad. "Girish Karnad, the Playwright: A Discussion". *Indian Literature*. 38:5 (September–October), 1995.

Nair, Rama. "Ritual as Self-Discovery in *The Fire and the Rain*". *Girish Karnad's Plays: Performance and Critical Perspectives*. Ed. Tutun Mukherjee. New Delhi: Pencraft International, 2006.

Paul, Rajender. "Girish Karnad Interviewed". *Enact*. No. 54 (June), 1971.

Rajagopalachari, C. *Mahabharata*. Bombay: Bharatiya Vidya Bhawan, 1951.

______________ . "Karnad's Heart of Darkness and Light" in 'Book Mark'. *Sunday Time of India*. Nov. 27, 2005.

Roy, Sumita. "Negotiating Ideological Spaces: Reading *Bali: The Sacrifice*". *Girish Karnad's Plays: Peformance and Critical Perspectives*. Ed. Tutun Mukherjee. New Delhi: Percraft International, 2008.

Sartre, Jean Paul. *Existentialism and Humanism*. Trans. Philip Mairet. London: Methuen, 1970.

Shankar, A. *Bharat Jyoti*. Sunday 11 March, 1962.

Suneel, Seema. "Karnad's *Yayati* Reconsidered". *The Plays of Girish Karnad: Critical Perspectives*. Ed. Jaydipsinh Dodiya. New Delhi: Prestige Books, 1999.

Umachandran, Shalini. "Powerful Plays". *The Hindu*. December 5, 2004.

3 Aesthetics in Folktales

Folktale is a specific genre found in the oral tradition and written form of a community. It expresses the primitive mentality of the people and their unified perspective of caste, class and gender. This is generally a literary form of the non-literary masses. Although in its later development there came legends and myths, folktales have some specific and linear differences from them. Both folktales and myths are male constructs and they deal with the natural and cultural phenomenons of a society. Folktales are patriarchal constructs and deal with the public culture of a region. They represent "primarily the male unconsciousness, fear and wishes" (Ramanujan 1994:12). Folktales neither adequately express inner feelings and experiences of women nor provide enough information about women's fears, anxieties and psychological problems. In folktales the voice of women and children is not recognised. They narrate the episodes of power games and real politik of joint families where the wonderful fantasies of women in different positions and their secret subterranean family life is expressed. Folktales have primarily a verbal composition and flourish through oral stories, jokes and varieties of word play among the people who mostly cannot read or write. Though its authorship is not known it transmits orally the human emotions, feelings, shocks and experiences with contemporary relevance. The households and domestics tell it for their repertoire about animals, jesters, men, women, fools, wisemen, different castes and occupations of people.

In Indian household folktales are not only told to make children eat more or put them to sleep but to keep the adults awake. It establishes an oral tradition to understand the treasures of cultures for the larger masses, mostly the illiterates. Folktales are potent enough to psychoanalyse the insights of the young and provide a psychological education to the young children. In India folktales generally deal with the ancient tales from the *Panchatantra*, the *Kathasaritasagara*, the *Jatakas*, and Hindu and Jain *Puranas*. They have often mythical elements and myths have also some folklorish elements. Folktales neither have strong contexts nor do they have strong elements of arbitrariness and universality like myths. Though they contain some elements of myth they do not have mythical dimension. They are devoid of religious meanings. Folktales are often called "folk mythologies or folk puranas" because they deal with the gods and divine agents who have their bodies without bodily functions. In human affairs practically they take part in rivalry, incest, betrayal, cruelty, forbidden feelings and ordeals of life in localised and domesticated matters. A.K. Ramanujan rightly remarks in his 'Preface' to *Folktales From India*: "A folktale is a poetic text that carries some of its cultural contexts within it, it is also a travelling metaphor that finds a new meaning with each new telling." In folktales everyday common incidents relating to human beings, animals and supernatural figures are expressed in fiction. In a sense folktales are the cultural artifacts which present the monolithic structure of the human mind.

Like myths folktales are of unknown authorship which have been transmitted orally and many of these tales have eventually achieved written form. Each folktale is interpreted in a particular way in a localised culture or dialects but it expresses a new aesthetic of meaning or cultural values. It is found that "Folktales include legends, superstitions, songs, tales, proverbs, riddles, spells, and nursery rhymes; pseudoscientific lore about the weather, plants, and animals; customary activities at births, marriages, and deaths; and traditional dances and forms of drama performed on holidays or at communal gatherings". (Abrams 105). Materials from folklore have been employed in traditional theatres. Using the folk elements in his plays Girish Karnad presents them in contemporay Indian situation. He has used his indigenous knowledge with the rich sources of folktales and folk beliefs which are kept alive by the rural folk and folk performers like Yakshagana, Bayalata, Bhavai, Nautanki, Terakooth, Veethinatakam, Ottandhullal, Chhau, Pala, etc. These folk performers make the people from rural and city areas realise the importance of folktales in social life. Through songs, music and dance, "They have also been the vehicles of expression of protest, dissent and reforms, the carriers of reform movements and the articulators of satire and social comment and thus the instruments of socio-cultural change" (Vatsyayan 3). Selecting a few folktales from national sources and regional sources he presents the function of various folk elements and their values in our social and civilisational space. In the dramatic performance of folk elements he presents the forces of nature, role of gods and goddesses, cosmic forces, and magic with satire, comment and influence on human life. In the dramatisation of folktales he applies his concepts in participatory and spontaneous reaction. Karnad's use of folktales are based on traditional beliefs and practices, and they carry the answers to contemporary socio-cultural problems and inequalities in terms of caste, class, gender and exploitation. Apart from this they establish the interdisciplinary study of religious, ethnic, cultural and various other aspects of life. The audience discover their own problems in the interpretative and presentational possibilities of his folk plays. The audience either fail to negotiate or overreact to certain extents with the incidents in them and make them realise in their mundane life. Aparna Bhargava Dharwadker rightly remarks, "The ideology of urban folk drama thus manifests itself most consciously in the treatment of femininity, sexuality, desire, and power; although the challenge to patriarchy is not absolute, women in folk drama find the means of exercising an ambivalent freedom within its constraints, unlike their urban counterparts..." (Vol. I: xxix).

Karnad reworks with the folktales which are quintessentially a new trend in Indian English drama. In the presentation of tradition and convention in Indian social life he revitalises them for the better purpose of human life. In the dramatic paraphernalia of his theatrical devices and use of masks, half-curtains, improvisation, music, mime and magic or miracle his folk plays present 'magic realism' upholding the nativce tradition. In choice of theme and treatment of magic realism upholding the native tradition. In choice of theme and treatment of magic realism he enunciates his ideas of contemporay reality which are essentially post-colonial. In treatment of folk elements he takes up the problems of identity crisis and individual's split persona. In his conscious attempt of manipulation of folk elements in his plays he associates them with Bertolt Brecht's notion of 'complex seeing', and mixes the high and low, superior and subaltern, human and non-human, and presents them in human characeristics. His plays present the 'charismatic realm of folk culture'. His folk elements have also useful pedagogical material. The use of folk elements are a part of his naturalistic theatre, and they evolve the aesthetic purpose of life while they speak enough to contemporary audience. As a social-realist Karnad presents the reasons and relevance of folktales as metaphors of humour life. Using the local and folk devices within the classical framework he generates opposing interpretations of the texts and discovers the world of the human and the non-human, the ordinary and the extraordinary, the narrative and the transgressive in "creative co-operation" (Kermode 19). Folklore is generally religious and often based on animism because the primitive imagination it carries extends its vision from the natural, in which it is steeped and with which it is saturated, to the supernatural, which to the folk mind is only an extension of the former. Folk belief, besides, being naive, has a touch of poetry about which works towards a psychic adjustment. Karnad rightly remarks on the folk theatre:

> The energy of folk theatre comes from the fact that although it seems to uphold traditional values, it also has the means of questioning these values, of making them literally stand on their head. The various conventions—the chorus, the masks, the seemingly unrelated comic episodes, the mixing of human and non-human worlds—permit the simultaneous presentation of alternative points of view, of alternative attitudes to the central problem. (*Three Plays* 14).

The folk tradition is inherent in the tradition of dramatic conventions. Karnad's plot and structure is derived from the folk tradition and therefore the elements of subversion and reflexivity are integral to his drama. The folk mind is syncretic rather than analytic. It absorbs all experience, and the sum total of it all is life, and the folk theatre presents such life.

Folktales are localised in a definite culture and dialect and carry the sign meaning for the national and international viewers. In them, "The signifiers, whether they are images or characters or episodes, or even so-called structures and analyses may be the same in different periods and regions, but the signification goes on changing"(Ramanujan 1994: xix). Using the folk elements in theatre is not new in India. In 'Bhasa' literatures there are good number of plays written on folk elements. In Indian English drama Girish Karnad uses these elements as powerful instruments for his plays. He says, "The energy of folk theatre comes from the fact that although it seems to uphold traditional values; it also has the means of questioning these values, of making them literally stand on their head" (Jain 2000:191). Reworking with myths in his plays like *Yayati, The Fire and the Rain* and *Bali: The Sacrifice,* Karnad has presented the human predicaments in epic grandure. But in *Hayavadana* (1970), *NagaMandala* (1985) and *Flowers: A Dramatic Monologue* (2005) Karnad has reworked with the folktales of Karnataka with new meaning and contemporary relevance. While transforming the oral environment to the presentational form on the stage Karnad popularises them with the narration of human predicament. Of course, for this he was highly influenced by the Natak Mandalis, Yakshaganas and Bayalata in his childhood, that further helped him to continue research on them in the writing of his plays.

After the treasure trove in Indian myths in his plays Karnad has made his creative trajectory into the folktales of India. Past always stands as an important aspect in Karnad's plays.' His importance on past is revealed through his research in history, myth and folktales. Reworking on them in the zest of a researcher and taste of a dramatist Karnad projects his contemporary reality in them. While history and myths have importance for their truth and universality, folktales are no more less important in their use as they evoke enough meaning for children and illiterate masses, and contribute to the study of society, culture and human psyche. *Hayavadana* (1970) is one of the best plays of Girish Karnad based on the sixth story of *Vetal Parchavimshika* which includes 25 stories in Sanskrit about King Vikrama and Vetala, and Somadeva's *Brihat Katha-saritasagar*. Karnad had also the privilege to go through Thomas Mann's story, "The Transposed Heads", which he makes as the archetypes for the story of his play. Introducing the theme of incompleteness and an individual's yearning for completeness and perfection from Mann's story based on *Vetala Panchavimshika* and *Kathasaritasagar* Karnad continues his discourse on individual's 'primary identification' and 'secondary identification' in the play.

Karnad draws his source from Thomas Mann's story and *Kathasaritasagar*, and has reworked on them in the plot and sub-plot of the play. "The theme of the play is an old one... man's yearning for completeness, for perfection. It's this yearning which makes people restless in this ordinary existence, and makes them reach out for extraordinary things.... But the idea of perfection itself is ambiguous" (Gandhi 68-69). He weaves the stories for his plot narrating the existential condition of his characters and their absurdity of desire for completness. Mann's story reveals that:

> The world is not made that spirit is fated to love only spirit, and beauty only beauty. Indeed the very contrast between the two points out, with clarity at once intellectual and beautiful, that the world's goal is union between spirit and beauty, a kind of bliss that is no longer divided but is whole and consumate. The tale of ours is but an illustration of failures and false starts that attend the efforts to reach the goal (Mann 168).

Kirtinath Kurtkoti writes in his 'Introduction' to the play:

> The plot of *Hayavadana* comes from *Kathasaritasagara,* an ancient collection of stories in Sanskrit. But Karnad has borrowed it from Thomas Mann's retelling of the story in *The Transposed Heads*. The Sanskrit tale, told by a ghost to an adventurous King, gains a further mock-heroic dimension in Mann's version. The original poses a moral problem while Mann uses it to ridicule the mechanical conception of life which differentiates between body and soul. He ridicules the philosophy which holds the head superior to the body. The human body, Mann argues, is a fit instrument for the fulfilment of human destiny. Even the transposition of heads will not liberate the protagonists from psychological limits imposed by nature (V).

In the main plot there is the story of the transposition of heads and in the sub-plot there is the story of *Hayavadana* ('haya' means 'horse', and 'vadana' means 'face') which means a horse faced man. Karnad reworks with the stories analysing the importance of body and head. He tells in an interview with Tutun Mukherjee about his discussion with Karanth on the absurdity and aesthetic purpose of the transposition of heads and its possibilities:

> I had told him the story of 'The Transposed Heads' and wondered if we could make a film. The tale from *Vetal Panchavimsati* had been used by Mann to address the question: after the heads have been attached to wrong bodies who would be considered the woman's husband? The tale answers that since the essence of a man is represented by the head the husband's head will identify the husband. Mann continues the logic to its ultimate end that since the head is the man, the bodies transform themselves to fit the heads so that men become exactly as they physically were at the start of the story. So the woman's problem remains unresolved....That's when the plot of *Hayavadana* began to take shape in my mind (Mukherjee: 38).

His introduction to the character Hayavadana is out of the discourse on head and body that ends in assertion and ambiguity. The theme initially interested him because it is about head and heart, psyche and body. Inventing the plot from the folktales Karnad heavily draws the rich sources of his native folk theatre and employs them in his play with ethical and psychological hypothesis.

Karnad uses the device of folk-theatre which frames "a world of inarticulate and non-human beings who create a typology of functional characters" (*Daedalus* 82). Weaving the folk forms like masks and music, stock characters and talking dolls in the convention of 'urban folk plays' he deals with the problems of human identity in a naturalistic way. Introducing an indigenous folk-form he critiques the mainstream culture in a classical framework and narrates the philosophical riddles about the nature of identity in the parable of conjugality and accidental disruption of human limbs. Karnad's ideology of folk drama manifests in the psychosexual relations of marriage and femininity, sexuality, desire and power. His woman protagonist takes an independent decision of choosing the head that rules the limbs and establishes the personal identity transgressing the constraints of patriarchy. We may call it woman infidelity and amorality. But the theme of the play determines the choice of head and body which have universal implications and complexity of choice between the two. While these body organs serve the purpose to fulfil individual's quest for completeness and identity, Karnad presents their absurdity and aesthetism in the portrayal of his characters. He writes in "Author's Introduction" to his *Three Plays*, "This is why characters in *Hayavadana* have no real names. The heroine is called Padmini after one of the six types into which Vatsyayana classified all women. Her husband is Devadatta, a formal mode of addressing a stranger. His friend is Kapila, simply 'the dark one"' (13). Refering to head and body which are necessary for human identity in the story of the play he writes about the simple riddle:

> A young woman is travelling with her insecure and jealous husband and his rather attractive friend. The husband suspecting his wife's loyalties goes to a temple of Goddess Kali and beheads himself. The friend finds the body, and terrified that he will be accused of having murdered the man for the sake of his wife, in turn beheads himself. When the woman, afraid of the scandal that is bound to follow, prepares to kill himself too, the goddess takes pity and comes to her aid. The woman has only to rejoin the heads to the bodies and the goddess will bring them back to life. The woman follows the instructions, the men come back to life—except that in her confusion she mixed up the heads. The story ends with the question : who is now the real husband, the one with the husband's head or the one with his body? (12-13).

With the introduction to the transformation of heads of two different bodies Karnad follows a technical device to make inanimate into an animate, natural into the supernatural, rational into ethical, and mystical into the magical. In the main plot he gives the complete picture of human beings and their quest for perfection. This illustrates modern man's universal predicament and existential dilemma in his choice for head or body. In the sub-plot, "The device of folktale helps the playwright in transcending the limitations of time and place" (Goel 1999:209). With his superb and ingenious skill Karnad employes the conventions of folktales and motifs of folk theatre through masks, curtains, mime, songs, the commentator-narrator, dolls, horseman, the story-within a story facilitating the mixture of human and non-human to create a queer magical world. The play focuses a realm of incomplete individuals, magnanimous gods, of vocal dolls and mute children, a world of longing and frustration, ecstasy and misery of human being.

The play focuses that human body has a composite structure of different organs. But of all its beauty, charm and physique it has a complex structure of mind and emotion. Both the stories the playwright incorporates in the play deal with the shape of body and scope of mind. In Mann's story Shridaman and Nanda are two bosom friends. Although Shridaman is a Brahmin by birth and Vaisya by profession, Nanda is a cowherd by birth doing the work of a blacksmith. While the two friends are travelling together Shridaman sees a girl Sita and falls in love with her onesidedly. Nanda takes it lightly and laughs at his friend because he had already fallen in love fifteen times before. But this time Shridaman is serious in his love for Sita. He engages Nanda to act as a messenger of love for him. With Nanda Shridaman sends his proposal to Sita who accepts him as her husband.

In her traditional role playing "Sita is married to Shridaman, who is cerebral, delicate, and sensitive, but she feels an intense physical attraction for his friend Nanda, who is visceral, strong, and emotionally crude" (*Collected Plays* Vol. I : xxv). A few days lates Shridaman, Sita and Nanda a travelling to the house of Sita's parents by a cart. Unfortunately they lose their way in the forest and arrive at a Kali temple. As they halt there Shridaman is overpowered by his devotion for Kali and goes inside the sanctum to express his obeisance. Beset with in a strange and incredible urge he offers himself to the deity by sacrificing his head. When he is late Nanda goes in search of him and finds his friend's body inside the sanctum. He is terribly shocked at his friend's death thinking that Sita would charge him of murdering him in order to win her. At the loss of his friend and fear of Sita's probable charge Nanda kills himself there with the same sword. Losing her husband and his friend Sita finds herself in wilderness. In frustration and helplessness she blames her fate and makes up her mind to hang herself there. But Goddess Kali grants life to the two dead bodies with a diretion to her to join their heads. But in excitement Sita fixes the heads on wrong shoulders. It poses a problem for her as to whom to acept as her husband. When the advice of hermit Kamdaman is sought for Sita's problem his decision goes in favour of Shridaman's head. The body with Nanda's head decides to become a hermit. Sita lives happily with Shridaman for some time but pines for Nanda. She is not able to forget Nanda and goes in search of him into the forest with her son Andhak. Sita finds him in the forest and stays with him for a night. Next morning when Shridaman arrives there he quarrels with Nanda. They fight and kill each other. With their death Sita thinks of performing *sati* to improve her image and the image of her son. She enters the funeral pyre of Shridaman and Nanda and performs *sati*.

The second story that the playwright incorporates from *Brihat Kathasaritasagar* is quite similar to the story in *Vetal Panchavimshika* with few alterations in place names, and names of the characters and their castes. It deals with the story of prince Dhavala who has married Madansundari, the daughter of King Suddhapata. The marriage of Dhavala and Madansundari is performed in the temple of Gouri in the city of Shobhavati. Once Svetapata, the son of King Suddhapata is going along with his sister and her husband to his own country. On the way, while they come across the temple of goddess Gouri, Dhavala goes to pay homage to the deity. In devotion and irresistible urge he sacrifices his head to offer it to the goddess. As he is late Svetapata goes inside the temple, and he finds that Dhavala has cut off his head and offered it to the deity. Svetapata also followes the path of Dhavala. When the husband and brother of Madansundari sacrifice themselves before the deity for their own causes and reasons she takes the decision to sacrifice herself before the deity in shock and grief. Goddess Gauri appears before her and preventes her from doing this, granting life to the two deceased persons. She asks Madansundari to fix their heads on the respective shoulders. In the hurry and excitement she fixes the wrong heads on them. But soon she realises her mistake that raises the questions on individual ethics and problem of incest which Vetala asks King Vikram,. "Who is Madansundari's husband?" The King answers, "Of course the person with Dhavala's head on his shoulders".

Karnad begins the story of his play where Vetala's ends. He develops it with few alterations. Drawing the theme of completeness and question of identity from two stories he presents the part of the human body, "what is considered the best in man, the Uttamanga, the human head" (Kurtkoti vi). The play begins with the Sutradhara, Bhagavata, like the stage manager in classical Sanskrit drama who invokes Lord Ganesha, the destroyer of obstacles, remover of all hurdles and crowns all endeavours with success. Lord Ganesha is called in many popular names as

Vighneshwara, Vakratunda- Mahakaya, Lord and Master of success and perfection, Image of purity and holiness, and Mangalamoorty signifying an "embodiment of imperfection, of incompleteness" (1). He is a paradoxical symbol of identity with the elephant's head on the human body, a broken tusk and a cracked belly, one who sits on a mouse, decorates himself with a snake, and the husband of Riddhi and Sidhi. He has a crooked face and a distorted body. In spite of these disparities in his physical features he is worshipped for completeness and perfection in life. Being engrossed with the Ganesha myth and engaging Bhagavata to communicate between the divine and human the playwright writes 'Author's Introduction' to his *Three Plays*:

> All theatrical performances in India begin with worship of Ganesha, the god who ensures successful completion of any endeavour. According to mythology,Ganesha was beheaded by Shiva, his father, who had failed to ercognize his own son (another aggressive father!). The damage was repaired by substituting an elephant's head, since the original head could not be found. Ganesha is often represented on stage by a young boy wearing the elephant mask, who then is worshipped as the incarnation of the god himself.

> Ganesha's mask then says nothing about his nature. It is a mask, pure and simple. Right at the start of the play, my theory about masks was getting subverted But the elephant head also questioned the basic assumption behind the original riddle: that the head represents the thinking part of the person, the intellect (13-14).

The Ganesha myth is beyond human comprehension and human logic to analyse body and mind, the shaping part and thinking part of a man. Karnad's adjustment of two stories from ancient sources in the play evokes some eternal questions of the Ganesha myth—What is a complete human being? Which limb identifies a man? Which limb is important than others and why? The image of Lord Ganesha contributes to the structural unity of the play. Lord Ganesha's complex symbolic connotation of the elephant-headed Lord, whose divine form appears to be so ridiculous and absurd because of its elephant trunk which is a unique organ, symbolises great adaptibility, sensitiveness, strength and discriminative power as they are signified by his tusk and trunk. Lord Ganapati is "beyond the three gunas" (*Sattwa, Rajas* and *Tamas*). Ironically his identity of incompleteness is worshipped for completeness and this arouses existential angsts in the play. Lord Ganapati as 'Gunapathy' (the master of all the three *gunas*) represents a perfect blend of three different worlds of experiences—the divine, the human and the animal. He suggests a major development in action of the play as well as the central theme of completeness of being.

In Karnad's play Devadatta (literally means the God-given) and Kapila (literally menas the dark and earthly one) are two friends living in the city of Dharmapura where King Dharmasheela rules. Devadatta is the son of Revered Brahmin Vidyasagara (literally means the ocean of learning). He is fair in colour, comely in appearance; unrivalled in intelligence, logic, has love for poetry and wit for which the mightiest pundits of the kingdom do not dare to face him in debates. He is the apple of every eye in the city of Dharmapura for which "every parent of every girl in the city is only waiting to catch" (14) him. But Kapila is the only son of the ironsmith Lohita (literally means reddish which reverberates the name of the great sage of Samkhya school of Indian philosophy), and is to the King's armoury as an axle to the chariot-wheel. He is dark and plain. He has no equal in the state in dancing, strength and physical skills. In spite of their varna, caste and colour differences both have "one mind, one heart" (2). The Dharmapurans think them as mythical Lava and Kusha, Rama and Lakshmana, Krishna and Balarama. Devadatta falls in love with a Vaishya girl Padmini (literaly means one of the six types of women as classified in Vatsyayana's *Kamasutra*) whose face is like a white lotus, beauty is as a magic lake for which Devadatta says: "I swear, Kapila, with you as my witness I swear, if I ever get her as my wife, I'll sacrifice my two arms to the goddess Kali, I'll sacrifice my head to Lord Rudra" (14). Padmini is beautiful, agile and the quick-witted daughter of a rich merchant. For Devadatta Padmini is the beauteous women of Indian myth like Yakshini, Shakuntala, Urvashi and Indumati. Kapila becomes a messenger of love for Devadatta and conveys his friend's love to Padmini. Karnad's alteration of names from the original stories is his own creation. "This device of giving his characters generic names also helps Karnad to dovetail the characters into the Bhagavata's narration, for stories in their oral, narrative style are mostly—since they are designed to drive home a moral—about representative characters" (Raykar 180).

Bhagavata is omnicient and has omnipresence in the play. He is intimately involved with every character, intends to draw the attention of the audience, able to step out of the play and explain the action with insightful comments. He is the Tiresian-witness presiding over the everyday reality that keeps turning into the 'problem' of the play. He focuses on the *Sattwa-guna* and *Raja-guna* in Devadatta and Kapila who stand for Apollonian reason and Dionysian instinct, culture and primitive nature, brains and loins, mind and body, spirit and flesh. The friendship between the two friends provides a psychoanalysis between Devadatta's Apollonian order and knowledge, and Kapila's Dionysian impulse and physique. M. Sarat Babu rightly observes:

> According to psychoanalysis human mind is divided into three organs; the *id*, the ego and the super ego. The id consists of instinctual drives and always seeks gratification irrespetive of external reality and cultural values (pleasurable principle). The ego perceives and responds to external reality (Reality principle). It, being the leader, tries to satisfy the *id* and the super ego within the limits of external reality. The superego irrespective of external reality and biological impulse (the *id*) contains ideals, values and morals and urges the ego to lead an ideal life. When the ego wants to be ideal under the pressure of superego, the mind starts functioning independent of the body. This naturally leads to a split between the mind and the body. Consequently they become strangers to each other. This is, the experiences of the body do not reach the mind, and the feelings of the mind do not spread through the body. The ego which causes this self-alienation is called Apollonian ego in which the soul leaves the body.... On the other hand when the ego wants to be natural or really human and when the superego accepts the biological reality (the *id*), the mind and the body work together. There is perfect harmony between them. The mind feels the bodily experiences and the body rocks with the feelings of the mind (Dodiya 1999:226).

Kapila becomes instrumental in the marriage between Padmini and Devadatta irrespective of the differences of caste and backgrounds of the two families where the goddess of wealth sweeps the floor, and the goddess of learning is a maid. He remains close to Devadatta after his marriage and becomes true to Padmini and shows his loyalty, faithfulness and obedience. The trio become close like mythical Rama-Sita-Lakshmana, and they appear as the admiring citizens of Dharmapura. The Dharmapurans believe that some merits in the present life have helped Devadatta to win the hands of Padmini, but the merits of his past seven lives have heped him to win a friend like Kapila. Irrespective of their sociological, intellectual and psychological differences the two friends appear as two brothers.

The study of psychic features of the characters is an important aspect of the play. In their portrayal the playwright projects their strength and weakness and their quest for completeness. Padmini desires to go on a trip to Ujjain after her marriage. Both Devadatta and Kapila accompany her on the way. While Devadatta remains absentminded, enjoying the beautiful scenery beside the River Bhargavi where Poet Vyasa had his hermitage, Kapila remains loyal and sincere to Padmini all along the way. In order to satisfy Padmini's desire for Fortunate Lady's flowers Kapila climbs the tree. Padmini wonders at Kapila's masculinity and prompts to Devadatta to see this "Celestial being reborn as a hunter" (26) and "How he climbs—like an ape. Before I could even say 'yes', he had taken off his shirt, pulled his dhoti up and swung up the branches. And what an eternal shape! Such a broad back—like an ocean with muscles rippling accross it—and then that small, feminine waist which looks so helpless"(25). She encourags him to see, "How his body sways, his limbs curve.... It's his strong body—his many muscles.... I had never ever noticed them all these years" (26).

The pilgrims' progress to Ujjain ends in failure. While they come across the forest and make their halt at a place Devadatta decides to visit the Kali temple, Kapila and Padmini plan to visit the Rudra temple. As Padmini moves with Kapila, Devadatta feels miserable. He marks Padmini's impulsive weakness towards Kapila. In his agonised heart and ratiocinative mind he says, "Goodbye Kapila, Goodbye, Padmini. May the Lord Rudra bless you. You are two pieces of my heart—live happily together. I shall find my happiness in that" (28) Devadatta's existential dilemma between the love for Padmini and Kapila's leaning towards Padmini makes her more miserable. Devadatta visits the temple of Kali in order to keep his promise which he had made before his marriage to Padmini. Imploring goddess Kali he says, "Bhavani, Bhairavi, Kali, Durga, Mahamaya, Mother of all Nature I had forgotten my promise to you. Forgive me, Mother. You fulfilled the deepest craving of my life—you gave me Padmini—and I forgot my word. Forgive me, for I'm here now to carry out my promise" (28). With worldly wisdom, with beautiful wife and faithful friend Devadatta has forgotten his promise to the deity. He takes out his sword and sacrifices his head before the deity. When Kapila and Padmini returns from the Rudra temple Kapila goes in search of Devadatta and finds his truncated head in the Kali temple. In love and bewilderment for his deceased friend Kapila moans:

> Oh my dear friend, my brother, what have you done? Were you so angry with me? Did you feel such contempt for me—such abhorance? And in your anger you forgot that I was ready to die for you? If you had asked me to jump into fire, I would have done it. If you had asked me to leave the country I would have done it. If you had asked me to go and drown in a river I would have gladly done it. Did you despise me so much that you could not even ask me that? I did wrong... I couldn't think—and so you've pushed me away? No, Devadatta, I can't live without you. I can't breathe without you. Devadatta, my brother, my friend (30).

This expresses Kapila's love and commitment which Devadatta neglects and leaves him for good. In order to avoid Padmini's impression that he has killed Devadatta for her hands Kapila follows in his friend's path. As both the friends become late Padmini goes in search of them and finds them dead. In helplessness she laments: "What shall I do? Oh, Devadatta, what did I do that you left me alone in this state?... And you, Kapila, who looked at me with Dog's eyes—you too? How selfish you are—how unkind. What shall I do now—Where shall I go? How can I go home?" (31). She is under the impression that both have fought and died for her and this will impress the people to call her a whore. A.B. Dharwadker rightly remarks: "In Mann's version, the husband beheads himself... out of jealousy and despair; the friend follows suit out of guilt and fear; and the pregnant wife prepares to die in order to avoid ignominy for herself and her child" (*Collected Plays* Vol. I : xxv-xxvi). In shame, helplessness and frustrations she tells the deity, "I can't show my face to anyone in the world," and points the sword towards her breast to make her an offering. Her devotion turns the situation into a miracle as Goddess Kali tells her "I'm pleased with you," and asks "What do you want?" (32). When Padmini desires to get back their life the goddess instructs her, "Now do as I tell you. Put these heads back properly. Attach them to their bodies and then press that sword on their necks. They'll come up alive" (32). In excitement and confusion Padmini joins the heads on the dead and bodies boon becomes a bane. This further complicates the problems in her life. The development of incidents in the life of the three unfortunate friends reveals how Devadatta desires Padmini to be his muse which she is not content to play. She has her own desire for recognition and affirmation for her selfhood through Kapila also.

With the joining of heads, Kapila's body with Devadatta's head and Devadatta's body with Kapila's head rise up. For Padmini it poses the problem of whom to accept as her husband. Before transformation they were friends but now they are "blood relations" and "body relations" (35). She laments in her choice of loss in gain and gain in loss, "What have I done?... What should I do?... I—mixed up your heads—I mixed them up!"(34). The two friends look at their bare bodies without blaming anyone and blame each other for their love for Padmini due to their past memories. Devadatta's head with Kapila's body claims Padmini as his wife. He argues before Kapila's head with Devadatta's body, "According to the Shastras, the head is the sign of a man" (36), the personal identity depends on the head. He says, "when one accepts a person in marriage, with the holy fire as one's witness, one accepts a person, not a body. She didn't marry Devadatta's body, she married Devadatta—the person" (37). He claims that "of all the human limbs the topmost—in position as well as in importance—is the head. I have Devadatta's head and it follows that I am Devadatta" (37). He views that "It's natural for a woman to feel attracted to a fine figure of a man..." (38). Kapila equally claims, "This is the hand that accepted her at the wedding. This is the body she's lived with all these months. And the child she's carrying is the seed of this body" (36-37). He says, " Padmini must come home with me,... She's my wife.... I have Devadatta's body now" (36). He rejects Devadatta's quotes from the scriptures and claims Padmini as his wife. The difference arises when Devadatta's head speaks of his rights and Kapila's body speaks of his reasons. Their claim for Padmini in respective viewpoints begins in a conflict but ends in a discourse.

Devadatta had a fair face, fragile body and intelligence but Kapila had an unpleasant face, elegant and muscular body with great bodily strength before their transformation. But after transformation "Devadatta-Kapila possesses the ideal mind as well as the body, while the other hybrid being, Kapila-Devadatta, is deficient in both respects" (*Collected Plays*. Vol. I : xxvi). On the other hand Padmini is beautiful, intelligent, assertive and witty. She invests her feminist agenda transgressing the social norms, and makes a "vain attempt to unite Man as intellect and as flesh in order to further her creative purpose". In her temporal and spatial division, and mind/body dualism Padmini chooses "the husband-head and friend-body".

She prefers the advantages of beauty and brain in him. When she decides to go with Devadatta Kapila tells in frustration that the people of Dharmapura will recognise his body with Devadatta's head. Padmini who was one time fascinated for Kapila's body and his masculinity discards him from her mind and tells Devadatta : "It's no use arguing with this rascal" (37). It raises some ethical questions on Devadatta-Kapila tangle and Padmini's choice between Apollonian order and Dionysian tendency—"Whose wife is she?" (36). "Can Padmini's fancy be taken as the solution?" (39). Can Padmini's joining of heads in excitement and confusion be taken as her deliberate choice for the best man? Can the evangelist take it a result of divine will? Can a woman's choosing of head or body be taken as her existential problem? Padmini's predicament is the predicament of every modern woman who in her love and choice for man's Apollonian mind and Dionysian body prefers Devadatta's head with Kapila's body. Her quest for perfection is marked with the appreciation of the science of synergisation.

Bhagavata gives a solution to all the questions by citing King Vikrama's answer to the question of demon Vetala. He says all the three unfortunate beings go to a great *rishi* in search of a solution to their problems. The *rishi* remembering King Vikrama's reply to the Vetala gives a solution: "As the heavenly Kalpa Vriksha is supreme among trees, as is the head among limbs. Therefore, the man with Devadatta head is indeed Devadatta and he is the rightful husband of Padmini" (40). The decision of the *rishi* clearly indicates that the head commands and moulds the body according to its choice, need and temperament. This comes true when Debadatta's Apollonian head slackens his Dionysian body after transformation. But in case of Kapila his Dionysian tendency fails to train his Apollonian body. Similarly Padmini's choice of "a perfect man" with brain and body raises bio-ethical questions. If Padmini asserts her right to accept Devadatta's head with Kapila's body the ethical hypothesis distorts it. She finds that the transposition of heads soon establishes the metamonphosis of their body elements. About their nature of body and identity of personality Kirtinath Kurtkoti remarks in the 'Introduction' to the play:

> Initially, Devadatta—actually the head of Devadatta on Kapila's body—behaves differently from what he was before. But ever so gradually he changes to his fomer self. So does Kapila. But there is a difference. Devadatta stops writing poetry while Kapila is haunted by the memories in Devadatta's body. Padmini who, after the exchange of heads, had felt that she had the best of both the men gets slowly disillusioned. Of the three, only she has the capacity for complete experience. She understands but cannot control the situation in which she is placed. Her situation is beautifully summed up by the image of the river and the scarecrow in the choric songs (vi).

Devadatta's body loses its charm without wrestling, swimming and visiting gymnasium after transformation. Similarly Kapila's head fails to command his body for making it strong. If on the one hand Padmini expresses her role of a *Pativrata* (a woman devoted to her husband), Devadatta loses her body glamour due to the effect of his brain and Kapila becomes a loathsome person for Padmini losing his attractive body on the other. In mental agony he blames his fate that his body is no more recognised by other. It creates a *vairagya* or dispassion in him. He takes renunciation from the glamours of life and goes into the forest for ever. His dispassion arising out of personal disillusionment with a situation is an accidental *vairgya.* It is because after his transformation he is no more able to sustain his life for a sensual enchantment. He realises in a momentary disenchantment and extreme self-abnegation what Buddha or Shankara had done in a self-consuming 'mind-reality'. Padmini is also not happy with the "Fabulous body-fabulous brain-fabulous Devadatta" (43) that becomes soft steadily. She enjoys her time only with two dolls brought for her from the Ujjain fair by Devadatta. As soon as Devadatta's body starts "going soft again" (49) she craves for Kapila's body. In the mechanical conception of life the playwright hypothesises the philosophy of head and body, emotion and impulse, and ridicules the moral problems which is both psychological and physical.

After enjoying her life with Devadatta, a "good mix" of head and body, "the better half of two bodies" (57) Padmini feels bored. As Devadatta's body goes soft, the notion, "The head always wins" (55) becomes a misnomer. Padmini analyses her past and present impression on Devadatta and Kapila. She has come in contact with "Kapila with Devadatta's body! Devadatta with Kapila's body! Four men in one life time" (56). Her illusion for body beauty and mind's philosophy becomes a delusion when the technical aspect of life of Devadatta and Kapila gets affected by the law of nature. She fails to forget Kapila's body. Her impulse dominates over her intelligence. When she goes in search of Kapila in the forest she finds him as if in illness. He narrates to her the transitional effect on his body after the transformation. He tells about its naturalistic effect to Padmini:

> When this body came to me, it was like a corpse hanging by my head. It was a Brahmin's body after all—not made for the worlds. I couldn't lift an axe without my elbows moaning. Couldn't run a length without my knees howling. I had no use for it. The moment it came to me, a war started between us (55).

In the forest Padmini tries to impress Kapila by showing him her son, "Yes. And yours.... Your body gave him to me" (54). Kapila advises her, "Go back. Back to Devadatta. He is your husband.... A pair coupled with the holy fire as the witness. I have no place there, no peace, no salvation.... I beg of you. Go" (57). Padmini realises that by saving them she has done a great damage to them. She regrets, "It's my fault. I mixed the heads up. I must suffer for it" (57). It is for her Kapila has become "an outcaste" (58) and both the friends enjoy the "mad dance of incompleteness" (57).

Devadatta goes in search of Padmini into the forest after his return from Ujjain fair. He finds Padmini with Kapila in the forest. This enrages him. In anger and reconciliation, love and despise he endures the unendurable. When Kapila proposes, "Couldn't we all three live together—like the Pandavas and Draupadi?" Devadatta nurtures the idea of their self-annihilation better than the idea of sharing one woman. He thinks of the only possible solution now is that the two friends must kill each other and thus cut the Gordian Knot. In love, anger, compromise, wisdom, wildness they are disturbed and decide to bring an end to their life. They fight like lions and kill each other like cobras, and die in each other's arms. Sitting beside their dead bodies Padmini says, "If I'd said, yes, I'll live with you both.... You forgave each other, but again—left me out" (62). She becomes helpless with the death of Devadatta and Kapila. In guilt and repentance she expresses her last wish before Bhagavata for her child which biologically belongs to Devadatta's head and Kapila's body, and exhibits the qualities of Kapila in its violence and unintelligible activities:

> My son is sleeping in the hut. Take him under your care, Give him to the hunters who live in the forest and tell them it's Kapila's son. They loved Kapila and will bring the child up. Let the child grow up in the forest with the rivers and the trees. When he is five take him to the Revered Brahmin Vidyasagara of Dharmapura. Tell him it's Devadatta's son (62).

Padmini realises that her love for the two has caused a disastrous effect. Her love for Devadatta and lust for Kapila have finally led them to death and her to perform *sati*. Expressing his raction to Padmini's performing of *sati* Bhagavata says:

> Thus Padmini became a sati. India is known for its Pativratas—wives who dedicated their whole existence to the service of their husbands—but it would not be an exaggeration to say that no *Pativrata* went in the way Padmini did. And yet no one knows the spot where she went *sati*. If you ask the hunting tribes who dwell in these forests, they only point to a full-blossomed tree of the Fortunate Lady. They say that even now on fullmoon and on new moon nights a song rises from the roots of the tree and fills the whole forest like a fragrance (63).

Padmini endures what she endeavours in love and lust for the two. Her decision for *sati* "wages a war against the patriarchal order of command and contentment" (Dhanaval 28). This shows that "Padmini's quest for perfection is not satisfied till the end and she decides to perform *sati*. She knows that she will not succeed in attaining completeness in the next birth too. She invokes Goddess Kali and says that other women can die praying that they should get the same husband in all the lives to come but she does not even that little consolation" (Goel 1999: 209). Padmini's choice of death through *sati* allows her to assert her will "partly due to the realization that her accepting two husbands,... would not solve the problem so long as they themselves could not reconcile themselves to the idea" (Raykar 185).

Karnad fuses the supernatural and folk elements in the main plot and sub-plot of the play. In the main plot while transposition of heads take place in the sub-plot he deals with a Kannada folktale, the story of Hayavadana's struggle for completeness. It is apparent that "Karnad diffuses this human 'tragedy' by placing it alongside two other realms of experience—the divine and the animal" (*Collected Plays* Vol-I: xxvii). In "Author's Introduction" to his *Three Plays* Karnad writes:

> The story of this horse-headed man, who wants to shed the horse head and become human, provides the outer panel—as in a mural—within which the tale of the two friends is framed. Hayavadana, too goes to the same Goddess Kali and wins a boon from her that he should become complete. Logic takes over. The head is the person: Hayavadana becomes a complete horse. The central logic of the tale remains intact, while its basic premise is denied (14).

Hayavadana's mother, once a very beautiful girl, is the princess of Karnataka married to a white stallion. M.K. Naik rightly remarks, "Hayavadana's parentage (he is the offspring of the union of a celestial being in an equine form and a princess) symbolically suggests the combination of the three elements of the divine, the human and the animal in his make up" (Mukherjee 139). Hayavadana narrates about this:

> My mother was the Princess of Karnataka. She was a very beautiful girl. When she came of age, her father decided that she should choose her own husband. So princes of every kingdom in the world were invited—and they all came.

> From China, from Persia, from Africa. But she didn't like any of them. The last one to come was the prince of Araby. My mother took one look at that handsome prince sitting on his great white stallion—and she fainted.... Her father at once decided that this was the man. All arrangements for the wedding were made. My mother woke up....she said she would only marry that horse! (8).

The princess marries that horse and gives birth to Hayavadana, a horse-man, neither a beast nor a human being. After living with the horse for fifteen years one fine morning his mother discovers that the horse has turned into a beautiful celestial being. It reveales that he was a *gandharva* cursed to be a horse by God Kubera for some act of misbehaviour. Enjoying human love for fiteen years he is released from the curse and gains his original self again. When he asks the princess to accompany him to his Heavenly Abode she wants him to remain as a horse again for her. The *gandharva* is angry and curses her to be a horse herself. This makes her live as a mare who, after the effect of the curse, gallops away without thinking about Hayavadana. From that day Hayavadana lives as a half-man and half-beast with his *gandharva* human identity without any divine power. He is not happy with his condition. "Unlike the god (Lord Ganesha), Hayavadana canot endure to remain mixed up; unlike the humans, he does not possess a prior self that can reassert itself. But as in the human world, the head determines identity, even if that means the triumph of the animal over the human: Hayavadana achieves wholeness by relinquishing his human characteristics, and turning completely into a horse" (*Collected Plays*. Vol. I:xxvii). He desires to get rid of his horse's head and become a complete man. He takes interest in social life, nationalism, civics, politics, patriotism and socialism. Being a horse-man he sings the natinoal anthem and patriotic songs like *Jana Gana Mana, Jhanda Ooncha Rahe Hamara* and *Sare Jhan Se Accha Hindustan Hamara.*

Hayavadana narrates his existential problems with his animal head because he is neither accepted in the human world nor in the animal world. In order to shed off his horse head he has made up his mind to do some *punya* and abolish the error committed in his previous birth. For this he has made his pilgrimage to Banaras, Rameswar, Gokarn, Haridwar, Gaya, Kedarnath, the Dargah of Khwaja Yusuf Baba, the Gretto of Virgin Mary; and has visited magicians, mendicants, maharishis, fakirs, saints and sadhus. But he has not progressed spiritually in his attempt. Bhagavata has advised him to visit Goddess Kali on Mount Chitrakoot and enjoy the power of her divine grace. In the play Karnad has introduced this sub-plot to narrate the act of Hayavadana's mother that runs parallel to Padmini's existential dilemma in the main plot. While in the story of *Hayavadana* his mother asserts her right through becoming a mare rather prefering to go to her *gandharva* husband's heavenly abode Padmini prefers death by performing *sati*. Both Padmini's son and Hayavadana do not have their choices but they suffer for their parents' act. The only benefit Hayavadana enjoys is that he speaks the language in a human voice. He prays to Goddess Kali, "Mother, make me complete". "I have become a complete horse—but not a complete being!" (68). With a quest for completeness and purgation he tells about his extreme decision, "if you don't help me I'll chop off my head!" (68).

Karnad makes a fusion of folklore and myth in the play. He presents the story of Devadatta-Padmini-Kapila from ancient folk classics, and narrates about the greatness and role of divine beings like Lord Ganesha, God Rudra, Goddess Kali, the presiding deities of Hindu pantheon; and the *gandharva,* human beings and animals on the other. His introduction of Bhagavata, the co-ordinater and interpreter among them, serves the purpose of God, man and animal. Combining the myth and folklore he says in a conversation with Tutun Mukherjee:

> It is true that after *Hayavadana* there was a rise of interest in folk forms.... It was all very educative. But the basic thing I discovered was that the subject of the play has to be the human spirit. Using folk elements as mere aesthetic device to ornament the plays with songs, dance and colour was meaningless for me. The technique had to be intrinsic to the plot. Let me make it clear here, elements from "folk" performances can not be used to cover sloppiness of either the dramatist or the director (40).

Hayavadana has no transformation. When all his attempts to liberate himself fail he returns as "a complete horse". Bhagavata gives him the responsibility to go and tell Revered Brahmin Vidyasagar that his grandson is returning home in triumph. The play ends with a prayer and Bhagavata reminds the audience about the unfathomable mercy of the elephant-headed Ganesha, who "fulfils the desires of all—a grandson to a grandfather, a smile to a child, a neigh to a horse" (71). The play becomes enjoyable for the congregation of gods, *gandharva*, human beings and animals.

Naga-Mandala is one of Karnad's best plays that depicts the man-woman relationship in their conjugal life. Narrating the several stages of this relationship which the young couple experience in their adolescence Karnad presents their belief in the *naga* as a supernatural being that tries its best to make the female and male characters to live harmoniously within the family fold. During 1987-88 Karnad was the visiting professor and Fulbright Scholar-in-Residence at the University of Chicago when he had the privilege to go through A.K. Ramanujan's works on folktales. He had also the privilege to listen two to oral tales of Karnataka from him. Although the energy of these folktales is to uphold the traditional values and to eliminate socio-cultural evils, "He does not specify exactly which stories they are, but equivalent stories are found in practically every Indian language. The first is obviously the traditional tale of a cobra turning into a man at night and visiting a married woman and the second is based on the popular belief that a night-long vigril in a temple can ward off death" (Naik and Narayan 202). At the age of 46 Karnad heard these two oral tales from Ramanujan about a *naga*-lover's "magical visits in the form of the husband are thus virtually overdetermined by the familiar folk logic that beauty and innocence must triumph without the overt violation of moral norms" (*Collected Plays*. Vol I. xxx). With his imagination of truth and fiction, and myth and reality in the tales he got creatively quite enervated to write the play. Recollecting his memories with A.K. Ramanujan he writes:

> *Naga-Mandala* is based on two oral tales I heard from A.K. Ramanujan. These tales are narrated by women-normally the older women in the family while children are fed in the evenings in the kitchen or being put to bed. The other adults present on these occasions are also women. Therefore these tales, though directed at the children, often serve as a parallel system of communication among the women in the family (Jain 2000:193).

In the play he uses these two tales narrating the erotic ignorance of his woman protagonist with her morbid concept on sex that it is mean and sinful. He deconstructs the cononised socio-cultural programming of sex roles on the one hand, and displays the vulgar male power, male promiscuity, gender bias and religious fanaticism on the other.

A *naga's* transformation into a man is unacceptable but shape-shifting or transformation is common in myths and folktales. Cultural anthropologists use this technique for a magical remedy to establish happiness in family life. Karnad uses this shape-shifting technique while "The two folk-tales are deftly blended in presenting the two allied themes of the nature of art and the relationship between art and imagination on the one hand and mundane reality on the other" (Naik and Narayan 203). *Naga,* the King Cobra, is worshipped in many parts of India. Chiefly in South Indian states it is worshipped by the women desiring children. The Naga is a cultural sign in local myths and cultural narratives in local literatures (verbal and written). One believes in the aesthetics of animal and human shape in togetherness which is beautifully terrible and terrifyingly beautiful. In India, "Nagas are closely associated with Lord Shiva, who is known in Indian mythology for his liberally granting the prayers of his devotees" (Kumar 150). The Shaiva Lingayats of Karnataka worship the *naga* which is depicted as Shiva. They believe the Naga as a phallic symbol which performs its role as per Lord Shiva's nature. On Naga Panchami, the festival that falls in the month of Sravana on the fifth day of the first half of the lunar moon, women pour offerings of milk and cereals into snake pits. Karnad presents this snake culture in South India that has left an indelible impression in his mind. Concentrating his imagination on this cultural practice he presents a *naga* as the protagonist of his play which appears like an animal but acts humane and divine. In this context Pranab Joshipura rightly remarks:

> In our Hindu mythology, the Naga represents several images. In South India, many houses have their own shrine which is often a grove reserved for snakes, consisting of trees, festooned with creepers, situated in a corner of the garden. Snakes are also the symbols of human maleness and strength. Nagas are sometimes portrayed as handsome men, or as half-man and half-snake, the top half using the torso of a man, the lower half a coiled snake (Dodiya 257-258).

A cobra is supposed to be closely associated with Lord Shiva who grants the boon to his devotes and rescues them from frustration. A *mandala* is a complex pattern belonging to *tantra* or occultism, representing the intricate working of the vital energy. In the story of the play it is presented as a trinagle and a square, a traingle within a square. The three points of the triangle are Rani, Appanna and Naga, and they illustrate the eternal triangle of an adulterous situation. *Nagamandala* means the 'coil of the cobra', a charmed circle of verbal or linguistic codes of establishment that prescribes certain codes for *moksha* or liberation for a believer in conservative sense. The *naga* worshippers believe that any suppression or repression of this code can become subversive and cathartic. However, in the socio-cultural belief the Naga is the sign, the *mandala* is the signifier, and tradition is the signified one. Conceptualising the role of the *naga* in Hindu tradition M. Sarat Babu remarks:

> Mandala is a tantric concept indicating inner concentration, a source of energy. Naga-Mandala is a magico-religious, ritual involving Naga, the snake-god of Hindus who grants the wishes of the devotees, especially the wish for fertility. In the play, Naga grants Rani all her wishes which she does not express openly. She grows mentally and becomes a confident lady. She is cured of her frigidity. She gets a devoted husband. Her husband's concubine becomes a life-long servant-maid for her. She begets a good son. Naga, in addition, makes Appanna's heart fertile with love and affection for his wife. At a higher level of symbolism, Naga represents a cultural leader who is instrumental in bringing about a socio-cultural reform (Dodiya 248).

Although snake worship is extensively found in the *Mahabharata*, the *Bible*, Brahminism; Buddhist, Lamaistic and Javanese writings Karnad presents the role of the *naga* in the South Indian cultural practice in the plot of the play to conceptualise the human and non-human worlds and examines the issues of adultery and chastity which the patriarchy frames to make a woman loyal to her husband.

Karnad explores the implicitiness of folk elements in the complexities and contradictions of conjugal life. He makes the play a critique of human psyche in marital relationship. He writes in "Author's Introduction" to his *Three Plays*:

> The position of Rani in the story of *Naga-Mandala* can be seen as a metaphor for the situation of a young girl in the bosom of a joint family where she sees her husband only in two unconnected roles – as a stranger during the day and as a lover at night. Inevitably, the pattern of relationships she is forced to weave from these disjointed encounters must be something of a fiction (17).

Projecting this traditional theme in the two folktales he initiates Bertolt Brecht's sense of alienation (*enfuhlang*) and estrangement (*verfremdung*) in the psychological construct of his woman protagonist. He upholds the traditional values in the presentation of a cruel husband's absolute superiority over his wife. In the interplay of two folktales he experiments the human nature and psyche, and presents them in the subject matters which are paradoxically trivial and serious, ordinary and absurd, extraordinary and cricumstantial, horrible and ludicrous, tragic and comic. The play presents about a failed playwright who is cursed to death, because he has sent so many people to sleep in the theatre. But he is helped to stay awake by the story, a personified woman character who narrates the story of the play recounting the exciting narrative of a cobra and a married woman, Rani. She is neglected by her husband, Appanna, who locks her up in the house day and night. In an interview with Tutun Mukherjee, Karnad says:

> *Naga-Mandala* combines two folktales. The framing story describes the gathering of the flames in a dilapidated temple after the lamps in the village homes have been extinguished. The gossip of the flames is over heard by a playwright who is condemned to die unless he can keep awake the whole night. The story the playwright hears is about a woman, her husband and her snake-lover. When I heard the folktales, I was captivated. I wondered if a woman in such circumstances would commit a deliberate adultery. Would she accept her secret lover? The conservative Indian attitude will neither permit nor tolerate this, of course. So how does she face the fact that the perosn who visits her at night, who is her tender lover, is not really her husband? What kind of truths or half-truths do we tell ourselves to avoid facing a stark and unpleasant reality? That was the inception of the play in my mind (2008:42).

A *Naga* acts as a human being in the play. It appears "more a symbol of sexual energy than of common sense" (Dhanavel 42). In the plot he probes into the female and male growth into selfhood and their mature adjustment with special roles fixed for them by the traditional society. Appanna marries Rani and brings her to his home. Rani, the only daughter of her parents, justifies her name for living like a queen in her parents' house. But her real problem starts when she marries young Appanna. who "reduces her daily life to a featureless existence without companionship or community" (*Collected Plays*. Vol-I:xxx).

The play begins in the inner sanctum of a ruined temple. The woman narrator, New Flame, tells the story to other flames. Inside the sanctum a man sits and hears the female voices outside the temple. He hides himself behind a pillar and watches how several flames enter the temple giggling and talking to one another in female voices. When the lamps are extinguished in the village houses the flames gather at this remote place in the outskirts of the village and spend the night together and gossip in the temple. But the man who shelters here in the night watches how the tiny flames enter the premises and talk to one another. All the flames have come here from different households and gather here to gossip for their entertainment. Interestingly the Flame is a female storyteller sharing her observation and experiences with others. In the structural device of the play:

> The story of the flames comments on the paradoxical nature of oral tales in general. They have an existence of their own, they are independent of the teller and yet live only when they are passed on from the possesor of the tale to the listener. Similarly the status of a tale becomes akin to that of a daughter, for traditionally a daughter too is not meant to be kept at home too long but has to be passed on (Joshipura 261).

The audience become sure of their identity as the New Flame tells in the "Prologue": "At night when the old man had gone to sleep, the Story took the form of a young woman and the Song become a Sari. The young woman wrapped herself in the sari and stepped out, just as the old lady was coming in"(25). The flames are the metaphors for women in the village who come and gather at this place in the night to tell stories and sing songs for their entertainment.

The identification of the flames with young, sprightly and 'vocal' women, and the stories that they tell each other are a brilliant device used by Karnad for creating a particularly female context and content in the 'man-oriented' folk-tale. "He brings within the play the strong association between the oral narrative tradition and women's sub-culture, existing within the patriarchal societies. Woman tell many of these folktales, myths and legends, and in their telling often reinvent and transform them... the female experience expressed in female narratives is woven within the folktale as the 'flame' tells her story to the professional, male playwright" (Gupta 250-51).

The man as a stranger enters into their converation and tells the flames, "I must not doze off during the tale. If I do I die. All your telling will be wasted"(26). He listens to a story that has escaped from a woman's head and promises with a vow not to have anything to do with the theme, plot and acting. The Story narrates the story of *Naga-Mandala* before the audience.

Naga-Mandala is based on the myth of chastity and fidelity of woman. At the centre of the story Naga plays an important role in husband-wife relationship symbolising for fertility and Rani as the symbol of life principle and continuance of life. Combining the human and non-human worlds Karnad focuses that chastity is such a value invented by patriarchy and forced upon women to accept it. The functioning of patriarchal restrictions in the spontaneity of love not only restricts and weakens its naturality but also becomes pernicious in its functioning like a safety valve. Chastity is one of the most powerful and invisible cultural fetters that has enslaved women for ages. Patriarchy frames the concept of chastity and prescribes it in a morbid thought that sex is mean and sinful. Parents and elders enslave their daughters by teaching them the importance of chastity and any negligence to it causes an irreparable loss to the name and fame of their family. It is often believed that death is preferable to the loss of chastity or in fear of cultural excommunication in the society. In the play both Appanna and Rani are the victims of their sexuality. While the husband spends his nights consciously with a prostitute neglecting his wife, she spends her nights desperately with the Naga paramour in ignorance. The loveless life of Appanna and Rani reveal how culture codifies the rules to establish a man's full control over the woman's body. But a woman's body matters much when she realises that motherhood confers a purpose and identity with which her culture has nothing to do.

Rani dreams romantically enough after her marriage. But to her misery she is perplexed and nonplussed with Appanna's attitude. She is in despair due to Appanna's treatment of her. She lives in her house very mechanically with his instructions. She meets him only in the noon time when he comes for his lunch. He is emotionally underdeveloped to provide happiness to her. Rani feels her failure on two fronts: being deprived of her parents' love just after her marriage and dreaming of the future with Appanna. She feels mierable thinking that the wild beast and reptiles even share their emotion but her husband being a human being fails to express it to her. In loneliness and alienation she sobs in his locked house and obeys him without any question. She never dares to question him as the questioning of a wife of her husband is considered an offence in the socio-cultural tradition. On the other hand she obeys him with loyality when he tells her, "Do as you are told, you understand?"(28). Reacting to Rani's miseries C.N. Ramachandran remarks : "*Nagamandala*... dramatises the agony and helplessness of a woman in the Hindu society in which she can see her husband only at night. In fact, the picture of Rani, shut up in a huge house for most part of the day and night alone, and who, in the end, has to go through barbaric ordeals in a severe indictment of a male-dominated Hindu society" (29). Appanna's extramarital relationship and deliberate negligence of Rani presents how she is used as a disposable object by her husband. She is the victim of patriarchal culture which supports the male dominance over woman. Karnad rightly remarks; "This reveals the position of Rani... for instance, can be seen as a metaphor for the situation of a young girl in the bosom of a joint family where she sees her husband only in two unconnected roles – as a stranger during the day and as a lover at night" (Jain 2000 : 194). Presenting the Rani-Appanna-Naga relationship in the play Karnad focuses on male assumption of keeping full control of woman's body, in the institution of family and notion of chastity.

In the Rani-Appanna relationship body matters and mind revolts because man experiments with the woman's body and woman expiates herself through her sufferings. Rani is ignorant about woman's predicament in a male–dominated society nor she is acquainted with the present predicament before her marriage.

A.B. Darwadker rightly remarks, "Marriage for Rani means the loss of the secure world of childhood and parental love, and she has to reimagine that world in her fantasies merely to keep herself from psychic collapse" (*Collected Plays*. Vol. I : xxx). Her miseries multiply in her everyday life as Appanna does not stay with her and never utters a syllalle to her more than required. In despair and helplessness she tells to Kurudavva, "I'm bored to death"(31). Kurudavva, the old and blind woman of the village, is a close friend of Appanna's mother. Kappanna, her only son like the mythical Shravan Kumar supports her in her old age. She shares her motherly affection with Rani after her first meeting with her in her confinement. Kurudavva regrets over Rani's misery when she comes to know about her suffering from Rani. The irony is that the man who dares to destroy another woman's chastity desires to preserve his own wife's chastity in an act of devilry by locking her in his house. Through Appanna Karnad mocks at the male ego and man's framing of the notion of chastity. Kurudavva regrets at Appanna's callousness and neglect of Rani's beauty, and plans to liberate her from her existential suffering. She appears as an angel for Rani and plans to liberate her from captivity. She becomes instrumental in Rani's psychological evolution. She prescribes a 'solution' to Rani for her problems. She gives her a piece of magic root that she had received from a mendicant to win her lover in her youth. In the self of a surrogate mother she tells Rani, "Take it! Grind it into a nice paste and feed it to your husband. And watch the results. Once he smells you he won't go sniffing after that bitch. He will make you a wife instantly" (34). In her existential dilemma Rani dares to do it as a necessity but soon retreats from her decision in the thinking that it will make Appanna sick. As a Hindu wife Rani cannot betray her husband's faith. She dissuades herself from doing this with an impression that it is a betrayal to her husband but prefers to do it with the reasons that it will bring her husband to the family-fold.

The idea of the application of magic root on Appanna in the hope of changing his nature gives a sudden twist to the play. While Rani's attempt to apply this is out of a positive thinking for enjoying her conjugal bliss, it reveals the betrayal of her mutual faith in her husband in a guilt consciousness that complicates her life. She never dares to revolt against Appanna, rather nurtures her secret desire to change him from a lecherous one to a devoted husband. The experiment of the magic root complicates her existential problems with the thought that magic is the manipulation of psychic action. When she mixes the paste of the magic root in the curry before serving it to him she finds its colour changed into deep red. In excitement, restlessness and apprehension of danger to Appanna's life she pours it out into an ant-hill near her house. This may be an error of her destiny, "But an error of destiny leads both of them, and, subsequently, the entire story towards a literal disaster. Can we call this disaster a part of human destiny, or a result of human error, or owing to a thirst is a matter of debate" (Jashipura 258). In its effect, the paste of the magic root quickly works on the Naga in the ant-hill and he falls in love with Rani.

Naga, the King Cobra, gets impressed with Rani's beauty, loveliness and long black tresses on her head. For Naga, Rani appears like a Yakshya (Naga) woman. It appears as an *avatar* and comes forward to rescue Rani from her distress. It enters Rani's room through the drain of the bathroom during her sleep and caresses her in its transformed shape of Appanna. This becomes its regular practice and it visits her every night. Sympathising with Rani for her predicament "Naga here functions as a male sex surrogate in curing Rani of frigidity" (Babu 243). In the daytime Appanna comes only to take his lunch and after this he goes to his concubine. He insults, punishes and mistreats Rani for no mistake. He is a male chauvinist who gets pleasure in punishing and exploiting Rani's innocence. He has an utter contempt for her only and only lust for the concubine. His insensitiveness to Rani's sensibility goes against his personal ethics that doubles Rani's misery. The aphrodisiac paste that Rani throws on the ant-hill makes Naga come to her rescue. In the dichotomy of male ethics between Naga and Appanna Rani is exploited by Appanna in the daytime and expiated through Naga in the night. But in love-hate relationship between Naga and Appanna she proves her eternal feminine endurance to her callous husband's oppression and caring for Naga's consolation for a marital bliss. A.B. Dharwadker rightly remarks in the "Introduction" to his *Collected Plays*: "Rani is willing to accept that the brutish husband of the day turns into the ardent lover at night because those are the conditions of her sexual initiation and emancipation" (Vol. II, xxx-xxxi).

Appanna's absolute male superiority over Rani weaves the theme of patriarchal tyranny, female sexuality, adultery and chastity in complex human experience. Rani is shy of sex. She is brought up in the patriarchal atmosphere where the moral code approves that sex is mean and sinful, and compels her to abhor sex. She is concerned with her frigidity and confused with the male notions of woman's chastity and his fidelity. She knows that Appanna is a 'rotten husband' who insults her in the day time and caresses her in the night time. But she fails to understand the reality when Naga as Appanna visits her nocturnally and cajoles her. When Naga Appanna calls her a "tender bud", and "very beautiful" (39) Rani is surprised because she has never heard these kind words from Appanna. She gets confused between the double personalities of Appanna. In her mortal eyes and feminine perception she fails to comprehend the difference between the Naga-paramour and her husband Appanna from Naga lover in Apanna's shape. At the night when Naga-Appanna grabs her and cajoles her she says to him, "You talk so nicely at night. But during the day I only have to open my mouth and you hiss like a... stupid snake." In helplessness and despair she tells him,"what can I say if you behave like this?" (42). She feels sick of being alone. She tells Naga-Appanna about her loneliness and anxiety:

> You don't know how I have suffered.... But my real anxiety began as the evening approached. I would merely lie here, my eyes shut tight. What is there to see after all? The same walls. The same roof As the afternoon passed my whole being got focused in my ears. The bells of cattle returning home—that means it is late afternoon. The cacophony of birds in a far-away tree—it is sunset. The chorus of crickets spreading from one groove to another—it is night.... Every night the same anxiety. The same cold feeling deep within me! (50).

Their love continues for some days. Rani does not know that the alchemy of magic root has affected Appanna fully or partially. But she is sure that it has affected the chemistry of Appanna's love for her. In this context G.C. Behera rightly views: "This love between human and snake like that between Arjuna and Snake Princess Ulupi, between Bhima and Snake Princess Nagabala romantically celebrated in the *Mahabharata* is common in our myths preserved in collective consciousness, that lends credibility and comprehensibility to the story" (133). Both Appanna and Naga are two faces of one man—one seen at day, the other at night who symbolise the exploitation and double standard of man.

Appanna discovers Kurudavva and Kappanna at his house when he comes for his lunch. Appanna apprehends something fishy about their presence at his house. He brings a watch-dog to guard his house with the intention not to allow anybody to come near his house. But one day he discovers that the dog has fallen dead due to a snake bite. He becomes sure about the surreptitious visit and nuisance of the King Cobra that lives in the nearby ant-hill. Kurudavva has also discovered the cobra's sliding away through their bathroom drain and she advised to Rani to burn incense in a ladle to keep the reptiles out. This also makes Rani doubtful about Naga's subterranean visits. It condenses her doubt in one night when she discovers "blood on his (Naga-Appanna's) cheeks... and shoulders" (48). Although she has used ointment on his wounds she is terrified to see the reflection of a Naga's face in the mirror while bringing the ointment from the mirror box. But after the death of the dog Appana becomes wild with anger and plans to bring an end to Naga's life. About his decision the Story narrates:

> The death of the dog infuriated Appanna. He next brought a mongoose. The mongoose lasted only one day. But it had evidently given a tougher fight : its mouth was full of blood. There were bits of flesh under its claw. Bits of snake skin were found in its teeth.

Rani faints when she sees the dead mongoose. That night he does not visit her. There is no sign of him for the next fifteen days. Rani spends her nights crying, wailing, pining for him. When he starts coming again, his body is covered with wounds which have partly healed. She applies her ointment on the wounds. But she never questions him about them. It is enough that he has returned. Needless to say, when her husband comes during the day, there are no scars on him (49).

The long alienated life of Rani in her house has a psychological effect on her life. In male ego and aggressive psyche Appanna curtails Rani's liberty. This reduction of liberty affects the natural growth of Rani's psyche. He keeps her in confinement without sharing food and love. His cruelty expresses his patriarchal bent of mind.

Habit becomes an evidence and magic becomes a reality in Naga's nocturnal visits to Rani. She is married but "deprived of her personal and familial needs" (Dhanvel 32). Through sexual initiation and fulfilment she desires her emancipation from Appanna's patriarchal control. She discloses before Naga Appanna, "I am pregnant.... We are going to have a baby.... I hid the news from you all these months" (50). Maternity gives Rani added strength, a sense of superiority and responsibility awaiting her. Her maternal satisfaction encourages Naga-Appanna's but it weakens him how to save her from blashphemy. In happiness and uncertainty she tells him, "Now a third life joins us!" (51) and asks him, "It doesn't make you happy?" (50). Naga-Appanna becomes serious about Rani's future child. He thinks of her progress from frigidity to fertility and psychological evolution from a girl to a wife to a mother. She says in assertion, "I was a stupid, ignorant girl when you brought me here. But now I am a woman, a wife and I am going to be a mother. I am not a parrot, not a cat or a sparrow... why do you change like a chameleon from day to night"? (51). Her happiness does not last long. Her wifely faithfulness and loyallty are questioned by Appanna when he comes to know about her pregnancy. Appanna accuses her of committing infidelity and asks her how it could be possible when he had not slept with her since their marriage. His male ego hurts him. He questions Rani in anger, "Aren't you ashamed to admit it, you harlot? I locked you in, and yet you managed to find a lover! Tell me who it is. Who did you go to with your sari off?... You shame me in front of the whole village, you darken my face, you slut-!"(52). In anger and with a motive for revenge he says, "I swear to you I am not my father's son, if I don't abort that bastard! Smash it into dust! Right now..." (52) and brings a huge stone to throw at her womb. But fortunately Rani and her baby in the womb are saved due to the hissing of Naga at a distance which makes Appanna withdraw himself from violent action. This also helps Rani to run away from the spot and lock herself in her room. Appanna's harassment and violent action make her think now that it would be better if she had remained barren.

Rani is disillusioned with Appanna's nature. She is worried for his playing double roles in her life. In the daytime he becomes cruel to her but at night he cajoles and consoles her. In belief and disbelief, truth and half-truth, appearance and reality she fails to distinguish between Appanna and Naga-Appanna. She gets confused when Appanna goes to complain against her before the village elders. Appanna accuses her of committing adultery and demands punishment for her. Rani thinks as if her pregnancy has doubled the risk of remaining barren. In the night when Naga-Appanna visits her she asks him, "Why are you humiliating me like this? Why are you stripping me naked in front of the whole village"? (53). She knows that the village elders will sit for her trial to punish her. The thought of the traditional method of trial to hold a red hot iron bar or plunging her hands in boiled oil in order to prove her innocence and chastity doubles her misery. She says in shame, frustration and despair, "I would have killed myself. But there's not even a rope in this house for me to use" (53).

Rani earnestly implores Naga Appanna, "Now you can go and withdraw the complaint. Say my wife isn't a whore" (53). But adding further to her humiliation and misery Naga-Appanna tells her, "the Village Elders will sit in judgement. You will be summoned. That can not be avoided" (53). He advises her to trust in him and opt for a more difficult trial, i.e., snake ordeal, "Like the mythical *Agnipariksha* of Sita in the *Ramayana,*" (Kumar 146) and prove her chastity. Introducing this classic chastity test from the folktales Karnad mocks at the traditional test of truth in his individual talent. The mythical Sita had come through the ordeal of fire because she was truly chaste and faithful. But here Rani's coming through the ordeal of handling a living cobra establishes her identity that is used to prove her as a *pativrata,* a faithful wife. The reversal is that in the *Ramayana* Rama has a classic rejection of Sita but in the play the wayward husband "has to accept the chastity of a wife who undoubtedly had a lover, and a child he knows he did not engender" (*Collected Plays* Vol. I : xxxi). Naga knows that the village elders will not object to this kind of trial for Rani as it is more difficult and risky than holding the red hot iron bar. In belief and half-belief Rani apprehends that she may die like the dog or the mongoose which her husband had brought to guard his house.

Rani's trial is like the trial of mythical Sita, Savitri and Draupadi who defied patriarchal authority by proving their chastity. Her test becomes a metaphor to mock at the male ego and gender superiority. Naga-Appanna tells her, "There is an enormous ant-hill under the banyan tree. Almost like a mountain. A King Cobra lives in it. Say you will put your hand into the ant-hill... And pull out the King Cobra and take your oath by that Cobra" (53). Naga-Appanna trains Rani to tell the truth in confidence failing which the cobra will bite her. When Rani gets worried as her private self is going to be disclosed to the public, Naga-Appana advises her that truth will preside and evade the evil. He tells her, "Don't you worry. Your huband will become your slave tomorrow. You will get all you have ever wanted" (54). On the trial day when Rani is summoned to remain present before the village elders, Appanna complains against her infidelity, "since the day of our wedding, I have not once touched my wife or slept by her side. And yet she is pregnant" (55). The whole village anxiously waits to see Rani's trial. When they ask her to take an oath for her chastity by holding a red hot iron bar or chosing to plunge her hand in boiling oil, she moves a step forward and opts to go through the snake ordeal. They advise her to think twice before taking such risky trial and desist her from this trial as it doubles the risk on her life and her unborn child too. Her choice for snake ordeal surprises the villagers. She pulls out the cobra from the ant-hill and holding it in her hands says gainsayingly that she has touched two in her life: "Yes, my husband and this King Cobra. Except for these two, I have not touched any one of the male sex. Nor have I allowed any other male to touch me. If I lie, let the Cobra bite me" (58).

The villagers have expected the trial scene to be a mourning scene. The expected mandate becomes a miracle when the cobra does not hurt her rather slides up her shoulder and spreads its hood like an umbrella over her head. Swaying its hood gently for a while, it becomes docile and moves over her shoulder like a garland and slips back into the ant-hill. Rani only stares at it uncomprehendingly. The villagers now call her a 'Divine Being' and a 'Goddess'. Rani proves to be a goddess incarnate for revealing her divinity. But Appanna knows the truth. He knows that he has not slept with her nor has she become pregnant parthenogenetically like Kunti in the *Mahabharata*. The cobra is the actual husband of Rani which is unknown to others and the world is not ready to accept it. The cobra is more understanding and humane in the beastly form than Appanna the beast in human form. Rani's taming the *naga* makes her instantly an angel. The whole village adores her as the mother goddess. In realisation of truth about Rani's pregnancy and suspicion of the half-truth about her proving as a chaste woman he suspects his own sanity. With Rani's trial, "His own notions of the dominant male and the chaste wife are pulverized by the ironic situation" (Dhanavel 24). With trust in the *naga* miracle and distrust in Rani's pregnancy he says;

> Is the whole world against me? Have I sinned so much that even Nature should laugh at me? I know I haven't slept with my wife. Let the world say what it likes. Let any miracle declare her a goddess. But I know! What sense am I to make of my life if that's worth nothing? (60).

The truth is that both the husband and wife know each other's honesty but through the trial the husband is made to believe his wife's chastity which he knows well better than others. The private matters often cannot be assessed well by the public in the magic of a trial. In public pressure and private distrust Appanna accepts Rani as a goddess incarnate for her going through the snake ordeal. He is surprised and disillusioned with her miracle that changes his contempt to concept.

The villagers deify Rani when Appanna defies Rani's chastity. They declare Appanna a lucky husband. They fall at her feet and take them in procession in a palanquin. They appreciate Appanna for marrying Rani due to his merits done in the past ten lives. They sought Rani's blessings. When the villagers leave them at their house and disperse Appanna suspends her disbelief, falls at her feet and tells her, "Forgive me. I am a sinner. I was blind..."(59). Rani emerges from a very weak, frail and archetypal traditional Indian woman to an extremely bold one. The trial is "the test of her fidelity, after which her husband, a victim of metaphysical mystique himself will become her slave for good—is a lie which gives the lie to the lie or mystique itself" (Chari 236). She is elevated to the status of a living goddess, an object of veneration and worship. In fact, "The central issue fo the play is Rani's fidelity to her husband. When she, on oath, declares before the elders that she is faithful to her husband, she is both true and not true" (Ramachandran 26-27). Rani realises that Naga is not an illusion but a reality and through it she attains a state of heavenly bliss. It is only due to Naga that she is "apotheosised into a divine goddess incarnate" (Goel 2007:49). Naga's transformation to Appanna is the "reminiscent of Satan's becoming a snake and then Satan again in the Christian mythology. The only difference between the two is that mythical Satan gets transformed into a snake with the ill intention of misguiding Eve, the mother of mankind, but in *Naga-Mandala* Cobra takes the shape of Naga (Appanna) out of love and affection for Rani" (Kumar 144). Due to her innocence and simplicity she fails to distinguish the difference between Appanna and Naga-Appanna. But this impoverishes her condition in frigidity. Through the snake ordeal she proves her extraordinariness. The village elders advise Appanna to spend the rest of his life in her service. The Story estimates her new life:

> So Rani got everything she wished for, a devoted husband, a happy life. She even got a life-long servant to draw water for her house. For Appanna's concubine was present at the trial. When she saw Rani's glory, she felt ashamed of her sinful life and volunteered to do menial work in Rani's house. In due course, Rani gave birth to a beautiful child. A son. Rani lived happily with her husband, child and servant (59).

> Rani is happy at last in her silent struggle to win over her husband. Seeing the change in Appanna she realises that "Every hope of opression has a ventilator of freedom" (Dhanavel 28).

The play evokes an impression how a traditional society is gender biased. When Appanna visits his concubine and inflicts all kinds of cruelties on Rani the village remains silent but when Rani enjoys her motherhood the village makes a hue and cry over her chastity. The village never questions on Appanna's integrity in the light of his relationship with his comcubine. But when Rani's pregnancy comes to light it compels her to go through a trial to prove her chastity. It is ironical that the village is callous enough to Appanna's lecherous and extramarital relation and becomes jubilant enough to see the mockery of a woman in the trial. The public trial of Rani "leaves the audience to reflect on the efficacy of the social laws which discriminate a woman from a man and which demand a wife's faithfulness even to her callous husband"

(Jalote 274). Although Appanna is ashamed of his sinful life in the past his reconciliation with Rani becomes possible for Naga. He accepts her as a chaste woman under the public pressure. With Rani he makes an uneasy homecoming in his accepted belief suppressing the truth. The reconciliation does not provide him a recession from his worries. This evokes a question on how a woman can fail to realise the love of her real husband and the other in transformed shape as no two men make similar love. Therefore the Story rightly remarks revealing the complex nature of woman, "No two men make love alike... when her (Rani's) true husband climbed into bed with her, how could she fail to realise it was somehow new?" (60). The efficacy of woman's chastity and husband's loyalty without emotional attachment is emphasised in the play. If neither Appanna, Rani nor Naga is chaste why then should social laws discriminate a woman compelling her to go through a public trial to prove her chastity. The snake ordeal of Rani expresses the miracle and mystery of human nature. All Appanna, Rani and Naga know what is truth and how much they are honest in their fidelity but they willingly suspend it for the future of a family.

Naga-Mandala has two endings. This is because the play is based on two Kannada folktales. In his narratorial skill and dramaturgical presentation Karnad sets these two endings to the play. In an interview with Tutun Mukerjee he says; "There are two endings for *Naga-Mandala*. In one, the snake dies. In the second ending, the writer is asked to do something to change the tragic end of the snake-lover. So, the woman lets down her hair and asks the snake to hide in her lock" (43). After the trial Rani enjoys her conjugal bliss with Appanna. Although she differentiates between Naga's love and Appanna's love she suspends the former in disbelief and surrenders to the later in compromise for her future.

Naga is happy that Rani wins over Appana. But he regrets that he has lost his love for Rani. For Rani's happiness Naga does everything. His sympathy for Rani is changed into love. Sitting in the ant-hill in alienation and melancholy Naga recollects his memories with Rani, "I have given her everything. Her husband. Her child. Her home. Even her maid. She must be happy. But I haven't seen her.... It is night. She will be asleep. This is the right time to visit her" (61). Naga visits Rani through his familiar way at the usual hour. He discovers Rani sleeping next to her husband by the side of her child and keeping her head on Appanna's shoulders. Naga is not able to believe his eyes at what he sees there. He gets besotted with Rani when he sees her,

> In another man's arms? In another man's bed? Does she curl around him as passionately every night now? And dig her nails into his back? Bite his lips? And here I am a sloughed-off-skin on the tip of a thorn... No. I can't bear this. Someone must die. Someone has to die. Why shouldn't I kill her? If I bury my teeth into her breast now, she will be mine—mine for ever. (Moves to her swiftly. But stops). No, I can't. My love has stiched up my lips. Pulled out my fangs. Torn out my sac of poison. Withdraw your veils of light. Flames. Let my shame float away in the darkness. Don't mock, gecko. Yes, this King Cobra is now no better than a grass snake. A common reptile. That's what I am and I had forgotten that. I thought I could become human. Turn into my own creation. No! Her thighs, her bosom, her lips are for one who is forever a man. I shed my own skin every season. How could I even hope to retain the human form? For me—yes, only her long locks.... They are right for me. I shall summon my magical powers for the last time—to become the size of her tresses. To become so thin, so small that I can hide in them, play with them, swim away in their dark flow (61-62).

For her skin and hair Rani appears in her sleep like a snake woman and a temptress to Naga. Naga enters into her tresses and commits suicide in it. Rani wakes up from her sleep due to the heaviness of her hair. As she combs her hair she and Appana discover a dead cobra falling out of it. Naga as the true lover of Rani has strangled itself in Rani's hair. Naga's *harakiri* surprises Rani. She mourns over Naga's death. In tearful eyes Rani picks it up and presses it to her cheeks. In willing suspension of disbelief Appanna knows that by her trial Rani has escaped from the inescapable truth but appreciates Rani: "You are no common person. You are a goddess" (63). Rani thanks their good lot that they have been saved because the cobra has spared their child and has given the gift of life to their son as a father. For this Rani expresses her desire, "A cobra. It has to be ritually cremated....When we cremate this snake, the fire should be lit by our son.... And every year on this day, our son should perform the rituals to commemorate its death" (63) what a son does for his own father to which Appanna agrees.

The second ending of the play reveals that Rani feels pain again in her hair. The pain is so powerful that she feels like pulling out her hair. This time when she combs her hair a live cobra falls out and writhes on the floor. In fear and nervoursness Appanna runs away for a stick when Rani tells it, "'He'll kill you. Go. Go away. No! Not that way... what shall we do? Why did you ever come in here, stupid? (Suddenly). My hair! Of course. Come, quick. Climb into it.... . Now stay there. And lie still. You don't know how heavy you are. Let me get used to you,....' It went that way—toward the bath room" (64). Rani's hair is the symbol of her wedding bliss where the cobra lives happily for ever.

In suspension of belief and appreciation of disbelief Appanna accepts Rani's superiority. For Naga's blessing on Rani patriarchal Appanna no more subjugates her. Karnad concludes that faithfulness and loyalty sweeten the conjugal happiness. Any authoritarian attitude to it spoils the happiness in both the lives. Loss of mutual faith is often regained with the benevolent public interference as Naga did for Rani to win over her husband. Thus, "*Naga-Mandala* exposes the secular and spiritual maladies of the society" (Dhanavel 24). The play ends with the disappearance of flames one by one in the morning. The man only sits alone in the inner sanctum of the temple and bows to the audience and goes out. Further "The play calls for destroying all boundaries, including those between the author and the reader, the read text and the heard performance" (Prasad 25).

Flowers (2005) is Karnad's first dramatic monologue written in English. Drawing a traditional world of folktale in the play Karnad attempts to focus the story of a very introspective, chauvinistic and confessional priest who is marked for his endearing innocence, and love for his shrivelled wife and a sensuous courtesan. It is also his first play on the story of self-realization and penance that works on male rather than female desire registering a small but important shift in his dramaturgy. Projecting the priest's sexual awakening in the home of the courtesan Karnad turns his world of ossified routine life upside down and begins to project his lifecycle of falsehood and concealment that culminates in the lie about the *lingam* sprouting hair. Karnad's authorial imagination is highly accelerated with the closeness of Hindu concept of eroticism and devotion. He deftly draws "the core event of the Shivalinga sprouting hair, but recasts the legend as a conflict between religious devotion and erotic love, undergirded by the priest's guilt at his daily betrayal of his wife" (*Collected Plays* Vol. II: xxxi-ii).

The play is a monologue based on the legend of Veeranna who belongs to the Chitradurga region of Karnataka. Before its theatrical effectiveness in the play the legend is incorporated from Kannada writer, T.R. Subbanna's (known as TaRaSu) novel, *Hamsageethe* (Swan Song) published in 1952. The title of the novel literally means the 'swan song' of the protagonist, Venkatasubbayya whom Subbanna inserts in the tale of Veeranna, the *archaka* of the Hidambeshwara temple. About the legend narrated in Subbanna's version Aparna Bhargava Dharwadker writes in the "Introduction" to his *Collected Plays* (Vol. II):

> The married priest has passionately in love with a mistress to whom he takes the offerings from the temple after the evening prayers. One day the *palegar* (chieftain) discovers a hair in the *prasada* and demands an explanation from Veeranna, who claims that the hair belongs to god. Challenged by the chieftain to prove the truth of this claim, the priest in turn challenges god to display hair or accept his head in punishment, and enters a meditative trance to the accompaniment of Venkatasubbayya's song. When the chieftain arrives the next day to expose Veeranna's lie, the Shivalinga has indeed sprouted long silken hair, and when (urged by the singer) he pulls out a tuft to test its authenticity, blood begins to ooze from the crown of the *lingam*. Overwhelmed by a sense of sin at having injured the deity, Veeranna beheads himself in the sanctum (xxxi).

But in the play Karnad probes into the priest's mind which oscillates between the rational and intuitive, the empirical and the transcendental. In the theatrical presentation of priest's desire for tradition and religion he experiments religious devotion and erotic love, and introduces new paradigms of poetic and sensual imagination in the story of a Brahmin priest's selfrealisation and penance.

The play evokes the figure of Praneshacharya, the priest and the 'crest jewel of vedantic learning' in U.R. Anantha Murthy's novel *Samskara*. While Praneshacharya in Murthy's novel is the spiritual leader of a community rather than a caretaker in a local temple, Karnad's priest in the *Flowers* is a temple priest of Chitradurga area undertakes a journey within. Karnad says:

> It is also true that *Samskara* is seminal to our understanding of casteist Brahminism in Karnataka, so much so that it is impossible to think of Brahminism in any other terms... Anantha Murthy has explored it so imaginatively, beautifully. The influence of that one book has been very strong. However, this particular story belongs to the Chitradurga area (Mukherjee 54).

Analysing both the works Apanna Bhargava Dharwadker finds:

> Praneshacharya's liaison with the untouchable prostitute Chandri precipitates a sexual and spiritual crisis that is still unresolved at the end of the novel... in *Flowers* the priest's sexual awakening in the home of a courtesan Ranganayaki turns his world of ossified routine upside down, and begins the cycle of falsehood and concealment that culminates in the lie about the *lingam* sprouting hair (*Collected Plays,* Vol. II: xxxii).

In both the cases the protagonists sublimate their sexuality into religious fervour, and find sudden release after a lifetime of repression in an illicit union. The two protagonists have their extended crisis in accelerated form but their thought of spirituality and act of renunciation gives way to sensuality, resistance to temptation and purity to pollution.

In the play Karnad recasts the legend as a conflict between religious devotion and erotic passion. He highlights the spiritual and aesthetic intensity in priest's worshipping and beautifying of linga which is transferred to the body of the Ranganayaki. Karnad mingles the spiritual with the carnal which is short lived in the miracle of the Shivalinga and confirms the power of the priest's worship. In the portrayal of the priest's act of involvement in sensual and spiritual affairs he establishes his direct contact with actuality, passion for love and sex, the *linga*'s mysterious quality and his religious experience that communes with God. Narrating a triangulated contest between the priest, the courtesan and the chieftain as the undercurrent of oppositional strands both within the psyche and outside it the playwright sets a landscape of emotive response. About the setting of the play Aparna Bhargava

Dharwadker observes:

> The monologue is... a recounting of the nameless priest's experience as he prepares to drown himself in the temple tank. As in Karnad's earlier folk-based plays the relationship in *Flowers* form a pattern of tringulated desire, this time between a man and two women. The drama highlights the spiritual and aesthetic intensifying with which the priest has devoted himself to the task of worshipping and beatifying the *lingam*—an intensity that is transferred to the body of the courtesan-mistress. This mingling of the spiritual and the carnal is short-lived, however. The miracle of the Shivalinga confirms the power of the priest's worship and marks him as one of the chosen, but it also ends his life (*Collected Plays* Vol. II: xxxii).

Although the play presents a story it is not a story and the playwright assesses the spiritual and sensual intensity with divine miracle in the experience of a single narrator. The monologue is a lengthy speech but short of a play. It focuses on the speaker's revelation of his memories at a significant moment in his life, emotional weakness, resolution and spiritual strength. Assessing the private thoughts of the priest about his sensual intensity and divine miracle the playwright makes it a discourse on sensuality that breeds spiritualism at certain point of time in one's life. Analysing the theme of eroticism and spiritualism in relation to his other folk plays Janhavi Acharekar remarks:

> A dramatic monologue by a priest torn between his erotic love for God on the one hand and that for the courtesan Chandravati on the other; caught between love for his wife and that for his mistress; between passion and duty. "Flowers" smells of Karnad's previous themes. It echoes the sexuality of "Nagamandala" and the conflict of "Hayavadana". And like all his other works, it draws inspiration from Indian history and mythology. Set in a distant mythological past, this play, derived from a folktale from Chitradurga, shares the landscape of Karnad's previous plays. And to the playwright, who lived in a village with no electricity until the age of 14, growing up as he did on stories or 'harikathas' as the only means of entertainment, this is the borrowed landscape of his childhood (5).

The monologue expresses the everyday rituals of the priest of a Shiva temple and his emotional involvement with the courtesan Chandravati, his spiritual involvement with the *linga* and detached life with his wife.

The priest in the play is Karnad's narrative voice who represents his two spatial units of male principle outside the temple—the priest's home and that of the courtesan. His home is the mundane world where he lives with his wife, two children, and aged parents who need his support. In such an environment he is denied of privacy and love-making with his wife. On the other hand he worships the *linga* with maximum efforts to decorate it with flowers requiring different emotions and skill which provide him a sense of pride and power. The priest lives with his dual selves—the self of a *grahyastha* and the self of a *sanyasa*—and torn between his desire for sensuality and quest for spirituality. The mundane subdues his spiritual and the spiritual safeguards his mundane. The house of the courtesan is the sensual world where he is emotionally involved with the courtesan that affects his act of worship of the linga and its ritualistic performances. The everyday life of his spiritual involvement with the *linga* is disturbed by his sexual desire for the courtesan, Chandravati. While his involvement with the *linga* is culturally inseparable, with Chandravati it is emotionally inseparable. He is deeply involved with the linga, his "step wife" (244) and spends hours with the ablution of milk, ghee and oil on its slippery surface, and devising new ways to decorate it with flowers. On the other hand he is emotionally attracted for the courtesan who acts as "a force which lures the male and which has to be conquered or dismissed before a full realization can take place of the principle" (Jain 347).

The temple is a public universe through which he has his recognition. Here he talks to *linga,* sings to it, discusses recent political developments and decorates it with flowers. The priest takes a full hour at sunset to get ready for the *pooja*. His wife attends to the basic ritual requirements such as jossticks, camphor and placement of wicks in silver plates for *aarati*. His decorating of flowers to *linga* is innovative. The Chieftain, a great devotee of Lord Shiva is an admirer of his floral efforts who only accepts a single flower as God's *prasada* after *pooja* and touches it to his eyes, sticks it behind his right ear and rides home. His everyday routine duty in the temple has been disturbed on a Shivaratri day when he explored the physical contours of the courtesan at the time of her visit to the temple. He says:

> She came into my life during the Shivaratri celebrations, which go on for a week. During this period, the Chieftain comes down for the pooja in the morning and once he leaves, there are the usual things of devotees, milling at the door of the temple to offer coconuts to the linga. I crack every one of the coconuts myself and return the halves as prasada, with a petal or two and sandal paste in it... I love doing it for the linga but... people shake their heads in admiration at my passion for the lord... I was too tired to look at faces and desperate to finish the day. I mechanically took the coconut she offered, broke it, placed the *prasada* inside and turned to hand it back. She was bending, holding the *pallu* of her sari spread out in front of her. The upper half of her bosom was uncovered and as I dropped the shells in her sari, I saw the mole. On her right breast, just near the cleft. I looked up at her. There must have been something unusual in my movement, for she looked up too and caught my eyes. For a moment we stared at each other and then she turned away.... During the rest of that week, I started the day impatient for a glimpse of hers (245).
>
> This prompted the priest to pick up some flowers from the *linga* after the departure of the Chieftain and proceed to courtesan's house where she was living with an elderly woman. He was of the impression that "she is a courtesan... and so perhaps not beyond reach. But I was a poor priest and had nothing to offer her" (245-46) except the flowers. He got infatuated for her and said, "I wanted her. I had never lusted for a woman before and so felt emasculated by his sudden weakness. Yet I could not control the fire raging in my loins.... I started the day impatient for a glimpse of hers" (245).

With the *linga* he could be playful but with the courtesan he has a totally different experience and enjoys an awakening of sensuousness. In a guilt consciousness and desire for *moksha* she pleads before the *linga*, "I am mad stupid. I am mad... But help me, please or at least forgive me" (246). In his state of helplessness he surrenders before the *linga* for a piety and at the same time he longs for Chandravati's naked skin.

The courtesan is always in the company of her mistress, a much older woman. The priest cracks a coconut, ties the halves in his shoulder cloth and leaves for her house. Every day they have a quick meeting of their eyes. But the priest has no privilege to register her features although she is receiving the *prasada*. He notices the mole on her face, brilliant eyes, straight nose and lips which look like thick petals. The sensuous appeal of her body, use of her perfumes and his constant touching of her body during *pooja* pose a challenge to his spiritual integrity. It is significant that the priest worships the *linga* with flowers in the daytime and worships the body of Chandravati with the same flowers at night. In sensuousness he never bothers that it is inauspicious to visit Chandravati during her menstrual seclusion in her mistress's cavernous house.

The decorating of the *linga* with flowers expresses priest's best filigree skill in his spiritual experience and visiting the courtesan in the night reveals his subteranean motifs in detachment to *linga*. He develops a derison for his wife which establishes a conflict between devotion for the *linga* and desire for sensuality. He becomes a torn self in his worshipping of the *linga* and weanig for Chandravati. He develops a psychic conflict between spirituality and sensuality. His devotion and fear for sin make him conscious of his *grahastha dharma* and *dharmic karma*. But it cannot stand due to the fluidity of his imagination for Chandravati. In a mad desire for her he says:

> I had to undress her—she would not help me. Sometimes the knot of her breast-cloth was tied into such a mischievous knot that I threatened to cut it with a knife... and of other times the cloth fell off without warning at my merest touch, leaving me staring breathlessly at her bare bosom. When I finished decorating her, I would lay her down and kiss the more (250-251).

The priest's sensual consuming of courtesan's body forces him for his self-discovery. His mental landscape is marked with the imagination of sacred and profane which exist as parallels, not as continuities or interactive practices.

One day the Chieftain does not come to offer his *pooja*. This encourage the priest's sensual appeal. He collects the flowers from the *linga* and goes to Chandravati's house to decorate her with the same flowers. But when the Chieftain informs about his coming with a sudden fire of canon on the hilltop the priest is horrified and leaves Chandravati's house immediately, collecting the same flowers from her body. He narrates the situation when he is drugged with sensuality for Chandravati:

> The tranquility of the night was shattered by the canon. It was barely more than a distant thud and it didn't even raise a ripple in her sleep. But I had spent years training my ears to catch its faintest reverberation and responded to its peremptory summons instantly. I sprang into action. Frantic, I started pulling out the flowers from her hair and piling them on my shoulder cloth.She sat up, groggy and dazed, yelping in pain as I snatched at the flowers. 'He is coming'. I said without wasting any time on looking at her. 'I must rush'. Every moment was precious. I rapidly calculated in my mind that I would have half an hour to set things right once I reached the temple and hoped my wife had not slept through the canon shot (255-56).

Just before his royalty's coming he decorates the *linga* with the same flowers. This act of using the same flowers to worship the divine *linga* and the human Chandravati goes against his priestly ethics. His desecrating and defiling of the *linga* is a sin in Hindu belief. The priest is morally afraid of the *linga* as has decorated it with the "illicit flower" (257). He is mortally afraid of the Chieftain as he discovers a long hair from the flower while he is receiving it as *prasad*. He is shocked when the Chieftain says, "I didnt know god had long hair" (256); this threatens his priestly sainthood and everyday existence. He blames his lot for his misdeed and takes it as a divine disgrace. In diffidence he pleads before the Chieftain to create confidence in God. He says that it is "possible under the circumstances. If we believe that God has long hair'... 'He will have long hair' " (257). The Chieftain places the flower back in the plate and leaves without exhibiting any contemptuous annoyance and insolent response with an instruction to prove it on the next new moon day.

The fear of sinning and fear of self-destruction establish a sudden transgression in the priest's self from profanity to spirituality. He realises that the long hair discovered in the *prasad* was from Chandravati. But this circumstantial incident that creates suspicion in the Chieftain's mind affects his sacred pristly integrity. The incident not only brings him shame and fear but also illuminates his renewed devotion for the *linga* again. He locks up the door of the inner sanctum and sets down cross-legged in front of the *linga* and does his meditation for a *mukti* (a freedom from public humiliation and authoritarian punishment). His association with the *linga* is from childhood. He hopes that it would save him from humiliation. He knows that the temple was his favourite shrine. It provides sustenance to his family and preserves his identity and reputation. Being repentant of his guilt and in realisation of the importance of *linga* he says:

> I had disgraced myself and trembled at the thought of facing the world in that state. I didn't know what God could do. I had created a situation which was now beyond even. His tinkering. But there was nothing else for me to do except surrender to Him. For twelve days, I cleansed my existence of everything, every name or person, except the *linga* (258).

The fear for the loss of his priestly status promptes him to worship the *linga* with renewed energy and ritualistic demonstration. He narrates the rigours of his meditation, "As soon as the Chieftain left, I dispatched my wife home and asked her, from stepping into the temple precincts. Then I locked the door of the sanctum and sat down,... in front of it and prayed" (257). In remorse he weeps for disgracing the *linga* and desecrating the shrine. Surrendering to Him for twelve days he wants to cleanse his disgraced self.

On the day of his trial the crowd gathers there to see the priest's fate. The Chieftain arrives in the evening. The priest knows that he has had his association with the *linga* from his childhood and He would not desert him during his troubles. The Chieftain asks falteringly, "should we test?" (258). The inner sanctum is dark and open. He takes it an ordeal as if ordained by God. Although the thought of the hair on the *linga* is churning in his mind he is feeling miserable with the thought of this miracle. Having completely failed to manage the situation he says:

> I was in a stupor, from hunger, from lack of sleep and from a complete sense of desolation. I dully wondered why they had all come. What did they expect to see? My public humiliation? What did the Chieftain hope to see? Why had he joined the charade? Indeed, what had I hoped to achieve by asking for a grace period? (258).

God's miracle surprises all. God is good and becomes kind to the priest. With his final prayer in the sanctum, "the long and thick hair that come cascading from the linga hiding it completely" (258). As one of the Brahmin courtiers of the Chieftain move to pull out the hair and bring the tuft for inspection of the Chieftain there is blood on his fingers. In nervousness, "The Brahmin ran back to the *linga,* felt for the spot from where he had plucked the hair and collapsed, crying hysterically, 'It's bleeding. It's bleeding. I have wounded God' (259).

The Chieftain falls at the feet of the priest, begs for his forgiveness and seeks his blessings. Now no one, not even the Chieftain, his wife and the public dare to question his honesty and integrity. He gains the status of a state saint. The soldiers protect and guard him at the approaches to the temple. He gains his reputation and credibility that is at stake due to the Chieftain's discovery of a hair from the *prasad.* When he returns to his usual everyday duty in the temple he prays to the *linga* with devotion. To his misery and surprise he finds, "The hair is gone but the wound is still fresh where the Brahmin had pulled out the tuft" (259).

The playwright has projected the two aspects of the priest's character. While his devotion for God is challenged by the Chieftain for his doubt over the priest's sensuous affair with a woman, the aspect of his family life is revealed in his relationship with two women—his wife and Chadravati, the courtesan. The extramariatal relationship with the courtesan paralyses and pollutes his marital bliss and dislocates his concentration from the object of worship. His priestly profession was psychologically affected by his attraction towards Chandravati. After the trial he is unable to live happily either with his wife or with Chandravati as his wife informs him, "she is gone. She and her old woman left town the very next day" (259). The priest was all appreciation for the courtesan and had humiliated his wife. Now he repents for his tainted self. He feels "Guilty of cruelty to the two women" (260). He says, "I am guilty of gross dereliction, of scarilege... why then should God cast His vote on my behalf?... Such grace is condescension even it comes from God. Why am I worthy of this burden He has placed on my shoulders?" (260).

The play ends with a dramatic resolution of conflict between spirituality and sensuality. The two in the form of physical passion and spiritual devotion merge as do notions of the male and female do. The appearance of Scorpio, the eighth sign of the Zodiac, crawls out of the recess in the third step towards the priest which corresponds to J.E.Cirlot's notion of a "span of man's life which lies under the threat of death.... It is also related with the sexual function" (280-81). The monologue is "a poignant soliloquy that questions and debates relentlessly even as it shares with the audience, the character's anguish in conflict" (Acharekar 5) for using the flowers to worship the *linga* in a cultural practice and decorating the courtesan in sensuality to gain her favour.

Karnad's *Hayavadana, Naga-Mandala* and *Flowers* explore the traditional world of folklores. Working with the ancient folk sources from regional and Sanskrit folk classics he has made us aware of India's rich tradition and culture. The folktales he has chosen as archetypes for his plays are not merely the stories told to the children to go to bed but they focus on the values and their implications to adore the adult mind. Though they deal with the human follies and foibles, the role of divine beings in human affairs, the world of realism and make-believe, and the rich culture of India are embedded in them. *Hayavadana* presents the myth of Ganesha, the embodiment of imperfection and completeness in Indian culture; the love story of Devadatta, Padmini and Kapila; and the story of Hayavadana. He has merged myth and folktales in dealing with human problems. *Naga-Mandala* presents the suffering of a newly married woman who is neglected by her husband for his extramarital affairs. Narrating the existential plight of the woman protagonist, and ill-treatment and attrocities of her husband the playwright presents a miracle in which a *naga* out of its love comes forward to rescue her in real life. In both the plays divine beings, human beings and animals are the role players. But when they play their roles in existential dilemmas, physical and psychological spatiality most of their actions and situations appear quite magical and like miracles. *Flowers* is different from the two. It can be read as a monologue, story, long soliloquy and confession of his protagonist who is torn between the sensual and spiritual, mundane and divine. Focusing on a contrast between the protagonist's lust for eroticism and longing for spiriritualism Karnad presents his Hindu conviction in the two that go side by side. Karnad guesses that folktales are not mere gossips of the common and illiterate masses rather they whisper to the larger audience about the treasures of India's great tradition and culture.

Works Cited

Abrams, M.H. *A Glossary of Literary Terms*. New Delhi: Cengage Learning India Private Limited, 2005.

Acharekar, Janhavi. "Of Love and Conflict". *The Hindu Magazine*. 130: 15 (April 15), 2007.

Babu, M. Sarat. "The Concept of Chastity and *Naga-Mandala*". *The Plays of Girish Karnad. Critical Perspectives*. Ed. Jaydipsinh Dodiya. New Delhi. Prestige Books, 1999.

______________ . "Dionysian ego in *Hayavadana*". *The Plays of Girish Karnad: Critical Perspectives*. Ed. Jaydipsinh Dodiya. New Delhi: Prestige Books, 1999.

Behera, Guru Charan. *Appropriating Folk Culture: A Study of the Post-Independence Indian Drama*. New Delhi: Authorspress, 2008.

Brown, Norman O. "Apollo and Dionysus". *Life Against Death*. London: Routledge and Kegan Paul, 1959.

Chari, A. Jaganmohana."*Hayavadana* and *Nagamandala*: A Study in Postcolonial Dialectics". *The Plays of Girish Karnad: Critical Perspectives*. Ed. Jaydipsinh Dodiya. New Delhi: Prestige Books, 1999.

Chinmayananda, Swami. "Shri Ganapati-Vinayaka". *Glory of Ganesha*. Bombay: Central Chinmaya Mission Trust, 1987.

Cirlot, J.E. *A Dictionary of Symbols* (1962). Trans. Jack Sage. London & New York: Routledge, 1988.

Dhanavel, P. *The Indian Imagination of Girish Karnad*. New Delhi: Prestige Books, 2000.

Aparna Bhargav. "Introduction" to Girish Karnad's *Collected Plays*. (Vol.I). New Delhi: Oxford University Press, 2005.

______________ . "Introduction" to Girish Karnad's *Collected Plays*. (Vol.II). New Delhi: Oxford University Press, 2005.

Gandhi, Krishna. "Hayavadana". *Enact*. (Aug-Sept). 1972: 68-69.

Goel, Savita. "*Folk Theatre Strategies in Hayavadana*". *The Plays of Girish Karnad: Critical Perspectives*. Ed. Jaydipsinh Dodiya. New Delhi: Prestige Books, 1999.

______________ . "Girish Karnad's *Naga-Mandala*: Levels of Transformation". *Indian Drama in English: An Anthology of Recent Criticism*. Eds. C.L. Khatri and Kumar Chandradeep. Jaipur: Book Enclave, 2007.

Gupta, Santosh. "*Naga-Mandala*: A Story of Marriage and Love". *The Plays of Girish Karnad: Critical Perspectives*. Ed. Jaydipsinh Dodiya. New Delhi: Prestige Books, 1999.

Jain, Jasbir. "*Flowers: A Dramatic Monologue*: Patriarchal Power and the Nature of Sacrifice". *Girish Karnad's Plays: Performance and Citical Perspectives*. Ed. Tutun Mukherjee. New Delhi: Pencraft International, 2008.

Jalote, S.R. "Epic-Theatre Revisited: A Study of *Naga-Mandala*". *The Plays of Girish Karnad: Critical Perspectives*. Ed. Jaydipsinh Dodiya. New Delhi: Prestige Books, 1999.

Joshipura, Pranav. "*Hayavadana* and the Interminable Quest for Perfection". *The Plays of Girish Karnad: Critical Perspectives*. Ed. Jaydipsinh Dodiya. New Delhi: Prestige Books, 1999.

______________ . "*Naga-Mandala* Reconsidered". *The Plays of Girish Karnad: Critical Perspectives*. Ed. Jaydipsinh Dodiya. New Delhi: Prestige Books, 1999.

Karnad, Girish. "Theatre in India". *Daedalus. Fall*. 1989.

______________ . "Author's Introduction" to *Three Plays*. (*Naga-Mandala, Hayavadana, Tughlaq*) Delhi: OUP, 1994. (All textual references are made to this edition).

______________ . "In Search of a Theatre". *Creating Theory: Writers on Writing*: Ed. Jasbir Jain. New Delhi: Pencraft International, 2000.

______________ . "*Flowers: A Dramatic Monologue*". *Collected Plays*. (Vol. II). New Delhi: OUP, 2005. (All textual references are made to this edition)

______________ . (Interview) "In His Own Voice: A Conversation with Girish Karnad". *Girish Karnad's Plays: Performance and Critical Perspectives*. Ed. Tutun Mukerjee. New Delhi: Pencraft International, 2008.

Kermode, Frank. *The Sense of an Ending*. New Delhi: OUP, 1985.

Kurtkoti, Kirtinath. "Introduction" to Girish Karnad's *Hayavadana*. Calcutta: OUP, 1975.

Kumar, Nand. *Indian English Drama: A Study in Myths*. New Delhi: Sarup & Sons, 2003.

Lacan, Jacques. *The Language of the Self: The Function of Language in Psychoanalysis*. Trans. Anthony Wilden. Baltimore: Johns Hopkins University, 1968.

Mann, Thomas. *The Transposed Heads*. Trans. Lowe-Porter. London: Martin Secker and Warburg Ltd. 1955.

Murthy, K. Narasimha. *Modern Kannada Literature*. Bangalore: Pustakalaya Publications, 1992.

Naik, M.K. "From the Horse' Mouth: A Study of *Hayavadana*". *Girish Karnad's Plays Performance and Critical Perspectives*. Ed. Tutun Mukherjee. New Delhi: Pencraft International, 2008.

Naik, M.K. and Shyamala A. Narayan. *Indian English Literature 1980-2000: A Critical Survey*. New Delhi: Pencraft International, 2001.

Prasad, G.J.V. "Reality Imagined". *Seminar*. 384. August, 1991.

Ramachandran, C.N. "Girish Karnad: The Playwright in Search of Metaphors" *The Journal of Indian Writing in English*. 27:2 (July), 1999.

Ramanujan, A.K. "The Prince who Married His Own Left Half". *Aspects of India*. Ed. Margaret Case and N. Gerald Barrier. New Delhi: Manohar, 1986.

______________. ed. "Introduction" to his *Folktales from India*. New Delhi: Penguin Books, 1994.

Raykar, Shubhangi S. "The Development of Girish Karnad as a Dramatist: *Hayavadana*" *The Plays of Girish Karnad: Critical Perspectives*. Ed. Jaydipsinh Dodiya. New Delhi: Prestige Books, 1999.

Roy, Arundhati. "Transposing Realities". *The Hindu Magazine*. April. 14, 2002.

Vatsyayan, Kapila. *Traditional Indian Theatre: Multiple Streams*. New Delhi: National Book Trust of India, 1980.

4 Contextualising History in Contemporary Heteroglossia

History has always fascinated Girish Karnad like myth and floklore in his creative imagination. For him history is no longer a static background for a play; rather it is timeless, alive, absurd and mysterious in its entirety. History provides him with the elements of psychoanalysis, political praxis and revolutionary concepts with a shift from socio-political possibilities to pessimism. By writing historical plays he suspends the disbelief of the audiance and readers, and generates a new penchant for the protagonists in it. Rewriting history in the job of a historiographer he rather uncovers and discovers it in the contemporary consciousness. For him history does not have an autonomous existence as it has been to Shakespeare and Brecht, rather as a lover of historical personalities in Indian history he has projected their whims, temperaments, eccentricities, objectives, peculiarities as well as popularity. For him history not only appears full of events but also of ethics, discourse, universal law and ideologies as tools to liberate a society or the mankind from slavery, bondage and perils. By projecting the historical personalities and events in his dramatic oeuvres he has expressed his concepts as an objective chronicler and transcendent commentator. In the job of an investigator of a parenthesised period he has discovered the living plasmas of these dead heroes debating over them in painful speculations.

As a dispassionate lover of the protagonists in Indian history Girish Karnad dramatises them in their historical proper. In the job of a historiographer he rehistoricises them and their contemporary socio-political spatialisation. He makes a holistic approach to history as an objective chronicler. It seems that he does not like to convey a moral lesson from history rather cautions the nation unconsciously. Awakening his dead protagonists from their fossilised selves he reverberates them with his ideological genomes in post-colonial speculations. In the text of his historical plays he analyses his protagonists, their political, diplomatic, psychoanalytical and revolutionary concepts as a transcendent commentator. With an investigator's eye and reformist's zeal he has analysed the parenthesised periods of Indian history by delving these deads and makes a pleasurable imitation of history with moral imagination. In a debating manner he dramatises the dynamism of his protagonists in their situatedness. Writing a text on historical personages is not new in world literatures for its peripheral and canonical status as it helps to understand the great historical figures in transcendental and universal canons and paradoxes. Reading a literary text dealing with history in its context establishes the hierarchy of historical causes, events and its assured distinctions between the central and peripheral facts in history itself.

Karnad's historical plays are research oriented both on individual protagonists and on contemporary social, cultural, political and economic conditions of Indian society. Analysing definite periods in Indian history and the then prevalent situation he gives a detailed picture of the past for its relevance in the present. Karnad never claims as a reformist but his plays on Indian history convey a covert zeal to homogenise the Indian society. His historical plays—*Tughlaq* (1972), *Tale-danda* (1993) and *The Dreams of Tipu Sultan* (2004)—are first written in Kannada and then translated and trascreated into English. Although each of these plays deals with different periods of Indian history from twelfth century to nineteenth century an attempt has been made to critique them not in order of the chronology of their composition but in sequence of the incidents and events that they present.

Karnad's *Tale-danda* (1993) is a historical teleology on social conditions of north Karnataka in the twelfth century A.D. The play projects a socio-religious movement during the time of Kalachurya dynasty. Karnad has analysed his contemporary 'Mandir' and 'Mandal' movements as an objective chronicler in the 'historical givens' of the past carnivalising the *sharana* movememnt of to 1168 A.D. He has projected this *sharana* movement as a socio-religious one in its spirit and action that opposed idolatry, temple worship, and caste system in Hinduism which are the historical materials of the play. He says in an interview with Tutun Mukherjee:

> The play is inspired by the life and work of Basavana, a revolutionary poet-saint who lived in the city of Kalyan in Karnataka in the twelfth century. He has got together a remarkable group of poets, reformers, philosophers who created a courageous age of enquiry and social reform unmatched in the history of Karnataka. They opposed the caste system, condemned idolatry and temple worship, believed in the equality of sexes, believed in the progress of human enterprise. Naturally they attracted the wrath of the orthodox and the conservative people and the entire movement of Sharanas ended in chaos and terror in 1168. The idea was to use collective memory and historical inscription to build the plot (44-45).

Dealing with the ugly aspect of caste and religious intolerance during the social and political crises created out of Mandir-Mandal issues Karnad says, "When people all around us are slaughtered in the name of temple, I hear echoes from those times long past" (*Frontline* 76). Retrospecting the history in its sordid prospect he projects the mystery of caste and religion in the Indian social dynamics. The play is written on the backdrop of growing fundamentalism and communal frenzy in India. But contextualising the contemporaneity in history he presents an individual's endeavour towards communal integration during an epoch of violence. The play responds to a later movement in the political evolution of India-as-nation—the decisive shift in the late 1980s from secular to religious (specifically Hindu) nationalism.

History is the repository of knowledge. The pity is that mankind fails to learn this in its ignorance. Projecting the truth and universality that history conveys in its texts Karnad hyphenates the past and present in his study of the *sharana* movement in the Indian history of 800 years ago. Bringing the historical evidence into the contemporary reality he has analysed the contemporary events in heteroglossia for which makes M.K. Naik and S.A. Narayan to say that, ".... the putative parallel between Basavanna's radicalism and V.P. Singh's "Mandalism" is not projected effectively enough" (Naik and Narayan 204). But Karnad writes in the 'Preface' to the play:

> I wrote *Tale-danda* in 1989 when the 'Mandir' and the 'Mandal' movements were beginning to show again how relevant the questions posed by these thinkers were for our

> age. The horror of subsequent events and the religious fanaticism that has gripped our national life today have only proved how dangerous it is to ignore the solutions they offered (*Tale-danda*).

Throughout the play Karnad has presented the contemporary inter-religious (Hindu-Muslim) conflict in the intra-religous (brahmin-untouchable) conflict of the twelfth century history by interlocking movements of transgression and punishment. Dramatising the social elements, revolutionary concepts, humanistic faith and caste factors in totality as historical materials he has deconstructed history in the corrective doubts. Aparna Bhargava Dharwadker rightly remarks:

> The play's historical narrative centres on the twelfth century Virasaiva movement of religious reform and protest, led by the poet-saint Basavana, which flourished by a time in the city of Kalyan (in present day Karnataka) under the patronage of King Bajjala, but ended in violence when the new community translated its opposition to caste into practice by arranging a marriage between a brahmin girl and an untouchable boy. The focus on the hierarchial disunity of Hinduism, Karnad foregrounds the problems of caste and relegates the devotional, mystical and poetic features of the movement to the background (xi).

Though Karnad has not prescribed any magic balm for the ills and evils of caste inferiorisation and religious marginalisation he has conveyed his theoretical notion in favour of Aristotelian equality and Gandhian tolerance for the sustenance of the Indian nation. Highlighting the caste and class conflicts and a social awakening Karnad analyses these elements to solve India's quintessential problems.

Sociologically, parentage, caste and religion are not the right canons to judge a man in a multicultural society of the modern and post-modern times. These are rather the pseudo-ideological yardsticks of high caste pundits to deprive a few of their rights for emancipation from their socio-religious condition. The play presents casteism as a social stigma on the Indian society and a political necessity in its historical past and hysteric present. As a matter of fact:

> Caste appears in *Tale-danda* as the basis of Hindu socio-religious organisation across class division, and the play

> presents the philosophical dialectic of caste as well as practical consequences of the opposing positions. The Virasaiva communitarians (who call themselves Sharanas) have exchanged the boundaries of caste for the bonds of friendship, fellowship, equality, humanity, and social change. The radicalism of such fellowship inspires King Bijjala, especially because as a caste barber whose ancestors reinvented themselves as kshatriyas, he has found full acceptance only among the Sharanas (Dhawadker xi-xii).

In A.R. Shukla's view, Karnad "... brilliantly develops this delicate matter and handles the situation in a masterly way to achieve new dramatic heights" (292). In the background of the play Karnad deals with the historical elements like Sovideva's meddling with treasury, Basavanna's resignation from the post of Chief Treasury Officer, the death and funeral ceremony of Jagadeva's father, the intercaste marriage of pancham boy Sheelavanta to a Brahmin girl, Kalavati, Bijjala's abduction and death, Basavanna's Samadhi or union with God at Kudala Sangam and above all, Sovideva's coronation. In a wider perspective:

> The play shows how the higher castes resent Basavanna's iconoclasm, and how the resentment reaches its highest peak when one of Basavanna's Brahmin disciples gives his daughter in marriage to an untouchable. The culprits are severely punished and in the subsequent holocaust King Bijjala is dethroned by his orthodox son, while Basavanna dies in mysterious circumstances (Naik 45-46).

Karnad times the action of the play in 1168 A.D. and depicts a communal struggle in the city of Kalyan in north Karnataka when King Bijjala was the founder ruler of Kalachurya dynasty. There were great scholars, poets and philosophers in Bijjala's court. Basavanna, the great scholar, saint-poet and philosopher was King's treasury officer who faught with other brilliant people for a casteless and classless society. These people shed their castes and got initiated into a new faith *sharana* and became the devotees of Lord Shiva. The Sharanas are the 'marginal groups' and socio-politically 'others' subjected to slavery, insult, and genocide. They talked about God and denounced idolatry and social inequality in *Vachana,* i.e., the language of common man. They considered the humanbody as the abode of living God, and condemned all inhuman traditions in the Hindu Society. But in the play:

> Girish Karnad seems to treat the Bhakti Movement as a reform movement. Karnad seems to be inspired by the Western humanism which has developed since Renaissance. But the Bhakti Movement was actually inspired by a kind of mysticism, since spirituality has been involved it. Saints and rishis, earlier, saw God everywhere. So it was a sort of mysticism. It was never a movement. It was a spiritual perception opposed to the hierarchy of the high and low practised by the society, which has been an age-old spectacle in India. The saints of the Bhakti movement were not actually reformers, in the modern sense of the term. Theirs was a mystical movement, which as the implications of reform. It was not a reform movement (Joshipura 68).

Finally this movement of *Sharanas* ended in a disaster when the marriage of a Brahmin girl to a cobbler boy led to a terrible caste conflict.

Dealing with the different historical materials of this social and spiritual awakening Karnad has made use of the facts in M.Chidananda Murthy's *Basavanna* in National Biography Series published by National Book Trust and H. Thipperudra Swamy's *Basaveshwara* in the Makers of Indian Literature Series, published by Sahitya Akademi. While the biographers express their indebtedness to the historical sources such as Harihara's *Basavarajadevara ragale,* Palukurike Somanatha's *Basavapuranam,* Bhimakavi's translation of Somanatha's Telugu version of *Basavapuranam,* Lakkanna Dandesa's *Sivatattva Chintamani* and Singirasa's *Ambalabasava Charita,* Karnad has taken the historical materials from these books.

Tale-danda is a tragedy of an individual as well as the society. Karnad presents King Bijjala, a shudra, barber by caste, and a lover of Lord Shiva. By virtue of his efficiency he had become the founder of Kalachurya dynasty and married a kshatriya princes Rambhavati of Hoysala dynasty. He had proved his efficacy by manipulating the Brahmins. He confesses this before the queen.

> ... I am Kalachurya.... A barber... for ten generations my forefathers ravaged the land as robber barons. For another five they ruled as the trusted feudatories of the Emperor

> himself. They married into every royal family in sight. Bribed generations of Brahmins with millions of cows. All this so they could have the caste of Kshatriyas branded on their foreheads (14).

On the other hand, Karnad has traced Basavanna as a great social reformer, visionary, rationalist, socialist and pioneer of *sharana* movement who did his best to establish an egalitarian society devoid of caste, creed, colour and sex biases. He raised a war against idolatry system, inhuman traditions, gender inequality and orthodox practices with his sharana followers.

The *sharanas* are the devotees of Lord Shiva who prayed in their common *Vachana* language undermining the traditional Sanskrit language. The Brahmins felt it an attempt to insult God and to their caste hierarchy. The *sharanas* were of the belief that caste generates the class system in their society. *Sharana* ideology and Vachana language were the methods to establish a casteless, classless and egalitarian society. The orthodox Hindus, and chiefly the Brahmins vehemently opposed this move. In his romantic idealisation Karnad has analysed the *sharanas* as 'other' and 'marginals' in historical proper, their reduced status in socio-ethnic hybridity, inventiveness in economics and religous overviews. Karnad seems disturbed to see when the believers of monism monopolise public faith in private politics. Damodara Bhatta, Queen Rambhavati's priest defends the high caste cause in language, and says:

> Sanskrit is a language engraved on diamond, unchanging, austere. Eternal truths can be captured in its immutability. Kannada our mother-tongue, however, is pure flux. It changes from mouth to mouth, from caste to caste, from today to tomorrow. It is geared to the needs of squabbling couples, wheedling beggars, prostitutes spreading their saris out. It can only speak in inconstant moods. Its sensuality is addictive and the sharanas use it to pimp for their vulgarities (57).

The *sharanas* believe in the practice of *Kayaka* (work/production) and *Dasoha* (offering/distribution) in their revolutionary ideology to solve their problems. They believe that work is worship, make no extra demand, treat profits with contempt and are full of "economic enterprise" (24). They think "There is no caste among

Sharanas, neither Brahmin nor cobbler" (38) and "Caste and creed are phantom"(44). A hundred and ninetysix thousand *sharanas* in the city of Kalyan are initiated in to this new faith in a "delirium of communal oneness"(45). The orthodox think Brahminism is in danger and give importance to the demonic celebration of fire sacrifice and slaughter of animals before Vedic Gods which the *sharanas* call a "Brahmanical farce" (28). The *sharanas* as a community are "in-sufferable moralists" (15) overdosed with ethics, devotion and ideology of not to steal, kill, lie or rage. The low castes, downtroddens, destitutes and women, who face the horrors of caste and class distinctions are unable to escape from the coils of caste. They think *sharana* to be an enlightened faith, a religious order, potentially a new divine consciousness and a philosophical method for spiritual perfection in the name of Veerashaivism.

Basavanna, the pioneer of this reform movement, was born into an orthodox Shaiva Brahmin family. He had denied his parents the privilege of performing thread ceremony with a view to not discriminating among men and man against woman. He had professed a spiritual revivalism and emphasised the distribution of wealth for an equal material prosperity. He encouraged the low castes and untouchables to gain spiritual knowledge by learning forbidden scriptures like the *Vedas*, the *Upanishads*, the *Gita* and other Sanskrit texts. His aim was not to insult the Vedic tradition nor to desecrate Brahminism, the then, symbol of elite, erudition, eloquence and intelligence. With a radical thinking he had encouraged inter-caste dining and inter-caste marriages for an 'organic society'. Basavanna believed in the equality of the sexes, and propounded that the body can be distinguished but the soul cannot.

Karnad has presented Basavanna's multidimensional personality as an efficient accountant, mystic, spiritual pioneer, and revolutionary, employs his ideology to reform his society. His practice of Shivayoga establishes relationship between *Jeeva* (soul), *Jagat* (Universe) and *Shiva* (God) in his self-realisation, and in the infinite consciousness of Linga, the basic concept of Veera-shaivism. He propagates the humanitarian principles of Shiva culture for a casteless and classless society. In this context it can be said that, "His very idea of establishing egalitarian society is based on the concept of Ishtaling" (Virupakshappa xii), a symbol of social equality. His Linga philosophy is based on historical and modern scientific investigations that promoted Veerashaivism, a religious order of scientific spiritualism and practice of human values based on humanism. His promoting of *Sharana* ideology through his followers, the Shivasharanas, helped the common mases enough to realise God *Parambraham*, the Absolute Reality—*Sat* (Truth)-*Chit* (Consciousness)-*Ananda* (bliss) through Linga, the *Soonya*, (void) that conceals countless billions of universes in it.

Basavanna's philosophy is a blow to the very roots of *Varnashrama dharma* in the Vedic concept that divides the Sanatana Dharma into four major *varnas*—Brahmins (the functionaries of priesthood and education), Kshatriyas (administration and war), Vaishyas (trade) and Shudras (of productive work). The caste division is a historical blunder but an indispensable evil which Karnad inadvertently projects into the play. Damodara says how the "four Varnas flowed out of the primordial man; the Brahmin from the head, the Shudra from the feet" (55) and they are emanated from Brahma's mouth, arms, thighs and feet. Beyond this four *varnas* there lies the *panchamas* (menial workers) who toil to produce wealth for the higher castes. He does not like the idea, "A Brahmana may compel a shudra whether bought or unbought, to servile work; for he is created by the creator to be the slave of a Brahman" (Qtd. in *Dr. Babasaheb Ambedkar* 418). He exposes the idea of the orthodox, "One's caste is like the skin on one's body" (14) and agrees that "Caste sytem is not merely a division of labourers—which is quite different from division of labour—it is an hierarchy in which the divisions of labourers are graded one about the other" (Ambedkar 67). While professional efficiency, competitiveness and individualism were the chief motives of varna system, its oblique motive was to consolidate social deformity, inequality, exploitation and oppression by the upper castes in the social hierarchy. Karnad is very much critical of the Hindu concept that caste cannot be separated from the corporeal body and neutralised through reason. In dealing with the caste dynamics as a serious historical material in the play Karnad negates Manu and affirms Ambedkar.

The title of the play, *Tale-danda,* literally means 'beheading'. Karnad presents Bijjala as a truly secular king surrounded by his unfaithful son, Sovideva, Queen's priest Damodara and Brahmin advisor Manchanna. But the king depends more on a faithful saint-poet-philosopher Basavanna and his *sharana* followers who are committed to values, morals and economy of the kingdom. Sovideva dislikes Basavanna for his philosophy of monism and his idea of making a casteless and classless society. Damodara and Manchanna support his cause in the prospect of preserving their caste hierarchy. But Basavanna and his followers are committed to lofty ideas and radical steps to establish a casteless and classless egalitarian society by demolishing the "poison-house of varnashrama" (38) that stands like a "Banyan tree" in Sanatana Dharma. Thus arises a conflict between the conservatives and radicals. The inter-caste marriage between a Brahmin girl and a panchama (cobbler) boy in Act Two, Scene Five, bolsters the superiority of orthodox Brahmins who consider this radical step a sharana misdemeanour.

The inter-caste marriage is a *sharana* attempt to correct the wrongs of history. While the *sharanas* celebrate this touchable-untouchable marriage in jubilation the orthodox cannot see a Brahmin girl to be "a cobbler's Priestess". They cannot see Kalavati, instead of sitting on the deer-skin, to remain busy in skinning dead buffaloes and spend the rest of her time in the smell of leather and burning camphor. Retrospecting and prospecting the caste and the role of *varnashrama dharma* when Madhuvarasa, Kalavati's father, a Brahmin *sharana* says "I shall not hesitate to sacrifice my daughter's life to forward the cause of our great movement"(39), Basavanna warns:

> The orthodox will see this mingling of castes as a blow at the very roots of varnashrama dharma. Bigotry has not faced such challenge in two thousand years. I need hardly describe what venom will gush out, what hatred will erupt once the news spreads (38).

Again he expresses his apprehension over the future of the young couple. He says "It is a question of life and death for these children. From tomorrow the wrath of the bigoted will pursue them like a swarm of snakes, to strike as they pause to put up a roof or light an oven" (38).

The Bijjala-Basavanna relationship reveals a deep insight into the matter. Basavanna foresees an ugly prospect for the society while Bijjala suffers, like the old Duke in Shakespeare's plays, and fails to resist the *sharana* radical attempt in spite of his boldness.

Nor is he able to compromise with them knowing that the *sharanas are* "All hardworking people... from the common stock. They sit together, argue about God together, indifferent to caste, birth or station" (15). He finds himself between Scylla and Cherybdis. He realises *sharana* contribution and says, "A hundred and ninety-six thousand *sharanas*! They only have to lay down their implements. And markets after market in the city will close down. Streets will fall empty. Trade will collapse, the economy suffer a set-back" (48-49). He knows Basavanna's miracle for which "A Brahmin girl chooses to marry an untouchable and two hundred thousand people come out in support of it! That is the only miracle Basavanna has ever performed" (65). In honour and praise he says to Basavanna how the *sharanas* "light a lamp every evening in your name for having given them a new life" (20). Knowing all these virtues of sharanas and Basavanna Bijjala accepts this "absurd wedding" (49) as a secular and liberal king.

The orthodox do not see this as a good sign for the kingdom. Sovideva, Damodara and Manchanna, though failed in all fronts, succeed at last. Sovideva fails to meddle with the treasury accounts and fails to liquidate his father's confidence in Basavanna. The Damodara and Manchanna alliance fails to check the *sharana* "crime against Nature" (65). They influence the king to stop this infamous wedding. The King's order to stop the marriage is disobeyed by Madhuvarasa and Haralayya. Even Basavanna informs Bijjala that he would sit with the *sharanas* in front of his palace for the purpose. Bijjala loses his patience and orders to behead the *sharana* parents. He supports the cause of the orthodox as he realises that the *sharana* faith has affected every household life in Kalyan putting every "Father against son-brother against brother" (2). His character is paradoxical as he prefers uniformity and spiritual brotherhood against prejudices and communal differences on the one hand and tries to support the othodox cause on the other to satisfy the powerful. While Bijjala tries to satisfy both in his administrative strategy the kingdom lapses into a civil war over the cause of touchable-untouchable marriage.

Bijjala's order to kill the *sharana* parents is an extreme step that infuriates the *sharanas*. Secondly Sovideva makes Bijjala a captive. Basavanna's departure to Kudala Sangam makes the *sharanas* desperate. In order to take revenge on Sovideva, the young *sharana* leader Jagadeva sneaks into the palace with his followers. As he fails to find Sovideva he stabs Bijjala to death. Again in frustration Jagadeva commits suicide. The *sharanas* become desperate in their noble mision. Aparna Bhargava Dharwadker rightly remarks: "The movement of the Sharanas remains an oasis of reform and protest in a desert of orthodoxy, and their own opposition to caste is too self-conscious and obsessive, devolving merely into a desire to challenge brahminism at every opportunity" (xii). In comparision and contrast, "If Basavanna and Bijjala are two characters of the same self, it appears that Bijjala and Sovideva also share a similar splitting of self" (Dhanavel 47). With the order of Sovideva King's army mercilessly suppress the *sharanas*. Widescale violence, gruesome tales of rape, murder and looting are enacted in the city. But Sovideva orders his guards in a frenzy to annihilate the *sharanas*:

> Pursue them. Don't let them escape. Men, women and children cut them all down. Set the hounds after them... Burn the houses that give them shelter. Burn their books. Tear them into shreds and consign them to wells. Their voices shall be stilled for ever (90).

Quite opposite to his father's personality Sovideva defines the role of a king and the duty of his subjects to him:

> The king is father to his people and people shall love him and obey him like his offspring. No tongue shall wag against the king or his family or his retinue or his officers... women and lower orders shall live within the norms prescribed by our ancient tradition, or else they'll suffer like dogs. Each citizen shall consider himself a soldier ready to lay down his life for the king. For the king is God incarnate! (90).

In the estimation of this extreme attitude of the two youths, Sovideva and Jagadeva, one observes "It is Jagadeva who appears to show an element of wickedness but Karnad has clarified that Sovideva represents fascism not Jagadeva" (Murthy 134). Sovideva becomes happy when he learns from Manchanna that "The sharanas have lost their drive and in course of time are bound to revert to caste for sheer survival" but becomes apprehensive to know that "Basavanna is alive and we can take nothing for granted"(79).

Bijjala appears like an agnostic in Karnad's dramatisation. Like the secular and liberal rulers of contemporary India he does not like to mix up caste and religion with politics. But he becomes a victim of his liberal thinking, when his close associates including his son turn his enemies. He feels the importance of Basavanna's movement, as the, "need of a new religion, a religion which can treat all human beings equal" (Shukla 290). This tone is also repeated in the words of Prakriti, an untouchable Chandal girl in Tagore's *Chandalika* (1933) that "A religion that insults is a false religon" (Tagore 154). He realises Basavanna's words, "Violence is wrong whatever the provocation. To resort to it because someone started it first is even worse. And to do so in the name of a structure of brick and mortar is a monument to stupidity" (29). But with his death in the hands of Jagadeva, "King Bijjala is elevated to the level of a great martyr" (Dhanavel 47).

Like Basavanna, Bijjala understands that religion and God cannot be edificed on caste and class basis. No religion is understood in watertight compartment, and every commandment, Shariyat or Vedic mantra needs re-assessment in understanding the time and spirit of its philosophy in its contemporariness. Any feeling of caste and class distinctions negates the true spirit of religion. No religion is insular in its texts but universal in tone and in contemporary context. Projecting the caste dynamics of twelfth century Karnad regrets its effect on Indian society even today that causes social deformity. In the play he presents brahmin-untouchable marriage as "a classic example of the right deed done for the wrong reason, and the ensuing blood-bath destroys the very movement the union was meant to celebrate" (Dharwadker xii). Regreting the caste effect on contemporary Indian society, he says, "It seems 800 years have solved no problems. We are back exactly where we started" (*Karnad* 1992: 76). It seems that Karnad has denounced caste as a social stigma, and believes in Basavanna's words—*Guna* (aptitude) and *Karma* (function) in greater and better cause of Indian nationhood. In this context it is observed: "In changed context of post-independent India, such perception of Karnad is highly relevant because many people of 'low caste' origin are in responsible positions today. The implied suggestion is that they ought not to forget their social obligations to create a more equitable society, though it may require real self-sacrifice" (Dhanavel 134).

Karnad is of the view that Indian society is full of rulers like Bijjala, philospher reformers like Basavanna, and conservatists and radicals like Sovideva and Jagadeva. If ' Mandir' and 'Mandal' movements of late twentieth century India is similar to twelfth century *sharana* movement we have nothing to celebrate and appreciate our civilisation. There are still many Damodaras who glorify the high castes and traditions superstitiously:

> But civilization has been made possible because our Vedic tradition controls and directs that self-destructive energy. How large-hearted is our dharma! To each person it says you don't have to be anyone but yourself. One's caste is like one's home meant for one's self and one's family. It is shaped to one's needs, one's comforts, one's traditions. And that is why the vedic tradition can absorb and accomodate all differences, from Kashmir to Kanya Kumari. And even those said to be its victims have embraced its logic of inequality (56).

There are many Manchannas among the high castes who poison the state administration to get rid of this low caste nuisance reminding the authority of it. Manchanna prompts Sovideva to get rid of sharanas like king Mihirakula of Kashmir who got rid of Buddhist menace, and Pandya king got rid of Jain scoundrels. Singing the glory of high caste and tradition Damodara says:

> This marriage arranged by the sharanas was no triffle matter. On the one hand stands the Vedic Dharma, which has branched out in strength over the centuries and now shades the whole of Aryavarta. On the other, there is the sharana movement—a pestilence—but of a virulence not seen since the days of the Buddha (64).

The play is a tragedy based on caste and religious conflicts which predict the horror of death for imagined India. In the post-modern pan-Indian context Karnad forecasts the horrors of caste that creates communal hatred and a great havoc in our society and nationalism. It seems that Karnad conveys a message to his communal and superstitious countrymen persuading them to relinquish this avenging and revenging tactics, failing which the contemporary society will experience the horrors of the twelfth century society of Bijjala's reign. Thus by dramatising the particular incident and historical pesonalities Karnad has performed his duty as a social activist in the zeal of a reformist.

Girish Karand's *Tughlaq* (1972), a modern Indian English play, has the historicity of fact and textuality of history in its post-modern and neohistoricist discourses evolving macro-historical schemes like the powereffection, social relations, political reasons and conservative thoughts in its structure. An attempt to study the "historicity of text" and "the textuality of history" (Montrose 305) in Karnad's seminal work deals with the veracity of historical events and the contents of history in its universal significance. The historicity of the text has its autonomous existence in Indian history, but the phychoanalysis, political issues and revolutionary concepts are conditioned by a shift from political possibilities to political pessimism. For Karand, history is no longer a static background for the play; rather it is timeless, alive, absurd, and mysterious in its entirety.

Unlike the plays in Greek and Roman literatures *Tughlaq* describes the ideology and psychology of a great emperor during a specific moment in history. In the text of the play Karand (re)writes history by judging the past and instructing the contemporary world in its social milieu, and its purpose with historicity like Malraux, Camus and Orwell in a specific historical moment. By historicising the text Karnad has categorised social factors in the textuality of history. The historicity of the text can be real in Hegelian idealistic sense conditioned by Karand's textual representation, by reconstructing the past and present concerns. In the context he has projected historical 'givens' as a transcendent commentator and an objective chronicler. The textual traces of the past are promised on the notion that the past is available to us only in the form of textuality which is embedded in the present. For Karnad "the appropriation of history, the historicization of the past, the narrativization of society, all of which give... the accumulation and differentiation of social space, space to be used for social purpose" (Said 78). He does not think that historicity of text and the textuality of history are to be read on historical conditions and circumstances. Since every text is autonomous but not absolute in its hermeneutic reconstructions, the text of *Tughlaq* is only the reprocessing of the past, with emphasis on the political and social needs of the present.

Tughlaq can be a writerly text because history is (re)written in semiological, conventional, sequential and essentially everyday fashion. It can also be a readerly text in its discourse as history is the necessary component of its text-production and behind the dramatic text there lies the subterranean text, i.e., the "ghost text" of history. The text as a real story is written on the basis of historical records, presenting the problematics of history in contemporary equivalences. Karnad has imagined, mediated and arbitrated the real and actual of the historical situation and periodisation not as a historiographer but as a narratologist. Of course, in the views of Bakhtin and Foucault historical reading of a text is necessary for the hybridity of understanding that helps one to make an assimilation of history in contemporaneity. The text as a historical reality with its historicity is based on the annals, chronicles and the past events with a desire to raise socio-political consciousness. In the post-modern context it is necessary to evaluate how "historical events were treated as 'textual' phenomena while literary works were regarded as material events" (Eagleton 197) in the narrator's own prejudices, preoccupations, canons and paradoxes. Ensuring "Eternity and immortality" to the facts and events in the text, Karnad has played the role of a historicist. Embedding history in the socio-political context he has carnivalised, parodised rather than worshipped the characters in his ideological polemics, historical analysis and self-critical approach to his heuristic character in an attempt to specify the gulf between the past and the present.

History is always a process of making the real out of a static background. Like the works of Shakespeare, Sidney, Spencer and Marlowe, Karnad's *Tughlaq* has the canons of history in its literariness. Particularising the subject position as in Shaw's *Saint Joan* (1923) in the historical situation he has expounded that history itself is erased in an attempt to settle the historical genealogy in the literary text and historical discourse. Like the protagonists of the historical texts his protagonist is guided by an egocentric psychology and a survival-instinct. His Tughlaq is highly imaginative and ideologically overdosed in the conscious psyche of his strategies. Recurring thoughts, deterrent impulses, compulsive need for action (murder) and immense socio-political pressures on him create a nauseating disillusionment that needs a psychiatric help which his political analyst and spiritual progenitor, Najib, and the humble historian, Barani, fail to provide. Like every head of the state he suffers from a stress syndrome, a post-modern disease because of the imbalance of his pathological humours essential for his Nietzschean problems that regulate his nerve impulses. Karnad delineates history in its appropriation and the circumstances in which Tughlaq is displayed. Karnad has categorised the events of history and historical figures in visual images as if exhibited in the paintings of memorial complexes and museums with homage and nostalgia. The violence and vulnerability in history is skilfully deployed in the context of the text though the protagonist is consigned to a lunatic hell owing to his willing suspension of belief and his inherited insanity.

Tughlaq is an outstanding chronicle-play based on the historical facts focusing the integrated themes of philosophy, social theory and politics. It is "the first major post-independence play to engage with the Sultanate period (twelfth to early sixteenth century), which brought the 'golden age' of classical Hinduism to a decisive end, and introduced Islam as a dominant political and cultural force on the subcontinent" (Dharwadker 2005: xix). Karnad has no reason to chronicle or glamourize any particular historical period but has made us conscious of living in the present analysing a historical era in Indian history. As a dispassionate lover of history Karnad assimilates Tughlaq's fond theories of methodology that he had applied for humiliation and political enslavement of his subjects, financial logic and genuine idealism. He has made Tughlaq a valid image of the past and has portrayed him in the complex ideological historiography. The English production of the play had its tremendous success in 1970 for the portrayal of the most complex character of Indian history, responsible for the tragic suffering of his own and of a nation. The success of the play depends on history as its theme and politics as ideology. Further, the theme of the play is ingeniously linked with the people, religion and history of the Delhi Sultanate.

Karnad has the deliberate intention of displaying India since the time of the Sultans as a beautiful world of wealth, success, position and power. That is how "it's full of brainless people, people with not an idea in their head" (50) who promote their self-interest but not the welfare of the people in starvation, dirt, disease, famine and a number of other ills. Karnad has collected the primary historical source from Zia-ud-din Barani's *Tarikh-i-Firoz Shahi* (1357) who spent 17 years in Tughlaq's court. He understands how Barani "defines history as a source of instructive examples that promote virtue and discourge vice but, more significantly, as a form of knowledge essential for understanding" (Dharwadker 1995: 47). Adopting Tughlaq as the subject of history Karnad ascribes Sultan's political failures to calamitous errors and to a series of projects without harmony with the religious tradition of Islam, and to perversion of judgment.

Karnad's protagonist in the play is a faithful portrait and profile of the sultan, Mohammed bin Tughlaq (1325-51), a one dimensional man with multidimensional thought and behaviour, great scholar and most idealist ruler of medieval India. The historicity of the play in Karnad's textual production and histrionic presentation spans five years period from 1327 to 1332. Karnad has attempted to present the events of Tughlaq's reign in the light of his hasty idealism and unscrupulous exploitation of his decisions by his own treacherous followers. In the textuality of history Karnad has aroused a reader's response to assess Tughlaq as an idealist, an upholder of Islam and a philosopher who dreams to bring a change by galvanizing the fortune of his subjects with his ideology for they live in their narrow cocoons of selfishness, religious bias and treachery. The play displays Karnad's understanding of history with an insight into the inter-textual connection between history and creative mind. The rise and fall of Tughlaq as a visionary idealist is presented in his successful measures and failures, and in the missons of his struggle for a secular nationhood during the twenty-years of time which serves an excellent backdrop to the play. Even after six centuries Karnd presents the similar socio-political crises in the similar context in our post-colonial status and says in an interview:

> What struck me absolutely about Tughlaq's history was that it was contemporary. That fact that here was the most idealistic, most intelligent king ever to come on the throne of Delhi ... and one of the greatest failures also. And within a span of twenty-years this tremendously capable man had gone to pieces. This seemed to be both due to his idealism as well as the shortcomings within him, such as his impatience, his cruelty, his feeling that he had the only correct answer. And I felt in the early sixties India had also come very far in the same direction-the twenty-year period seemed to me very much a striking parallel (*Enactment* 54).

The abiding interest of the play lies in the study of "the ambiguities of Tughlaq's character" related to "philosophical questions on the nature of man and destiny of a whole kingdom which a dreamer like him controls" (Murthy viii, ix).

Tughlaq appears to be an idealist but in the pursuit of his glorious ideals he visualises to make his empire the envy of the world and perpetrates Machiavellian craftiness in his personality that demands our sympathy for his human side, praise for his statesmanship and blames for his failures in shaping a welfare state. Ideology is social apparatus in his scientific mind that makes him decisive to join the theoretical and practical reasons enjoying life in cognitive self-realisation and conative self-cancellation. In the text, Tughlaq is placed in the multiplicity of cultural and historical forces in man's struggle against failure throughout his life and topical limitations. He is divided between populist rationality and political reality, individual autonomy and inclined audacity, truth and falsehood, hypothesis and hypocrisy. His used, unused and abused capabilities can be analysed as a whole to be aiming at improving the human condition and ameliorating the life of his subjects in his intellectual efforts to achieve the absolute and a void the obsolete. As a ruler with authoritarian principles he aims at the socio-political development of his kingdom but acts by improvising his logic and institutionalising murder just to stabilise his reign. With depth and range, suggestiveness and richness, Karnad explores the historicity of the events and characters during Tughlaq's reign in his imaginative reconstruction. "Tughlaq is every man" (Rajgopalachari 21), a disillusioned idealist and an alienated protagonist who hopes to lead his people into a Utopia but fails especially which the idealist in him becomes impulsive to manage the unbridgeable gulf between aspiration and reality. In his micro self the macro possibilities threaten his religious and political austerity. In his royal self with an idealist's vision he thinks that a king is no king unless he is one with his people. In this context Nehru views him with grater historicity:

> He (Tughlaq) was a most learned and accomplished man both in Persian and Arabic. He has studied philosophy and logic, even Greek philosophy. He knew something of mathematics and science and medicine. He was a brave man, and was for his times quite a paragon of learning and a

> wonder. And yet, and yet, this paragon was a monster of cruelty and seems to have been quite mad! He came to the throne by killing his own father. He had fantastic notions of conquering Persia and China. (*The Glimpses of World History*, 214)

Describing Tughlaq's multiphrenia in Indian history, Karnad presents him in his historic attempts at correcting the mistakes of his predecessors which are rather turned in to Napoleonic blunders in his ambitious exercise of power and betrayal of conscience to make his kingdom a God's plenty and a heaven on earth. He is not "afraid to be human" (1) and does not like to "waste...time by sleeping" (10)

Karnad has not written the costume plays like his predecessors, rather he has attempted to relate a historical episode with modern sensibility in his *Tughlaq*. "The play has an interesting story, an intricate plot, scope for spectacle and uses dramatic conventions... to which theatre audiences respond readily" (Murthy vii). It is interesting to judge Tughlaq's elusive character as a tragic caricature that relates to the philosophical questions on the nature of man and the destiny of a kingdom which a dreamer like him controls. Karnad writes:

> My subject was the life of Mohammad Tughlaq fourteenth century sultan of Delhi, certainly the most brilliant individual ever to ascend the throne of Delhi and also one of the biggest failures. After a reign distinguished for policies that today seem farsighted to the point of genius, but which in their day earned him the title "Mohammad the mad," the sultan ended his career in bloodshed and political chaos. In a sense, the play reflected the slow disillusionment my generation felt with the new politics of independent India: the gradual erosion of the ethical norms that had guided the movement for independence and the coming to terms with cynicism and realpolitik.(*Three Plays* 7)

In Karnad's textual production Tughlaq appears far, superior to other kings because of his ideological and philosophical quest in a neurotic self that alienates himself in his psychic distance form Nature and command man forgetting that he is only a living organism. As analysed power corrupts human relationship, and alienates and dehumanises man. Politics is taken as a power-structured relationship that leads a man to be a tyrant and to cause sufferings. History repeats itself in the process of learning and experimenting, and politics as a sign is subjectified in his empirical instruction. The symbiotic relationship between the Titanic ruler and hits cringing courtiers attempts to gain his favour to climb the ladder of political power is always uneasy and shaky.

In an age of religious fanaticism and hostility between Hindus and Muslims, Tughlaq usurps power by involving himself in parricide in order to bring amity between the two for a lasting brotherhood. He desires justice to work in his kingdom without any subjugation of might or weakness, religion or creed. When suspicion and distrust are rife his broadminded religious tolerance seem foolish to the Muslims and cunning to the Hindus who suspect his very motives. In this kind of socio-political environment it is an irony that Tughlaq aims at the welfare of the state by practicing hypocrisy and dualism. His anguish is not understood and he is betrayed by those he loved and trusted. He employs a Hindu officer to watch the Muslim soldiers and a Muslim officer to keep watch on the Hindu soldiers. But he is not understood by the society around him because his ideals are far above the comprehension of his contemporaries and much in advance of his time. His broad-minded religious tolerance seems foolish to the Muslims and his very motives are not free from suspicion to the Hindus. In other words, the people in the society appear to be constantly on the lookout of betrayal, suspicion and infidelity. In such a kind of socio-political atmosphere he desires a society without opposition by paralysing public criticism. This helps him to enjoy the ideological celebration of hierarchy through exploitation and repression by dehumanising his subjects while alienating his self from these with an insane utopian vision.

Tughlaq is ambitious but unscrupulous to steer his kingdom's administration in the adverse circumstances and situations. His armchair administration and amnesia of taking precaution for his reform activities only invite frustration and the necessity of taking severe action. The idealist in him is restless and cannot sleep to fulfil his dreams. He suspects people around him as suspicion is a necessary apparatus for efficient administration and a necessary evil to rein the administration. But he is haunted by its violent cnsequences. Similarly, idealism is the essence of his life and for the sake of it he kills his father, brother and gets involved in a series of murders but at the end he realizes the futility of his far-fetched idealism. Idealism and ambition are complementary to him, and this helps him to consider 'duty' as above the personal relationship by dismissing the allegation of a parricide as a piece of gossip, and he manufactures lies for public consumption. His madness is due to contemplative enjoyment of active manipulation and control of power. This makes him find freedom and safety in his madness—the freedom of loneliness and safety from being not understood. His madness is a product of the abnormality and cunningness which have a therapeutic effect on his metaphysical reason.

Karnad casts his brilliant Oriental despot's biggest failures with his conflict between self and soul, and his dysfunctional state of mind in the textuality of history. He presents Tughlaq's self-defeating nature of politics that creates spatial division in policy making and practising it in reality. His ideology of secularism and strategic intelligence not only causes his loss of political innocence but also present him as an eccentric, insane, hypocrate, short-tempered and violent ruler. While his virtues make him 'an unattainable utopia' his vices in personal and public spheres invite his failures. He is little genuine at the interpersonal level and tries his best to impress his people by playing the role of a just benevolent dictator. Ambitions, action, anxiety, anger and anguish dominate his mind, and this alienates his egoistic self from society, individuals and religion around him. He is torn between his personal ideology and isms of the statecraft. His thinking is spiritual but suffering is spatial. He lives like an optimist but his options remain optical illusions in his existential suffering. Being dominated by the syndrome of aggressive energy he exists between oppression and domination in his suffering from the neutrality and paralysis of public criticism and opposition. The benevolent and innovative measures he undertakes by providing equal rights to Hindus, abolishing Jiziya, shifting capital from Delhi to Daulatabad and introducing copper currency presage his alienation from the public. He is unable to win the confidence of his people, and fails to foresee the flaws in his schemes. At the interpersonal level he is estranged from the individuals around him, but at the extra personal level he has a longing for them, and tries to bring them into the mainstream of his imagined kingdom as their saviour and a benevolent despot. As an ace schemer of his power politics he is torn between immediacy and intimacy and plans diabolically a clever strategy to get rid of "both his enemies-Sheikh Immam-ud-din and Ain-ul-Mulk at one stroke"(Gomez 115). His idealism is a kind of sophisticated scheme of socialism which cannot make Tughlaq the tyrant separated from Tughlaq the idealist. The type of government he visions and promises does not cover the legitimately constituted forms of political subjection in his designed repressive strategies. Living in the cocoons of his ideology he has captivated his self like a lion in the cage of a squirrel, and dares the carrions of his subjects in the name of reform. He thus appears in a state of physical suicide preferring to enjoy the coldest solitude in Nietzschean sense.

Karnad portrays Tughlaq as the first secular sultan of India even before Akbar. For him politics and religion are complementary to each other. He expects religion to guide politics but not the vice versa as "the oldest trick in the world" (42) and is very rigid to the amalgamation of the two. As a benevolent socialist he does not believe in politics as a means to achieving the ends of religion when Sheikh Imam-ud-din accuses him for putting religious men—the Ulemas and Sayyids behind the bar, and reminds him, "God has given you everything—power, learning, intelligence, talent" (20) but "you are trying to become another God"(21). Tughlaq retorts that an atheist can try to be God and cross accuses them who "try to indulge in politics" and says, "my kingdom has millions—Muslims, Hindus and Jains" (20). He admits, "there is dirt and sickness in my kingdom" but says, "why should I call on God to clean the dirt deposited by men?" (20). He philosophically defends himself, "I have never denied the words of God ... because it's my bread and drink"(20) nor "makes himself complete by killing the Greek in me ... by denying the visions which led Zarathustra or the Buddha"(21). For him God is not dead in the Nietzschean sense but like a Sartrean existentialist he buries the idea of God as a useless and costly hypothesis by banning prayer in fear of his life and in fear of sin. He knows that his consciousness for sin would become self-destructive and cause a mental collapse. Thus he takes the shelter of the philosophy of fascism before its inception by making his conscience a martyr, saint of immorality and captive of the hysterical cult of power. When the Sultan prepares for Kanauj, news arrives regarding the twin dangers—the march of Ain-ul-Mulk with his powerful army, and the arrival of Sheikh Imam in Delhi. Najib and Barani advise him to take support of Shihab-ud-din, the powerful prince of Samparshahr as an envoy to dissuade Ain-ul-Mulk from marching to Delhi with a plea that such a saintly person would not like to see Muslims slaughtered at the hands of fellow Muslims. Sheikh Shihab-ud-din, who resembles Tughlaq in the royal robes, rides the royal elephant on a diplomatic mission. As the enemy thinks of Tughlaq's coming for peace talks, his army succeeds with Tughlaq's superb strategic knowledge in killing two birds with one stone. Sheikh is killed and Ain-ul-Mulk's army is rushed in the trap set by Tughlaq. Tughlaq's staging of 'Macbethian high drama' to liquidate his enemies evokes the tragic ethos in the play.

The shifting of his capital from Delhi to Daulatabad is a historic feat in his idealistic vision. It is a step to mediate between the two communities for a peaceful co-existence. In meditation of power he says, "I'll have to admit I've been wrong all these years. And I know I haven't I have something to give, something to teach, which may open the eyes of history, but I have to do it within this life"(56). When Shihab-ud-din pleads not to move the capital to the unhappiness of people of Delhi Mohammad expresses his logic, "I have explained every reason to them, shown how my empire cannot flourish with Delhi as its capital. But how can I explain tomorrow to those who haven't even opened their eyes to the light of the day"(39). It is a geopolitical decision to satisfy the Hindus by providing effective administrative control and sustain his government's effective economic stability with a penchant for cultural integration and safety from the attacks of the foreign invaders. His dream is to perpetuate "greater justice, equality, progress and peace ... but a more purposeful life"(3) keeping his overwhelming futuristic vision in tact. He appeals to his people, "come, my people, I am waiting for you. Confide in me your worries .... Let's laugh and cry together .... History is ours to play with—ours not!"(10) and says:

> Justice works in my kingdom—without any consideration of might or weakness, religion or creed. May this moment burn bright and light up our path towards greater justice, equality, progress and peace not just peace but a more purposeful life.

> And to achieve this end I am taking a new step in which I hope I shall have your support and co-operation. Later this year the capital of my empire will be moved from Delhi to Daulatabad.(3)

When his decision is final he orders bluntly to his people, "Anybody who attempts to stay behind ... will be severely punished"(46) and tells to Najib "I want Delhi vacated immediately. ... Nothing but an empty graveyard of Delhi will satisfy me now"(44). On the other hand he justifies, "I came to Daulatabad first, and built this .... I supervised the placing of every brick in it and I said to myself one day I shall build my own history like this, brick by brick"(53). Looking back to the history he says, "Look at the past Sultans of Delhi. They could not bear the weight of their crown. They couldn't leave it aside. So they died senile in their youth or were murdered"(11). But the suffering of common people on the way of their transportation, their emotional attachment to their native soil was heedlessly neglected by his administrative machinery. When the sceptre of horror presides over Daulatabad he is turning to tradition and history and seeking an answer from them—in the blessings of Abbasid Khalif.

In statecraft reform without administrative precaution may become disastrous. The historicity of the truth in *Tughlaq* lies in the textuality of history. The introduction of copper currency in place of silver dinars is a failure of his idealistic vision due to lack of precaution. He knows that his subjects are afraid of him and would not dare to mistrust him but he fails to suspect the nature and instinct of men who get involved in counterfeiting the token copper coins. He knows that most Hindus remain involved in this foul business just to prove him a failure in his model role. He dares his enemies but does not dare his subjects and says, "I am not worried about my enemies, I'm only worried about my people"(11) in sheer helplessness. He is convinced of the public confidence in his private self that: if China has paper currency then his people will accept him as "They have faith in the Emperor's seal on the pieces of paper" (39). He is ignorant to realise that his confidence has drawn contempt on his kingdom, the hidden land of immorality. In order to keep his faith in his mission he invites Shihab-ud-din and some Amirs of Delhi who hatch out a conspiracy against him. He gives them a "long rope" in the form of asking suggestions, and convinces them to take an oath on the *Quran* to support his new measures. On the other hand he takes Ratan Singh, Shihab-ud-din's adopted brother into his confidence to betray them all and stabs Shihab-ud-din repeatedly in a frenzy and orders to behead the Amirs involved in the conspiracy. In his cruel exultation he orders to stuff their bodies with straw to be displayed around his kingdom. But in a very shrewd manner he changes such a volatile situation into his advantage by making a public statement that there was a rebellion in the palace, and while the nobles of the court tried to assassinate him during prayer he was saved by Shihab who died a martyr's death by defending him. He rather orders to organise Shihab's funeral in a grand manner to felicitate his shocked father for the sacrifice of his loyal son. To this politics with the dead Barani laments "Oh God! Aren't even the dead free from your politics?" (44). Karnad describes selfishness, treachery and betrayal in Tughlaq's state affairs as the "honey comb of diseases" (55) and Tughlaq has no cure for this.

By exploiting the situation and his subjects Tughlaq functions as tyrant and surpasses "the boundary situation" like the progressive protagonists of Albert Camus's *Caligula* (1947) and *Myth of Sisyphus* (1955) vacillating between the individual's longing for order and the irrationality that destroy the individuals. He applies cruelty and tyranny, to overcome his existential alienation, with an absurd imagination to revitalise his society through violence in a Nietzschean sense. He asserts his deliberate intention to persuade his people that "the tyrant doesn't deserve to be considered among the faithful" (36). Tughlaq considers every conceivable unscrupulous means to be justified to acquire and sustain power and authority. Referring to his cunningness and grandiose schemes Gomez writes: "If they failed to understand his reasons for proposing these schemes, he too fails to foresee their reactions to them" (Gomez 115). His intention to murder is revealed as a definite means to self-recognition and self-identity. He has adopted tyranny as a way of life, a means to an end, a vehicle to fulfil his mission in life. He dreams to build a new future of India by solving "all problems in the flash of a dagger" (42) and adopts the art of silencing dissenters like a contemporary demagogue, be it Hitler, Mussolini or Saddam Hussain. Tughlaq desires to build the foundation of his empire with an innovated idea of golden age syndrome by acclimatising his ideal democratic notions mingled with the catholicity of spirit which embraces diverse religions and cultures with a truly human attitude. Philosophically he dreams of the "salvation of society" and of establishing "the Kingdom of Heaven on earth" (14). In his imaginative complex psyche Tughlaq is represented as a "divided self" between his higher motives of idealism and his lower instincts of political ambition. Yet as an empiricist in his ideals he has striking opposites between the substance of power politics and the values in which power-politics is based. In imaginative reconstruction of significant events in the play "Tughlaq is more or less monomaniacal like Captain Ahab in the deadly pursuit of his dreams" (Dhanavel 2000:26) but "a megalomaniac halo surrounds the protagonist ... as he keeps on employing various kinds of inhuman trickeries to keep himself in power" (ibid. 34).

Exploitation of prayer for murder is an outcome of Mohammad's state policy to liquidate his opponents. He holds prayer very dear to his heart but he gets fouled when the prayer halls are polluted by the discussions of politics. He does not like to be merely ritualistic in performing prayer, rather like a realist says, "I had wanted every act in my kingdom to become a prayer, every prayer a further step in knowledge, every step to lead us nearer to God. But our prayers too are ridden with disease and must be exiled" (44). Prayer is meant to sanctify the mind, but ironically, it has become a dirty political game of Mohammad. At first he considers prayer as "pollution" (13) and bans it for seven years and later reinitiates it through Khalifa's grandson as a path to salvation. Applying this as a method of his statecraft and a bobby trap he realises it to be a regrettable sport. In the textuality of the play Karnad has allied prayer to parricide and murder. To Tughlaq religion is a personal matter as well as a matter of politics for the state control and struggles hard to preserve his ideals in tact against overwhelming odds. By joining religion and politics like the contemporary politicians and rewriting history for political ends he does not like to drag India to the Dark Age in the early fourteenth century by refusing to be another Charlemagne. His banning and introducing prayer reflect the inner drama of his intentions, ambitions and passions. It is also a diplomatic retreat to appease the Ulemas and Sayyids who often stir up people's religious sentiment.

Tainted politics and corruption in his kingdom make him to be tactful to murder one after another in desperation. Murder is a strategy used as a sign for interpreting his happiness. Barani appeals, "your majesty, there was a time when you believed in love, in peace, in God. What has happened to those ideals? ... Why this bloodshed? Please stop it" (56) assuming that this malaise has arisen from the rejection of God and fellowmen. Barani suggests to him to renew his relationship with God and neighbours, but Mohammed is unable to detach himself from this merry sport of violence and bloodshed like Shakespeare's *Macbeth*. His series of murders is an outcome of his Utopian passion for building an ideal kingdom, "a new world ... not found in the Arabs or ever the *Koran*" (21) but it is reduced to a "market of corpses"(55). Barani reminds him "you are known the world over for your knowledge of philosophy and poetry. History is not made only in state-craft; its lasting results are produced in the ranks of learned men" (55). He realises that the idealistic visions of his dream can never reach the stars unless they are rooted in the firm support of his subjects. In an existential dilemma he realises life to be a tale told by an idiot, full of sound and fury signifying nothing"(Macbeth, v, ii) and asks Barini, "why must this happen ...? Are all those I trust condemned to go down in history as traiors? ... will my reign be nothing more than a tortured scream which will stab the night and melt away in silence?"(43). Moralists may raise eyebrows on Tughlaq's cunningness to use prayer as a craft for state politics but had he not done so, his very existence would have been in peril. Thus he stands as a victim-turned-sinner owing to his prayer-politics tactics.

The main events in the play are based on historical episodes "in the life of a great emperor seen not only in relation to a particular period in India's national history but also in relation to a contemporary history" (Ramamurti 15). Being tired of his intelligent and tactful opponents—Sheik Imam-ud-din, Shihab-ud-din, Ain-ul-Mulk and Amirs—all men of vested interests ambitious for the throne of Delhi, he is compelled to act as a despot for a better "tomorrow " and "new future" when his stepmother point out his degeneration: "It's only seven years ago that you came to throne. How glorious you were then, how idealistic, how full of hopes. Look at your kingdom now. It's become a kitchen of death"(65) he admits "I killed them-yes-but I killed them for an ideal"(65). As she discloses her involvement in Najib's murder Tughlaq remarks "you are worse than an adulteress" and later says, "I want her stoned to death publicly ..." (67).

The play provokes one look at history through the lens of contemporaneity. At one level it deals with the Indian political scene in 1960s, and offers in ironic prophetic commentary on the ideology of secularism and he provokes that subverts that ideology in India's traditional and diverse society on the other. Karnad realises the rotten condition of Tughlaq's time to be synonymous with Nehru's vision of modern India in his attempt to Europeanise her socially and politically during his "era of idealism in the country" (Murthy viii). In the textuality of history he encompasses the imaginative reconstruction of Nehruvian socialism in the five myths of his legacy—a promoter of dynasty, betrayer of his master (Gandhi), an opponent to Vallabhabhai (a better choice for Prime Minister than Gandhi's selection to Nehru) and an autocrat and imposer of centralised 'Stalinist' model of economic development in India. On the one hand Karnad portrays the rights of Tughlaq on a vaster canvas and on the other hand delineates as man's struggle against failures to preserve his ideals, visions and dreams in imaginative reconstruction by overcoming topical limitations in Indian situation in early sixties. A.B. Dharwadker rightly remarks:

> The twenty-year period of Tughlaq's decline as a ruler also offered a 'striking parallel' to the first two decades of Indian independence under Jawaharlal Nehru's idealistic but troubled leadership, and Nehru appeared remarkably like Tughlaq in his propensity for Failure despite an extraordinary intellect. Yet the play was not meant either as an 'obvious coment on Nehru' or an 'exact parallel' of the present : rather, it addressed the emerging ambivalence of power relations in the political and public spheres which were based, for the first time in Indian history, on the principles of mass representation and enfranchisement (*Collected Plays* Vol. I : xviii).

Karnad examines history in the contemporary context raising the fundamental social and political issues prevalent in Indian society and polity for a better future. The play presents his disillusionment that his generation felt with the new politics of independent India and some understanding of its socio-political conditions. The historicity of the text in its understanding and analysis presents Tughlaq as a man of striking paradoxes who ascended the throne of Delhi as "a dreamer and a man of action, benevolent and cruel, devout and godless" (Naik 1982:262).

The text in its political permutations shows the interweaving of historical changes and politics from the past to the present and repeats its design from state to state. Karnad's fictional Mohammad evokes not one but several political figures of the colonial and post-colonial India as "basically concerned with the tragedy of limits of human power in a predominantly psychological context" (Naik 1987:138). By embodying Mohammad in radical impulses Karnad makes him "at once the Gandhi experimenting with truth, the Nehru aiming at cultural modernity and the Indira choosing self-destructive authoritarianism for her concept of national well-being" (Sengupta 169-70) in the style of her leadership to modernise and discipline India with a serious reformative zeal. Tughlaq's humility and self-questioning for public confessions of errors are "fundamental to Gandhi's political practice"(Dharwadker 1995:51). His desire for a transformative union with his people is a striking parallel to Nehru's dream to revitalise his citizens by his anxiety to give independent India a garb of modernity releasing their vast stores of suppressed energy and ability. With his 'disenchantment' of the Nehruvian decades for its accomodation of a new phase of corruption and violence as established during the Mughal and British imperialism Karnad thinks that this has become a general system in our political and public life. Thus making an uncannily accurate portrayal of the brilliant but authoritarian and opportunistic political style of Nehru and his daughter, Indira Gandhi, in the play he sets:

> ... the polarity between politics as the selfless extension of individual spirituality (Mahatma Gandhi) and vision (Jawaharlal Nehru), and politics as the self-serving, sometimes demonic expression of individual fantasies of power (evidenced in Indira Gandhi, Sanjay Gandhi, and, more recently in Sikh, Muslim, and Hindu fundamentalist leaders). These two models of political action in turn imply

> radically different relations between leaders and citizens, but by embodying both impulses within Tughlaq, Karnad also suggests an ironic identity between them (Dharwadker 2005:xx-xxi).

It appears that his altruism, benevolence, self-sacrifice, dedication to the public good and solitude for human race seem to be irrelevant in the context of the disorders of the time.

By evoking Gandhi, Nehru and their political heirs in contemporary time Karnad lends his protagonist of history to contemporary relevance. Although the historicity of the text helps to judge Tughlaq from the standpoint of contemporary India there are essential differences between the characteristic features of the fourteenth century and those of the twentieth century India. It is common knowledge that the chief architects of India's tryst with destiny despite "their innate idealism and commitment to the progress of the nation have more or less been reduced to more footnotes on the margins of contemporary Indian history"(Ghose 120). Karnad's interpretation of history in contemporary paradigms reveals the fact that there are many leaders akin to Tughlaq who failed to sustain their own visions in politics in spite of their honesty, integrity and model ideals. Tughlaq, by virtue of his kingship, feels it his duty to protect and govern his country and people. But he fails utterly in both. His failure is partly due to his characteristic limitations that prompt him to commit murders, cause urpheavals, upset the economy and violate moral codes. The other part proves him to be villainous for taking odd decisions, lacking practical knowledge about his contemporary reality and knowledge on human character. The outside factor is that the circumstances were not in his favour. Karnad develops Tughlaq as a parallel to Nehru, and his abortive ventures are quite similar to Nehru's favourite dream-plan which were not only futile but aggravated the existing maladies. He makes Tughlaq a caricature of the post-colonial monster who preys upon his own people under the guise of a saviour. Karnad converts the history of Tughlaq into myth to enumerate the idealistic personality of the great Indian leader whose vision became fatal to the society in postcolonial reality. Historicity of the text confirms that honest and clean politcians become disastrous for a nation. Keeping this in mind Karnd shows how the ever-increasing criminalisation of politics today is indicative of the failure of ideal role models to govern the country. He shows that mere idealism and unrelated understanding of time cannot only help a ruler in reaching the visionary heights. He presents that in power-politics dynamics all idealisms are only mirages. It is true that Tughlaq's tragedy lies in his failure to reconcile his idealism with the historical imperatives of the situation and events in which he finds himself to be only a pawn.

In the theatrical presentation of history, *Tughlaq* is not merely a political allegory but an absolute thesis on an interesting character, his nature, philosophy and destiny all linked with the people, religion and history. Tughlaq's tragic tale is symptomatic of the inherited complex problem of the Indian society. It strikes parallel between the political instability during the reign of Tughlaq and the social nostalgia of Delhi in the nineteen sixties. Tughlaq is a projection of two selves—one comprising his higher motives of idealism and the other his lower instinct of political ambition. His madness may be an outcome of his complex fear-psychosis but it has a steady progress in the process of self-consummation and self-realisation in search for human values. As Lear realises Cordelia-consciousness in his madness, the Sultan resigns his egoism and realises the greater God in his madness. When there is a rush of negative emotion he says to Barani, "Sweep your logic away into a corner ... all I need now is myself and my madness—madness to prance in a field eaten bare by the scarecrow violence.... I have a companion to share my madness now ... the Omnipotent God!"(85). The rotten condition of his kingdom helps the play to gain a tragic height though it fails to emerge as a "tragedy chiefly because the dramatist seems to deny himself the artist's privilege to present an integrated vision of characters full of conflicting tendencies" (Naik 1982:262-63) for a nemesis.

The play has a close parallel to the historical antecedents and photographic imitation of history presenting "at once an idealist and a crafty politician, a humanist and a tyrant, a man who has murdered sleep and yet not a Macbeth haunted by supernatural solicitations a man who thinks and broods too much and yet not a Hamlet incapable of action on guilty of delay" (Ramamurthy 42). Through different symbols like payer, rose, sleep and chess Karnad attempts to succeed in creating the right political atmosphere to understand history and contemporaneity. Through the symbols the morals and manners of the political world of power has been sensitively commented upon.

Reading of history as a narrative to the human subject exists outside the history in the text, and both are historically shaped without intervening in the process of history. The historicity of the text and the textuality of history are inseparable in their hermeneutic resonance. Karnad does not like to keep Tughlaq as a cosmetic mummy in the textuality of history, and so presents him as a living organism in history's timelessness knowing that "historical narration without analysis is trivial, historical analysis without narration is incomplete"(White 268). The text can be read as a discourse on historical narrative in the analysis of its historicity. History is (re)written from the vantage point of each new generation. Indian historians in the past and present, both Marxist and liberal, provide the scholarly interpretation of the Sultan from vantage points with a taste for nostalgia maintaining sharp distinction between the ruler and ruled. The historiographers present him like a mountain climber who has reached the point of no return where he can move neither forward nor backward in the heart-breaking spectacle of self crucifixion. The historicity of the text and the textuality of history imply to rethink history, the text, and the interaction between the two, to bring out that history is no longer merely static background but rather something timeless, living, and mysterious in its entirety, and speaking through many devices of which the literary text is one.

Karnad's *The Dreams of Tipu Sultan* (2004) is his third historical play after *Tughlaq* and *Tale-danda* based on the historicity of eighteenth century India. The play exposes the status of Tipu, his psychology, and the struggle for peace and strategic resistance of this great personality when the princely kingdoms in India were struggling for their individual hegemony, and the British were consolidating their empire. In the dramatisation of Tipu's dreams Karnad has projected the historical materials in his conscious endeavour without any prejudices, preoccupations, obsessions and conceived canons. Analysing history in the postcolonial perspectives he has presented his ideological polemics and objective point of view into the then socio-political paradigms. For him, " 'history is the vehicle of rational self-consciousness through which the incomplete human spirit progressively acquires an improved sense of its own totality' " (Gandhi 1998:105).

In the job of historiographer and in the self of a dramatist Karnad has carnivalised the dreams and dauntlessness of this great personality in a rhetorical and hysterical manner. In projecting Tipu as a great protagonist of Indian history with his survival instinct Karnad hypothesises Tipu's objectives. Conditioning Tipu's achievements, successes and failures in the 'historical givens' he has rescued Tipu from colonial imperatives. Analysing Tipu's patriotic past and the needs of his present in a rational and realistic way, Karnad has assessed Tipu's right to self-assertion, war stratagem, desire for his kingdom's sovereignty, and his diplomacy for trade and peace. At the same time Karnad projects Tipu's personal emotion, love for family and love for his subjects, secular attribute, far-sighted outlook which was akin to the Nehruvian outlook in the twentieth century and dreams for a prospective nationalism in his struggle for freedom from colonial humiliation and exploitation. The play on the one hand projects the imperial victor's 'contaminated' self that pollutes the ideological pollens of imperial politics and a rhetoric of psychological and emotional duress of Tipu in his existential essentialism on the other.

Karnad had his 'obsession' with Tipu which he had inherited from A.K. Ramanujan's unfinished novel in English on the subject. From Ramanujan he had come to know about Tipu's secret diary in which he had recorded his dreams. In 1987 Karnad located a copy of this diary at the University of Chicago's Regenstein Library. In 1990, he was among the public figures voiced his strong support for Sanjay Khan's tele serial *The Sword of Tipu Sultan*, on the grounds that Tipu needed to be given his due as a major figure in Karnataka history, a visionary, and a patriot. The historical portrayals of *Tipu Sahib* or *British Valour in India* put on at Covent Garden, London, 1791 and folk ballads on Tipu in Karnataka had also inspired him to make the play stageworthy. With these historical materials Karnad could understand India's colonial problems, the overdosed ideology of this philosopher-king, and the chess-board politics among the British, Marathas, the Nizam and Tipu. Karnad points out how the alliance of the evil had checkmated and decimated this powerful king. In 'the historical givens' and 'historical totality' Tipu's invincibility, authority, figural dimension and ambitious dreams are portrayed without any ideological aberrations and in a dispassionate distance. The play is a tragedy of a person as well as a nation, and Tipu is represented as the worst victim of the Anglo-French conflict and as the nexus of Indian princes with the British that made a steady headway towards the apocalyptic approach of British imperialism in this subcontinent.

The thought of writing a play on Tipu came to Karnad's mind when he was commissioned by the BBC for a play, in 1996, in honour of India's celebrating the fiftieth anniversary of her independence. While its Kannada version was staged in the precincts of Tipu's Summer Palace, Daria Daulat in Seringa-patam to commemorarte Tipu's two-hundredth death anniversary, in May 1997, its English version was broadcast on 15 August 1997 to mark the fiftieth anniversary of India's independence, perhaps in an attempt to caution the Indian nation states to remain aware of the dangers of foreign interference in India's affairs. The play is about the beginning of British colonialism in India, its crucial stages of military expansion and an Indian emperor's inescapable psychodrama. It dramatises Tipu's fabled persona as the Tiger of Mysore in a historical reconstruction demonstrating his dreams—partly narrated and partly enacted—along with his interpretations. The playwright narrates Tipu's four dreams in elegiac tone. Tipu shines as a proto-nationalist who resists English man's schemes to rob his land and believes in Englishman's belief 'in the destiny of their race,' and will to die in faraway places for the dream of England. In colonial historical parenthesis Karnad reconstructs Tipu's ambition for nation building; rational, calculating, pragmatic and ruthless British generals and their racist contempt; hostile Hindu and Muslim allies like Nana Phadnavis and Nizam of Hyderabad in their 'traitorous' collaboration; and others like prominent historian Kirmani, his family members and military officials. About the play A.B. Dharwadker rightly remarks in the 'Introduction' to Karnad's *Collected Plays* (Vol. II):

> It draws upon a range of historical sources to present convincing portraits of the principal characters, but creates an imaginative plot and resonant dialogue to contain their experience. It deals with a controversial protagonist who can be characterised in radically opposite ways, depending on the observer's view-point—as a heroic figure of anticolonial

> resistance (comparable to the Rani of Jhansi) in one perspective, and a treacherous but fallible (and even foolish) adversary in another (xxiii).

However, he conceived the thought in his understanding of the late eighteenth century socio-political milieu of India in a cartographic imagination in which everything was exhibited as it were, in the paintings at memorial complexes or museums. Karnad's sole aim, in this play, is to highlight Tipu's visionary zeal, political strategies, battlefield manoeuvres, modernising impulses and the populist trade and commerce policies. In the dramatisation of his protagonist he has achieved the artistic merit of the play.

Tipu was a great visionary, dreamer and utopian nation-builder. As a premature utopian of Indian nationalism he loses his political haemoglobin by interrogating the British imperialism in counter-hegemonic activity. In portraying him Kanad strictly adheres to the historicity without distorting the facts. In the context of the play a comprehensive layout is made on geographical regions,and the periodisation of the Anglo-French conflict in the backdrop. Presenting him in the vortex of a major transitional moment in Indian history, "Karnad also casts his protagonist in multiple and contradictory roles—as a beloved ruler, legendary warrior, loving father, and visionary dreamer, but also as the Machiavellian schemer who plots with the French against the English, the defeated soldier who enters into humiliating treaties with the enemy, and the gullible commander who is eventually betrayed by his own side" (*Collected Plays*, (vol. II: xxiv). The towering dimension of Tipu's stature is assessed in his political ideology, philosophy, and in his diplomatic relationships with the neighbouring kingdoms and foreign countries. Tipu was restless but not foolishly callous like his Indian counterparts when the West was establishing its strongholds, to dominate the East. Dramartising this dreamer's vision, humanism and dynamism, Karnad projects Tipu as a casualty of history for his zeal for nationalism and his strategy to tackle his enemies. He appears to be grieved for Tipu's decimation by his peripheral adversaries and British advantages to override him. Tipu's failure as a nation-builder and dreamer lies in his tightrope walking between bargaining for peace and batoning the enemies.

In 1803 Colonel Colin Mackenzie, the British Oriental scholar in the auspices of John Cmpany, summoned Tipu's court historian Mr. Husain Ali Khan Kirmani to translate his dreams. Though Kirmani was employed in the Job of a historiographer to narrate the topsy-turvy career of this great Sultan, it was very painful to him for the betrayal of his conscience and his loyalty to his one-time patron. Narrating Tipu's obsession with idealism, secularism and militarism, Kirmani presented the glorious achievements of his Sultan in the history of Deccan India. He presented Tipu's passion for the socio-economic potentiality and civilisational plenitude. Tipu's struggle to achieve these glorifies him in history, but it led him to suffer in the stature of an Aristotelian tragic hero. His bargaining for peace ultimately became a diplomatic snag in his policy which served as a tragic hamartia. Though Kirmani snubs this as a diplomatic failure he appreciates this as a strategic necessity from different ontologies, political praxis and historical exigencies. Karnad analyses them in a postcolonial hypothesis.

Tipu was called by his volatile English enemy Arthur Wellesley "the tiger of Mysore" (14). The British even after his death had not dared to chop off his whiskers as this tropical tiger had made them restless with his bravery, diplomacy and idealism. A serious researcher of history may neglect the relevance of his tie with the French to strengthen his ideological state apparatuses in his contemporary ambience but it is adjudged as a great strength of this dreamer. In England's territorial ambition the two British Governor Generals—Lord Cornwallis and Arthur Wellesley—had accused him dubiously as ambitious, disloyal and betrayer of friendship. In a dispassionate perspective it can be said if the British signed the Treaty of Versailles with the French to sort out their differences in Europe and Afro-Asian countries for the safety of their extended empire, it is merely a colonial bias to label Tipu's alliance with France a betrayal of faith. His passion for galvanizing his Sultanate with all amenities and successful foreign relationship shook his intolerant neighbours like the Marathas and the Nizam of Hyderabad with apprehension. It is obvious that Tipu had borne the envy of his neighbours as his late father Haider Ali had made them restless by occupying parts of their territories. But Tipu had tried his best to satisfy them without adding salt to their injury and without insulting the spirit of his father.

Tipu hated the English, as the English hated the French, in his motive hunting malignity in defiance of their repressive schemes. From the point of view of sovereignty, if the imperialist Governors dreamt their empire Tipu asserted his rights to translate his dreams into action. He admited of accepting two teachers in his life—his father Haider who taught him war, and the English who taught him trade. While he used the former's teaching to safeguard his territory, the latter's inspired him radically to start transcontinental business by sailing across the seas and not by riding camels through the deserts. In negotiating for peace with the British he tried to sort out all differences, but they rather accused him as the enemy of all mankind for joining his "hands with villainous French" (33).

With the self of a historian and the soul of a friend, philosopher and guide, Kirmani had a close association with Tipu in his evil days. Being torn between loyalty and "dispassionate distance" he narrates the last days of Tipu before Mackenzie. He presents Tipu as a great dreamer like Alexander and Napoleon who had met with their end in the course of translating their dreams into action. Tipu is one of the worst victims of destiny, in the proverbial saying, 'Man proposes God disposes'. In his artistic endeavour Karnad agrees with Kirmani's assessment of Tipu before Mackenzie.

Tipu was secular in spirit, modern in thought, much above than the thinking of his Indian counterparts and very defiant in his dreams for his reasonable vectors. While negotiating for peace he was never neglecting the interest of his state. He had appointed a Hindu Brahmin, Poornaiya, as Finance Minister, and had high respect for Hindu pundits, seers and astrologers. There were even many Hindu soldiers in his army. He believed superstitiously in Hindu astrology and the propitiousness of stars and planets. On his way back from Farrukhi near Salamabad he was mystified by the stone eyes of the female idols in a dilapidated temple, and turned to Poornaiya with the proposal, "We'll have the temple repaired, the walls rebuilt so that these seekers (devotees) after God are not disturbed" (19). Tipu's respect for other faiths and foreign envoys was expressed in his offering them situations in his Diwan-i-Aam and Diwan-i-Khas, and had made him popular at home as well as abroad. The Hindu seers, like the seer of the monastery of Sringeri, had offered them the blessings of Goddess Sharada.

The emperor of China had sent his envoy to Tipu's court to negotiate on silk business. He had also sent his delegation of envoys to France, Istanbul, China, Turkey, Arabia, Mascot and Iran. Through his successful foreign policy he had established a healthy diplomatic relationship with all the Islamic nations. Tipu had a dream to make his state capital a centre of trade and commerce by establishing industries of sandal wood, spice, ivory and silk. His "passion for trade" (26) and missions for scopes in the international marts was competitive in spirit with the British. While the British industries were established in a bandit-mode to exploit the natives Tipu's attempt to industrialise his capital was populist, desirably benevolent and ethically equalitarian. He had a great ambition to make his state a model one by designing Lal Bagh in the shape of Versailles and "stun the world" (27). He had negotiated with the French through his envoys to procure professionals like doctors, surgeons, smelters, carpenters, weavers, blacksmiths, cutters, watchmakers, dyers and gardeners to model his Lal Bagh and to train his men.

It becomes clear from Tipu's discussion with Ghulam Ali Khan and Osman Khan that in modernity and sophistication the French are much better than the English. He had the desire for inter-civilisational alliance between the French and his people. For civilisational plenitude and perfection he preferred 'hybridity' and 'mimicry' in his inter-continental diplomatic relationship. In order to negotiate with Monsieur Pierre Monneron of Pondicherry he had sent Osman Khan to convey his request to the French Governor General of Mauritius for his consent to send his delegation to France. His "Main objective is to explain to the king of France the situation in India. Particularly the state of French here" (24). He had the plan to convince the French King Louis XVI, "if the French don't wake up, the English will gobble up the whole of India" 24). Expressing his willingness to sign a "Treaty of Perpetual Alliance" (24) with the French he made a request to send ten thousand French soldiers to be placed under him to kick the British off from India. He made a request to the French king to send mechanics to make guns, cannons, pistols, and also varieties of trees and flower plants to beautify his capital. His request for newly invented machines like thermometer to help his hakim in treating the patients and for translation of different French professional books into Persian reveal Tipu's outlook as a great visionary.

Tipu's dreams situate him in a difficult position in history. It is true that Tipu's awakening is a premature outburst of India's mass awakening for independence. But his time was critical from the point of view of a socio-political transition when the West was slouching over the East, and the apocalypse of imperialism in its claustrophobic omnipresence was slowly devouring this subcontinent. He was the first Indian king to explain the British that they were not the only messianic harbingers of civilisation with the gifted power to prescribe limitations for the Indian princes rather like a Marxist anti-imperialist he challenged the imperial cause expressing his obligations to his subjects through his societal preoccupations and developmental projects. From time to time England was sending efficient Generals famous for their hawkish diplomacy, to consolidate their empire in India and they succeeded in decimating a powerful sultan like Tipu, and expelling the French from India for good. From each failure the British were learning a new lesson. Tipu had perceived that the English succeeded in India not only because of their superior weapons and warfare, but because of their ability to play off members of the native ruling elite against each other. In 1790, Tipu defeated Cornwallis who ran away with "his tail between his legs" (12). Although the English retreated realising it difficult on their part to capture Seringapatam, they diplomatically succeeded in compelling Tipu to sign the treaty for peace as the Marathas and the Nizam joined hands with them.

By signing the treaty Tipu committed a historical blunder. He was trapped in the British diplomacy. For the sake of six crores to pay to the British as war indemnity he mortgaged his two sons as hostages to Cornwallis. His twc years' war with the joint force of the English, the Marathas and the Nizam, and the seven years' peace accord with the English to clear up the indemnity had greatly affected his stature, economy of the state and morale of his army. In the binary of imperial psyche it might be Cornwallis's final attempt to mesmerize Tipu's valour and aggressive spirit or to allude him for a final defeat through the temptation "to use a psychological mechanism more congruent with the basis rules of the oppressive system so as to have a better scope to express one's aggressive drives. The temptation is equal to one's tormentors in violence and to regain one's self-esteem as a competitor within the same system" (Nandy 1986:354). It was a humiliation for him in the eyes of the Marathas and the Nizam. The mean and tricky imperial methods finally reduced this tiger to a cat. His overengagement in wars, and devising of counter-strategies by frequently changing the diplomatic atmosphere diminished his heroic spirit. On the other hand, he remained busy in his abortive attempts to unite his nagging neighbours, and this gave ample chance to the British to play the politics of divide and rule. This helped the British to denerve Tipu diplomatically first, and strategically next.

Tipu signed the treaty as he had no alternative to protest or retreat. He realised the evil designs of the British colonier how "colonization works to decivilize the colonizer to brutalise him in true sense of the word, to degrade him, to awaken him to buried instincts, to covetousness, violence, race hatred and moral relativism" (Cesaire 1972:13). All the four conditions laid down by Cornwallis—all the English prisoners by his majesty as well as his father Haider Ali to be released unconditionally; secession of half of his domain adjacent to the territories of the English, the Marathas and the Nizam; pay six crores of indemnity; and keep two of his sons as hostages to the English till the terms and conditions in the treaty are fulfilled. He was emotionally hurt and was unable to console his queen Begum Ruqayya Banu in the matter of hostaging his sons for peace. It seems that this kind of extreme action of Tipu might be due to his dyspepsia for idealism and love for his subjects.

While his stature was outwardly diminishing before his immediate enemies Tipu was losing courage even to stand before his queen. He sought refuge in prayer and recited Sufi Zikr when the spirit of his dead father appeared and reminded him of his being maimed. Tipu explained how he had become the victim of his destiny when his father accused him of sparing the British in their defeat, he explained that his trusted officers secretly negotiated with Cornwallis and he had no way out for other options. He says to his father's spectral spirit in self-pity, anger and helplessness:

> This land is ours and it's rich, overflowing with goods like the world hungers for, and we let foreigners come in and rob us of our wealth! Today the Indian princes are all comatose, wrapped in their opium dreams. But some day they'll wake up and throw out the Europeans (36).

He explained his situation before his father remorsefully, and also the reasons that made him a failure. He promised to his father to check the British from conquering, plundering, hostaging, and to restore his lost glory and dignity.

Tipu had realised that it would be difficult on his part to check the British nuisance. He made an attempt to unite the Indian princes against the British. He visited Hari Pant Phadke, the Maratha Commander-in-chief, negotiated with Nana Sahib, Chief of Scindia, Nawabs of Carnatic and Oudh, the Rajahs of Travancore and Cochin and Nizam of Hyderabad who had already signed the Treaty of Perpetual Peace with the English. He told them that his seven- and eight-year-old sons were prisoners then, but "make sure it's not your children next-time" (55). Karnad projects Tipu the first Indian king who had well understood the present and future of Indian princes as well as whitemen's burden in British imagined India.

The defeat of Cornwallis in the First Mysore War marked a stigma on the British crown which they tried always to wash off from the York Town. Tipu got his two sons released within two years. The Pitt's India Act emphatically instructed the Board of Control of East India Company to be more defensive rather than offensive while dealing with the Indian princely states. The Board was further instructed to shun the idea of conquering more territories in India. Tipu was unhappy with Pitt's Act since he was confined to a landlocked kingdom. Even though he had returned the lands acquired by him and his father to the Marathas they had joined hand with the British to fleece him by placing new demands. The Marathas had shared the territories of the western coast including Salem, Dindigul and the Malabar coast with the British for an enormous bazaar thus destroying Tipu's possibilities for trade with the French. Tipu knew it well, "sea is the key to power, to prosperity" (54) but the English-Maratha nexus had stifled all his commercial possibilities.

Tipu achieved no good results from the Treaty of Versailles, or from the Pitt's Act, or from his seven years treaty for peace with the English. He felt isolated more and more day by day. The final blow came when Richard Wellesley, the Earl of Mornington, came as the Governor General of India in 1798. Wellesley had a radical diplomacy for India in general and Tipu in particular. He made his predecessor Cornwallis, an "evangelical Christian" (56) responsible for giving Tipu so much scope for "building a trading empire on European model" (56) with the French, Portuguese and Dutch. He made his policy more aggressive while he came to know that Tipu had sent a delegation to Napoleon inviting him to attack India. He was deeply annoyed when he came to know about Tipu's dispatching of a secret delegation to Sir Malarctic, the French Governor of Mauritius, for a dispatch of ten thousand French and twenty thousand African troops to attack the English with his army.

Wellesley and Tipu both had realised that peace was a misnomer for them. While the latter was busy in silkworm industry and sandalwood forest the former thought "the longer the peace the stronger will Tipu become" (56). Blowing the bugle hot and cold at the same time Wellesley said, "We want Tipu's friendship. It gives us time to prepare" (58). While Tipu was having an upshot in power and prestige Wellesley planned to count the strategic milege and placed impossible conditions before Tipu by claiming other half of his kingdom and four of his sons as hostages. Now Tipu had no option except going for war. Tipu invited his ministers, *qilledar* and army chief to discuss the needs and essentialities of war. Kirmani recollects this melodramatic situation before Colin Mackenzie:

> We were halfway through our lunch, our sweat streaming into our plates, when the skies exploded. The English had launched their assault. The Sultan washed his finges and got up from his lunch. He buckled on his sword belt, took out an envelope from his pocket, sealed it and gave it to me: 'keep it till I come back'. (9)

As Kirmani reluctantly opened the seal of the envelope in the betrayal of his conscience he discovered "inside was a paper on which he had recorded the dream he had had the previous night. His last dream" (9) is that "God Almighty and our prophet will make me another Alexander ..." (20). He thought once "the Marathas and the Nizam on our side, we can chase the English into the sea any day" (64). Being disillusioned in the British cunningness and unreliable neighbours, he felt as if he were always haunted by the spirits of his dead wife Ruqayya Banu and of his dead father. He felt relieved in hopes and despair "God's will be done .... Territories come and go. We fight, we gain, we lose" (40).

By defeating Tipu, Wellesley wanted to focus the eyes of the world on Seringapatam and English prowess in India. On 4 May 1799 he attacked Seringapatam. Tipu's ministers, army chiefs and close men betrayed him in the battle front with alacrity. On that afternoon Tipu was killed in the battle. The history of Mysore tiger was closed and a new era dawned. The English boasted : "While the dreadful fate of the fallen ruler could not be contemplated without pain and regret, it should show the Indian princes the danger of inviting foreign invasion against the British power" (65). The English in India and England breathed their relief at last as "the tiger of Mysore had ... been hunted down" (15) and smiled slyly at the "dreadful fate of the fallen ruler" (65). Kirmani narrates the horror of the day before Mackenzie: "Doors and windows in the city had already been torn down by the British soldiers .... And through the night ... the soldiers' rampage seem like child's play ... within a night, all ... recorded facts became memory" (17). He told about Tipu's personal diary, "It was a diary in which my master had recorded his dreams. He had kept it concealed from his closest confidants" (17) with the *Arthashastra* under his pillow. The British found these two objects as the strength of Tipu. "The play begins and ends with memory: Kirmani and Colin Mackenzie serve as the chorus for a highly selective and reflexive history that unfolds cyclically, beginning with the day of Tipu's last battle and returning to it via crucial stages in his slide towards defeat and death" (*Collected Plays,* Vol.II: xxvi).

In the next 20 years the English annexed the Maratha territories, defeated Nizam and transported Tipu's sons to Calcutta in order to avoid further politial litigations. Kirmani rightly observes, "It was not Tipu's dreams but his predictions that came true" (65). Now Tipu's soul might be rising happily to his enemies' defeat and India's ability to make "the white plague depart" (64) in 1947. Karnad seems to proclaim in the play that this great warrior's "blood and tears dried up a long time ago" but his "wound remains fresh" (7). It seems that through this great warrior Karnad has reminded the Indian nation states about the dangers of inviting imperial powers and their meddling in India's integrity. In shock, pity, irony and obeisance he writes about our apathy and political amnesia for this great hero in the postscript of the play:

> When India became independent in 1947, the families of maharajas who had bowed and scraped before the British masters were granted sumptuous privy purses by the Government of India while the descendants of Tipu Sultan were left to rot in the slums of Calcutta (65).

Thus forging the facts, events and the life and career of this great warrior as the historical materials into his play Karnad has made *The Dreams of Tipu Sultan* a great success. The play appears to be a historical teleology in colonial taxonomy. Karnad has attempted his best to defend Tipu's marginalized status in his patriotic past and needy present in a post-colonial perspective dousing all colonial bias.

Karnad's historical plays are essentially the products of the historical texts, both official and unofficial, objective and subjective, and about dominant and subaltern. In the historical reconstruction Karnad has his self-evolution in the understanding of its personages and incidents. He introduces history in his dramatic praxis in order to express a positive concept incidents. He introduces history in his dramatic praxis in order to express a positive concept on Indian society and polity. Each of his historical plays presents his obsession with India's secularism, nationalism and patriotism. He knows that Indian history was written by the British but it evokes suspect in Indian mind.

Reinterpreting the twelfth, fourteenth and nineteenth century historical materials he draws his characters and events in our contemporary socio-political realities. *Tale-danda* deals with caste communalism and adverse effect of caste hierarchy in Kalyan. Contemporanising the theme and effect of caste communalism and religious intolerance between the *virashaivas* and brahmans in twelfth century Karnataka Karnad presents it a recurrent melodrama in modern India's secularised society. The marriage between a brahmin girl and untouchable boy not only make the two communities antagonistic but it generates the intrareligious conflict in Hinduism that promotes sectarianism and violence damaging the bonds of friendship, fellowship, equality, humanity and social ethics. The intercaste marriage destroys the intrareligious unity in Hinduism. Violence is wrong, whatever the provocation is. Karnad presents caste and religious violence which destroy the spirit of secular fabric of Indian society.

Tughlaq evokes certain modern issues in India's Post-independence socio-political realities. Presenting an ostensible narrative of mediaeval history he evokes his readers' and viewers' concern for the existing socio-political situation of India. The play caricatures Nehru's idealistic but troubled leadership at par with Tughlaq's political innocence. He presents Tughlaq's virulent idealism in political and public spheres, and his controversial personality that sounds empty of all morality.

The Dreams of Tipu Sultan is a complex poetic rehabilitation of Tipu. In the portrayal of this legendary Sultan Karnad presents India's first anticolonial resistance, and crisis in polity due to his internal dissensions and presence of powerful alien adversary. In the presentation of a major tansitional moment in Indian history, politics and culture he estimates Tipu's dreams and modernising impulses to shape Mysore in the 'new ideas' of Europe. The play carries the same potential like that of *Tale-danda* and *Tughlaq* in dealing with our contemporary problems that make history relevant even in the twenty-first century.

Works Cited

Cesaire, Aime. *Discourse on Colonialism*. Trans. Joan Pinkham, New York: Monthly Review Press, 1972.

Dhanavel, P. *The Indian Imagination of Girish Karnad*. New Delhi:Prestige Books, 2000.

_______________ . "The History and Myth of Girish Karnad's *Tale-danda*". *The Literary Criterion*. 35:4, 2004.

Dharwadker, Aparna, Bhargava. "Historical Fictions and Post-colonial Representation: Reading Girish Karnad's *Tughlaq*." PMLA 110:1(1995).

_______________ . "Introduction" to Girish Karnad's *Collected Plays* Vol. II. New Delhi: Oxford University Press, 2005.

Eagleton, Terry. *Literary Theory:An Introduction*. New Delhi: Doaba Publications, 1996.

Gandhi, Leela. *Postocolonial Theory: A Critical Introduction*. New Delhi: Oxford University Press, 1998.

Ghosh, Nibir K. "Girish Karnad's Tughlaq: History in the Future Tense". *50 years of Indian Writing*. New Delhi: IAES, 1999.

Gomez, Christine. "Karnad's Tughlaq as an Alienated Protagonist." *The plays of Girish Karnad*. Ed. Jaydipsinh Dodiya. New Delhi: Prestige Books, 1999.

Joshipura, Pranav. "*Tale-danda* : A Problem Play". *Indian English Drama: Critical Perspective*. Ed. Jaydipsinh K. Dodiya and K.V. Surendran. New Delhi: Sarup and Sons, 2000.

Karnad, Girish.. "Discussion" *Enactment* 54, 1971.

_____________ . (Interview) "Where is the Tradition?". *Frontline.* (September 25) 1992.

_____________ . *Tale-danda.* New Delhi: Ravi Dayal, 1993. (All textual references are made to this edition)

_____________ . "Author's Introduction" to *Three Plays.* New Delhi: OUP, 1995.

_____________ . "Discussion with U.R. Anantha Murthy and Prasanna". *Indian Literature* (169) New Delhi: Sahitya Akademi 38.5 (September-October), 1995.

_____________ . *The Dreams of Tipu Sulatan* and *Bali: The Sacrifice.* New Delhi: Oxford University Press, 2004. (All textual references are made to this edition)

_____________ . (An interview with Tutun Mukherjee) "In His Own Voice: A Conversation with Girish Karnad". *Girish Karnad's Plays: Performance and Critical Perspectives.* Ed. Tutun Mukherjee. New Delhi: Pencraft International, 2008.

Murthy, U.R. Anantha, Prasanna and Girish Karnad. "Girish Karnad the Playwright: A Discussion". *Indian Literature.* 169 (September-October), 38:5, 1995.

Montrose, Louis Adrian. "The Elizabethan Subject and Spenserian Text." *Literary Theory/Renaissance Text.* Ed. Parker and Quint. Baltimore and London: Johns Hopkins University Press, 1986.

Murthy, U.R.Anantha "Introudction". *Tughlaq.* New Delhi: OUP, 1977. (All textual references are made to this edition).

_____________ . "The Limits of Human Power: A Comparative Study of *Tughlaq* and *Caligula.*" *Studies in Indian English Literature.* New Delhi: Sterling Publishers, 1987.

Naik, M.K. *A History of Indian English Literature.* New Delhi: Sahitya Akademi, 1982.

_____________ . "Cinderella Still: Recent Indian English Drama". *Littcrit.* 27:1-2 (June-December), 2001.

Naik, M.K. and S.A. Narayan. *Indian English Literature 1980-2000: A Critical Survey.* New Delhi: Pencraft International, 2001.

Nandy, A. "Oppression and Human Liberation: Toward a Post-Gandhian Utopia". *Political Thought in Modern India,* Eds. Thomas Pantham & Kenneth L. Deutsch, New Delhi: Sage, 1986.

Nehru, Jawaharlal. *The Glimpses of World History.* New Delhi: O.U.P., 1982.

Rajgopalachari, M. and N. Anil Krishna. "Karnd's *Tughlaq*: A Critical Note." *Indian Scholar.* 11:1(January), 1989.

Ramamurti, K.S. "Some Aspects of Indian Drama in English with Special Reference to *Tughlaq*." *Littcrit*. 5:1 (1979).

Said, Edward W. *Culture and Imperialism*. New York: Vintage Books, 1993.

Sengupta, Ashis. "Being and Role -Playing :Reading Girish Karnad's *Tughlaq*." *Indian Literatue* (213). New Delhi: Sahitya Akademi, 47:1 (January-February), 2003.

Shakespeare, William. *Macbeth*. Ed.D.Wilson. Cambridge: University press. 1947.

Shukla, A.R. "Caste and Religion in *Tale-danda*". *The Plays of Girish Karnad: Critical Perspectives*. Ed. Jaydipsinh Dodiya. New Delhi: Prestige Books, 1999.

Sundararaman, M.N. "Historical Plays in Indian Drama in English: A Glimpse". *Revaluations*. 1:2. (Summer) 1995.

Tagore, Rabindranath. *Three Plays*. Madras: Oxford University Press, 1950.

Virupakshappa, B. "Author's Note". *Basava and His Teachings* (2nd edition) Bangalore: Basava Samiti, 2002.

Dr. Babasaheb Ambedkar: Writings and Speeches. Bombay: Government of Maharashtra, 1987.

White Hayden. "The Value of Narrativity in the Representation of Reality." *Modern Literary Theory*. Ed. Philip Rice and Patricia Waugh. New York: Oxford University Press Inc, 2001.

5 Contemporaneity in Girish Karnad's Plays

Shifting the context of his plays from, myth, folklore and history Girish Karnad concentrates his dramatic imagination on modern man's post-colonial situation and existential angsts. It is significant that Karnad projects life and society in the real world which suffer from internal vacuity and external vanities. In some of his recent plays he has presented the contemporary human situation in varied manifestations. Portraying the contemporary reality in his plays he highlights morality on the one hand and negotiates with the essentiality on the other. Two of his most 'contemporary classics' are *A Heap of Broken Images* (2005) and *Wedding Album* (2009) which have their groundings in the technology-affected and culture infected-Indian society. While the former is a dramatic monologue the latter is an one-actplay of nine scenes. In both the plays Karnad presents the subjectives of life in the objectivities of purpose.

A Heap of Broken Images like many of Karnad's plays is first produced and then published. Although the title of its Kannada version is *Odakalu Bimba,* its first English title in the drafts of the manuscript was *Words* and then *Macaulay's Children*. In the evolution of its title the play presents a complex discussion on technology and accurate recapitulation of the classic grounds for the language debate. Karnad uses a new technique to analyse language and memory through the technological presentation. For him language is emotive (experessive), conative (impulsive), phatic (ideological), referential, metalingual and poetic. In the hypothetical assessment of language dynamics in India he presents that language is the major force through which the human individual is constituted as a structured and gendered subject. Karnad believes that language is the sign that identifies a person, defines a culture and unites a society or nation. It is the interpretative and repertoire tool that establishes relationship between the psyche and external forces. Every language promotes concept, responses and embelishes words for expression. Secondly, he gives a psychoanalysis of individuals' mental faculties, mode and instinct, reaction and how they cannot escape from the bondage of ideology. The play is a landmark production of Indian theatre. In an interview with Tutun Mukharjee he says, "When I returned to Bangalore in early 2004, I realized the extent to which technology pervaded and affected our lives. To me technology wasn't depressing at all. This was the age of image. We needed to understand its aesthetics and use it" (Mukharjee 2008:53). It seems that Karnad's dramatic career counteracts the premise in the play. The subjective purpose of the play is to present English as the necessary tool to bridge the literary and material success for the Indian authors, and English and the Indian languages are mutually exclusive medias. In the play he portrays very insightfully the issues of a class system in contemporary Indian literature that involves not only language but the genre. Incorporating his ideas in the play he says, "The idea for the play came to me when I heard Shashi Deshpande talk about the problems of the writers of regional literature. I was advised to change the title because it had a literary rather than general appeal" (ibid. 52). The play also presents playwright's impression about the tremendous technological advances. He focuses that language usually speaks man but now technology speaks man. He is convinced that technology could immensely change and affect the life style of the people specially in the cities like Bangalore and Hyderabad. He views that technology can speak to us and can become a tool to interpret us.

Selecting the contemporary themes on language and technology the playwright expresses his concern that globalization is killing regional languages although it has opened up job sectors through English language. In his obsession for Kannada and passion for English Karnad speaks his mind through his protagonist. In the brilliant presentation of his woman protagonist's character he has an accurate perception on the power of language:

> Globalization has opened up certain job sectors for which English is in demand. One must not forget the fact that English was learnt by the Indians during colonialism also for the purpose of getting jobs. So learning a language for entry into job market is a practical step.

> Globalizing may be displacing regional languages but only in their written and read forms. Actually, the opening up of the skies has given tremendous impetus to the proliferation of regional languages and the regional channels now occupy more space. The programmes are watched and the image speaks to more number of people—in the language of technology. The visual mode actually continues the tradition of performance which has never lacked a regional spectatorship. This is the cheerful aspect about what's happening. What may be getting lost is the written tradition. That was anyway unavailable to large sections of our populace; whereas they always had an attachment for the tradition of performance, which continues through television and films. Most of these spectators owe no loyalty to the written language of the region. Earlier one learnt to read and write in a language to get a job, one would now learn English to get a job. Those who moan the death of regional languages have been associated with the reading and writing tradition of the language.... Even when regional language in its written form dies, the performative tradition will breath new life into it spoken forms (Mukharjee 52-53).

In the structure of the stage and plot of the play Karnad presents on literary politics as:

> The central issue in the play (that) does not involve drama at all but the radically unequal status of fiction written in two contemporary languages, Kannada and English. The exclusion of Karnad's own life long form from the discussion is both an acknowledgement of the power of fiction in English and an imaginative leap into the world of other writers. The formal device of a character being interrogated by her own mechanically reproduced self, the crisp dialogue, and Karnad's fine ear for an up-to-date conversational idiom also make this a technically accomplished play (Dharwadker xxx-xxxi).

It is a one-woman play and technology is a character if not in flesh and blood. The stage is arranged with a row of television sets. As specified by Karnad the play was arranged in the Ranga Shankara Auditorium, Bangalore, with a tremendous zeal and enterprise of Arundhati Nag and her friends. It was a low stage as suggested in the *Natyasastra* with a semi-circular frontage surrounded by a rising gallery of seats.

The play is about a novel authored by the protagonist, Manjula Nayak. With the unexpected publication of her stunningly debut novel in English she feels how her entire Kannada literary fraternity is completely dismayed. Even some of her Kannada fellow writers and well-wishers are completely shocked and spit fire at her. The sudden shift of her literary creativity from Kannada to English has created resentment among them. She is accused of betraying Kannada for the sake of name, fame and fortune. Her novel has drawn the praise from the vast expanded audience. The play presents the conversation with her own image on the television in a very participating and non-performative way. It reveals her own self as an imposter who has passed off her dead sister Malini's novel *The River Has No Memories*. The shift of her autobiographical self from Kannada to English may be due to her self-fashioning out of some fascination but in reality she is accused of disregarding her mother tongue in dishonesty, desperation and cowardiceness. In her debate over language conundrums she presents how she has become the victim of language politics. Defending herself from language hegemonists and chauvinists she clarifies that her writing in English never pollutes Indian literary culture. She knows that English is already recognised as an Indian language if not an indigenous one. The value of it lies in her superbly accomplished autobiographical novel about a life long invalid who has 'breathed, laughed, dreamt in English'. The novel is all about a Kannada writer who tries to cash in on her dead sibling's talent.

The play is the monologue of a lady, Manjula Nayak, an English lecturer and a short story writer in Kannada. She is in her-mid thirties/ forties. As a Kannada short story writer she has established her name, fame and reputation. But as a novelist in English she has a sudden spurt in her writerly career. The novel *The River Has No Memories* has earned reputation from abroad, big advance, rave reviews. It has enabled her to visit seven prestigious American universities on invitations. It has given her the passport for identity in the global literary field, bank accounts, property, financial investments. She is known in India and abroad as a novelist of brilliance for which she has received fabulous advance from the British publishers. At the time of its launching in the US it was a major media event. In Britain it is a super hit.

Manjula is born to Kannada language, civilizsation and reality, and proud of her Kannada origin. But her shifting of creative self from Kannada language to English is not a betrayal to her mother tongue. She has no aberration to her mother tongue nor any adoration for English. She presents her arguments in defence of her sudden transition. She says that her novel is a spontaneous outburst in English and she is somehow able to intuit and emphasize with the experience of a crippled woman well enough to craft a masterpiece about it. But at last before her image all her literary justifications are discredited and she is exposed as a plagiarist. All her self-interested arguments for larger audience and making money are viewed by her critics as illegitimate pursuits of a writer. Her critics apprehend the contaminating effect of English and disapprove of her success.

The evening is important and memorable for Manjula as she is invited to the TV studio to share her feelings about her book to the viewers of the programme, "Literary Phenomenon of the Decade". The announcer of the Shree—TV Channel congratulates her for her best-seller. The viewers are informed by the announcer that Ms Nayak is going to address about her book and soon after this a Kannada telefilm based on this remarkable novel will be broadcasted. The announcer appears on the plasma screen against the logo of the TV Channel. Manjula's image appears as a character on the technical media. The viewers observe Manjula's image with its smiles and bowing to them. In the studio adjustment there are technological apparatus like elephantine lights, headphones, cameras and mike. Manjula sits with the earpiece and a lapel mike. As the announcer's image disappears on the screen Manjula introduces herself as Manjula Nayak officially known as Manjula Murty after her marriage to Pramod Murty, a software development engineer who now stays in Los Angeles. She identifies her creative self as Manjula Nayak saying that "There are some areas in which we must not let marriage intrude too much" (263). Before saying something about her book she says that it is very difficult on her part to say about it. But in the studio she is ready to explain about it on two recurrent questions which are asked to her in India and abroad. Presuming the viewers' mind she replies on the possible questions: (i) Why did she choose suddenly to write in English after having written in Kannada all her life? Does she see herself as a Kannada writer or an English writer? What audience does she write for? and (ii) gets ready to explain about the book on variation of her theme from public to private matters relating to her education, career, acquitance with others and about her creative self.

Manjula has prepared herself to deliver a fifteen-minute speech about her book. Her speech is a sort of 'objective correlative' to explain the phenomenon of her success to her viewers. The objects, events, and eternal facts present in the novel evoke the viewers' responses. The playwright models this Eliotian notion: "The only way of expressing emotion in the form of art is by finding an 'objective correlative; in other words, a set of objects, a situation, a chain of events which shall be the formula of the particular emotion: such that when the external facts... are given, the emotion is immediately evoked" (T.S. Eliot's essay "Hamlet and His Problems", (1919). In order to narrate the splintered self of the protagonist the playwright quotes a few lines from Eliot's famous poem *The Waste Land*:

> What are the roots that clutch, what branches grow
> Out of this story rubbish? Son of man,
> You cannot say, or guess, for you know only
> A heap of broken images, where the sun beats,
> And the dead tree gives no shelter, the cricket no belief
> And the dry stone no sound of water... (Lines 19-24).

The loss Eliot presents is due to the symbolical spiritual desolation and barrenness of the modern world that makes the civilization stand like a dead tree. The lack of spiritual values even makes the vegetation impossible and it does not provide any shelter for a cricket or any relaxation for human beings. In the title of the play Karnad presents a similar socio-psychological breakdown in human communication and relationship in the face of overpowering ambition and greed. His protagonist's self-revelation expresses her phenomenal success. The play is about a novel that exposes protagonist's own life in private and public selves. Karnad rightly remarks:

> Manjula Nayak is being interviewed on TV about her successful debut novel in English. She has written in regional language earlier but this one novel written in English has brought fame and money. When the reel interview is wrapped up, the real one begins.... Manjula's image appears

> on the screen and holds her captive with probing questions. Slowly fragmented and painful truths emerge. As layers of carefully cultivated poise peels off, the persona splinters (Mukherjee 2008:53).

While her private self reveals her plagiarism and opportunism for stealing her dead sibling's talent, her public self is occupied with the language conundrum for writing in Kannada and English. The public self of the protagonist reveals playwright's ideas on the problems of bilingual writers who often caste their choice for nativity in language consciousness, and tenacity of acquiring versatility and universality from other languages. Manjula's problem is similar to many bilingual writers' in India who in their care for regional language and choice for English are accused of neglecting ethic for choosing "between integrity and corruption, wholeness and fragmentation, rootedness and rootlessness, decolonization and recolonization" (Dharwadker xxviii). Manjula's novel is undoubtedly a surprise to the viewers. In its critical interpretation of language conundrums she presents an 'exact equivalence' of her psychic reflection. On the other hand by doing so she unravels her own self in the recollection of her memories. Her speech becomes a confession in which something personal is exposed and the 'objective correlative' is annihilated.

Manjula's speech content is very much debated. It is complex and emotionally charged. She explains that she is not anti-Kannada nor she has the desire to insult her mother-tongue. She has only presented the vernacular culture in foreign medium. The anti-English tirade continues by the vernacular zealots who in their schizophrenic attitude launch their verbal attacks on her with the words: "English is a medium of dishonesty" (264). She says that her attempt to write in English is not a betrayal to Kannada rather it is a matter of conscious choice for wider communication. She says:

> What baffles me—actually, let me confess, hurts me—is why our intellectuals can't grasp this simple fact! I have been accused of writing for foreign readers. Accused! As though I had committed a crime. A writer seeks audiences when she or he can find them! My British publishers said to me: 'We like your book because it's so Indian. We receive any number of manuscripts from India but they are all written with the western reader in view. Your novel has the genuine Indian feel!' (264).

In the globalised world everything global has become local and local has become global. So, loving the mother-tongue is good but there is no justification of saying that a foreign language is impure, dishonest and illegitimate. Loving a foreign language and writing in it if gives delight, earns respect and material success it is not an onslaught on the vernacular. In her argument Manjula expresses her love for her mother-tongue and justifies that she has committed no crime by writing in English. In belief and thought Kannada is like her genes inside her body but generating thought in English for her oeuvre has given her a new-found status. The personal feelings of Manjula on the plight of a bilingual writer in his/her socio-cultural dynamics evoke many debatable hypothesis in the contemporary literary perspectives.

Manjula hits back at her critics. She is disturbed by them as they call it for creativity or for money. The book has given her publicity, fame and glamour. The advance she has received for the book helped her to resign from her job and concentrate in writing. Having struggled through Kannada which she had been failing to achieve has been achieved from writing in English. For its meaningful response she has received *Artha*_(money) which causes jealousy among her critics. They talk about their authorial (creative) integrity in Kannada to which Manjula is cynical. When British publishers say that her 'novel has the genuine Indian feel' she wonders at the saying of "A pundit for instance (who) has stated that no Indian writer can express herself or himself—honestly in English" (264). She asks how many Kannada writers are honest in what they write—in Kannada. If for their genuinity and honesty they do not win awards, fame and publicity in Kannada writing it is not justifiable to condemn her immediately as a traitor. Narrating the irony of the situation she cites the high ethics of these votaries of regional literatures:

> Recently the President of the Central Sahitya Akademi—the National Academy of the Letters—(who shall remain nameless) declared that Indians who write in English do so in order to make money. That by writing in English they confess their complicity in the global consumer market economy. He of course spoke in English. Speaking in English, as you know, gives you the authority to make oracular pronouncements on Indian literatures and languages (264).

Manjula fails to understand the motive behind this language diplomacy. She simply accepts this as their 'grim anxiety' for money, fame, glory and jealousy which is hierarchal in tact but not in instinct. She is surprised at the intellectuals and her *gurus* whom she respects the most for their patting on her back and sharing her delight accuse her now of betraying Kannada and breathe fire at her. Her writing in English has upset them with the overt reason that she has committed a crime by betraying Kannada, and the covert reason is that they cannot bear with her ability to write in English and earn everything what they have failed in their life. She does what every bilingual author does but it doesn't mean that it pollutes her creative integrity and authorial honesty. If she shuts up her writing by listening them it will be a loss to her and loss to the world of creative literature. She does not like to be entangled in this vexed language conundrums. She desires to be a consumerist in her creative imagination rather than an anarchist in her fascination for the vernacular.

Concluding the language issues related to her writing of Kannada short stories and first English novel *The River Has No Memories* Manjula suddenly shifts her stand to the second question of the viewers on the background, theme and imagination which emphatically spin over in their mind. This part of the play reveals some of the challenging, personal and private matters about her career, marriage life, love for her disabled younger sister, Malini, and above all the emotional involvement of the three—Manjula, her husband Pramod and her sister Malini in her Jayanagar house in Bangalore. Manjula's speech deals with her private matters, about her career as a lecturer and writer. The thematic palimpsests of her novel, reveals her mind. It reveals her syncretic attitude to disseminate her inner feelings as a person and writer. In her existential reality she oscillates between duty, responsibility, loyalty, ethic; and emotional imperatives. In the role of a wife, a professional and a loving sister she has become ambidextrous to solve the problems in all aspects of her. In her human existence she tries her best to be a loving daughter, loving sister and loving wife.

The viewers are informed that Manjula's parents have died six years ago. Now she lives with her disabled sister who is confined to bed all through her life. Interacting with her Image on the TV screen she says in tearful eyes "I loved her" (268) because she was pretty. She says:

> She was physically challenged. Suffered from what is technically called, meningomyelocele—the upper part of her body was perfectly normal; below the waist, the nervous system was damaged. Completely dysfunctional. A series of operations, which started soon after her birth, reduced her existence to misery—she spent her entire life confined to the wheel-chair (265).

> She never asked for anything. Soon after her birth, the moment the gravity of her situation was realized, my parents moved to Bangalore. Took a house in the Koramangala Extension. She became... the apple of their eye. When she was old enough to go to school, a teacher came home to teach her English and Mathematics. Everything else, she read up for herself. History, Philosophy, Anatomy. She was hungry—hungry for life (269).

Manjula wonders at her thirst for life and thirst for knowledge. She thinks that she would have been as bright as her sister if she had received all that love and attention. But Manjula's parents had left her with her grandparents in Dharwad. She remembers them very affectionately but no substitute for parents. Usually in vacations she was going to Bangalore to live with her parents. She finished her college education and got the job in Bangalore. While she stayed with her parents she met Pramod, an intelligent, warm and lovable person. She fell in love with this noble and simple man of jokes for his fun-loving nature. By that time Pramod was working in software development. For his calibre he was demanded everywhere and now much in demand as a software wizard in Los Angeles.

Giving a brief chronicle of her life, career, love, marriage and creative self Manjula says how she married Pramod just in an instant analysis of his character. She not only found him good-looking and attractive but a fool who even did not try to save his self-respect in an incident before his marriage with her. She narrates how she came across this "odious character" (271):

> ...we met soon after I moved to Bangalore. He felt attracted to me. Didn't know how to convey it. So do you know what he did? I had a friend called Lucy. A close friend. He wrote a letter to her about me. And wrote me a letter about Lucy. Then he mailed her letter in an envelope addressed to me

> and vice versa. So I received this letter addressed to Lucy—moaning and groaning about how I tortured him. And I didn't even know he was interested in me. And of course Lucy received the other letter. He thought he was being absolutely clever—original. We went and confronted him. Lucy tore her letter to shreds and flung the pieces on him and stormed off. Melodramatically I felt sorry for him and said, "Idiot, every fifteen-year old tries that trick, convinced it's never been done before" (272).

This was the time when she was working full time as a lecturer in Jayanagar college. As her parents were staying in Koramangala she had some difficulties to commute between her parent's house and her college. Secondly she did not like Koramangala as it did inhabitated by non-Kannadigas who had no love for her mother-tongue and culture. For her love for Kannada language and culture she shifted her house to Jayanagar a walking distance from her college. She finally sold the big bungalow to Non-Resident Indians in Koramangala and settled in Jayanagar.

Manjula's early life and background becomes a narrative necessity that gives a sensitive presentation about her relationship with her husband and sister. After her parent's death Malini came to stay with them in their Jayanagar house. As Manjula was childless Malini became her child. Her father had left most of his money in Malini's name for her care. Malini's six years presence in her house critically improved her understanding of life, human relationship and standard in English. Time did not run well for her. As she was improving financially, she was the weakening emotionally. The Pramod-Malini issue and the Pramod-Lucy issue disturbed her more. She was shocked when Pramod agitated to receive the offer of an American Software Company. His delivering of polished and narrative jokes about his work, information technology, Bill Gates, Wipro and Infosys, and all his cyber jokes were no more becoming hilarious because of his inexhaustible gaiety with Malini that worried her. Rejecting the American Company's offer he opened a new office for himself away from her home. The cook and the maid were coming and doing their work in usual turns. But she smelt something insidious in the Pramod-Malini relationship. As she was out all day and had no time to watch them she marked Pramod and Malini had some better intimacy. She found Malini was becoming more charming by staying at home without exposure to the sun or wind. She had developed a soft skin. Most people in her situation would have grown fat, obese and developed diabetes due to weight and boredom in confinement but she was happy to stay with Pramod. In spite of this she had an attractive physique about which Manjula was jealous.

The play presents an equitable balance between love and jealousy on the one hand, and sympathy and duty on the other. Manjula was much disturbed by Pramod's weakness for three women—herself, Malini and Lucy. By and by Manjula realised her husband "basically a two-woman man". She called him "Tirupati Thimmappa" (273). Yet she was trying to discover their affairs for six years. She did not know what Pramod and Malini were talking about for six years during her absence. She could not believe that their declaring love for each other would take so much time. She tried to know what was going on between them in various experiments. She said:

> I tried various experiments. If I turned the key in the main door noisily enough before going in—sure enough I would find him at his table, studious, a picture of concentration. She would be deep into her book or her laptop, but never so absorbed that she couldn't give me that warm, welcoming smile. If I surprised them by entering silently, animated conversation would suddenly come to a stop—a guilty pause—before she picked the exact note effortlessly and continued, involving me too in their talk. It was always her. He was no good at subterfuge (277).

As a teacher of literature she thought every individual was guided by universal principles than by ethics in his/her existential situations. Manjula was worried for Malini's physical impairedness. She said, "She was paralysed below the waist. There was no possibility of any physical intimacy" (277) between them. But she thought their failure to declare love was creating a sensually charged atmosphere in her house. She projected it as an 'emotion recollected in tranquillity' and as a perfect 'objective correlative' in her novel. When she was in bed with Pramod she was imagining as if he was "fantasizing about having Malini" (278) instead of her.

The Image as the reflective part of Manjula's inner self and conscience was unravelling her mind layer by layer. It troubled her in various conflicting questions. Her replies to the technologically induced Image appeared alive on the plasma screen. With its transmission Manjula started speaking to it through her formal monologue. The Image as the product of stage apparatus interrogated the collective imagination of the non-participating audience on Manjula's psyche and her splitting self. It projected some light on her troubled psyche. Like an inquisitor the Image played a reflexive part of Manjula's mind and conveyed a ruthless probe into the conflicting emotions, impulses and desires of her mind. It appeared, "Karnad's use of the Image on the plasma television screen (and subsequently many images)... is not as a part of the general theatre technology but as an aesthetic and dramatic component integral to the plot and characterization of the play, totally determining and controlling its texture and structure. The Image becomes a performing intelligence, a mediated metaphor of the protagonist's mind" (Mukherjee 339). The Image steadily unravelled her private self compelling to reveal truths and facts about her psychological orchestra and the real world in 'an excellent performance' of the play. It was about her private self, her sister and her husband who all pretended in acknowledging their relationship. Manjula had a love marriage but this had not diminished her love for her physically impaired sister, her parents and love for writing. She found herself utterly in despair when she leant back in her chair after the college chore. Some of her living memories were the subject matter of her novel. While the theme was entirely personal, the characters and the plot of the novel were entirely fictional.

Manjula's novel was a narrative of her private life. It was written in beautiful English. She was obliged to her dead sister who had helped to improve her English. In her creative imagination she presented herself as "The sympathetic heroine. A villain as a counterpoint "(271). After Malini's death when she published Malini's manuscripts in her name she expressed her compliments in regrettable affection:

> The novel doesn't really do her justice. She was attractive—more attractive than me. Intelligent than me. And vivacious, which I never was. I accepted that. She radiated life from the

> wheelchair to which she was confined. I have always been reconciled to being the second best (269).

Her novel was an "objective self-analysis" (271) in English. In spite of her impairedness Malini had written the best-seller in English. In a smaller house at Jayanager "she breathed, laughed, dreamt in English" and that could help Manjula—"critically and financially" (271). Yet she discovered her "A villain as a counterpoint" (271) because one day when she returned home she found:

> A furious battle was raging.... They (Pramod and Malini) were squabbling like a married couple. It was about ethics. He was arguing that any system of ethics demanded a single universal principle applicable to everyone.... She was horrified by this. Different human situations called for different principles on which to act. Ethical demands are ethical because they are conflicting, she said.... They were screaming their heads off. He said Hinduism knew no real ethics. She called Immanuel Kant a fascist.... So I stepped in. They saw me, a sudden look of guilty horror as though I had caught them making love (278).

Manjula wondered in this sensually charged atmosphere wherther her "quintessentially Indian husband" (279) was guided more by emotion than his love for her. She thought if this could be the universal principle of human emotion in Kantian philosophy, to her horror she said, "This isn't my home. I am an intruder here: someone external to the soul of this house" (278).

Narrating the chronology of incidents in her life, Pramod's career and Malini's death Manjula spoke about her book and its success in the global market. For her success she was questioned by the Image. She replied how she could write her novel of 350 printed pages at a tremendous pace and complete it within a couple of weeks of Malini's death and mail its typescript manuscript to a British literary agent collecting his address from the Directory of Literary Agents in the British Council. As the Image suspected her authorial authenticity for such a marvellous job of completing the book within two weeks of Malini's death she faced the viewers' jibes. It was a gigantic task that her book was worthy of the Guinness Book of World Records for writing one hundred and fifty thousand words in two weeks and ten thousand words a day. It was really a wonderful success since the journey of Noah's Ark and a record-holding success. This was not an inspiration but an insult to her emotion. She exploded at the remark of the Image calling it 'nasty'. She confessed, "I didn't write the novel. She did. She wrote it. Every word of it" (279). And "I published the novel in my name" (283). Malini had printed off the entire novel and arranged the pages, carefully. Before eighteen months of her death when her health began to collapse for her 'hammering away at the laptop', Manjula came to know that she was writing something. One may accuse her of stealing her sister's novel as 'a genuine mistake' or she was hating the cripple and waiting for her to die. But these were the events in her life.

Manjula's novel was a successful best-seller for its psychological and emotional analysis. She had not imagined her work would find the light of day. The novel was not the product of her imagination but it projected a canvas for self-introspection. She could never say " I won " (283) nor could assert her "total control" (280) over it. She thought that she had not stolen it knowingly nor had she plagiarised it. Her self was defeated before her conscience. She knew that she could keep the world in a blur but she could not make herslf blameless before her consciene. Unforgivingly she confessed that Malini had signed her manuscript with "M. Nayak but when she sent it to an English agent with her letter of self introduction as Manjula Nayak" and "the agent obviously thought we were the same person" (280). The plot of the novel was about Malini's emotional life and flattering portrayal of Pramod whom she had enjoyed for six years from her wheel-chair. Manjula suspected that it was an advantage for Malini's creative power to write such a brilliant masterpiece. Manjula spoke about that period of time in guilt consciousness when Malini was pinning down the details in 'coruscating prose':

> It was venomous. I was camouflaged as the first cousin and not sister. But it was me all right and the portrayal was rancorous. I was a shallow woman, a pretentious mediocrity, a gushy, convincing and devious relative who had taken her in for her inheritance.... The events were from life. They were accurately described. The conversations were recorded verbatism. I couldn't deny them (282).

The theme of the novel dealt with Malini's emotional craving for Manjula's nursing and the craze for emotional involvement with

Pramod. Although the plot was fictional Malini was the only character drawn from real life. In a fictional invention Malini presented her feelings, emotions and involvement with Manjula and Pramod. Being a Kannada writer, if Manjula's writing in English was a 'cardinal sin' and there was no *prayshchitta* for it in the eyes of the literary pundits, then publishing her sister's novel in her name was worse still. Now she felt as if her sister was challenging her to burn the script from beyond the funeral pyre. If she destroyed the masterpiece she would be condemned by the readers and "go down in history as a footnote in the life of a brilliant author" (283). The very thought of her crime and injustice endangered her authorial self. She thought as if Malini died for her advantage but in her death she was crucifing her authorial self every minute. Manjula was of the impression that she had succeeded in her fraud but now she believed Malini had won at the end.

Manjula's private life was affected for two reasons: the Pramod-Malini relationship, and her stealing and publishing of Malini's book in her name. Pramod was not ready to forgive Manjula for her cardinal sin that she has committed in her authorial self. He had smelt about Manjula's stealing of her sister's book from the email print off copy which she had received from the publisher as Manjula had sent it in Pramod's address. When the book saw the light of day, Manjula was inundated with invitations for literary tours, public advance, functions, cultural events and so on. But this made Pramod very unhappy not because of his gender superiority but for his hatred towards her concealment and stealing of her sister's book. She knew about the Malini-Pramod's 'full scale affair'. She disclosed her worries, "She despised me. Perhaps they both did. Perhaps she had turned him against me" (282). For this reason perhaps Pramod did not come at the time of her book launch in Los Angeles with the plea of not getting leave. Further his departure to the States after Malini's death had condensed her suspicion about his relationship with Malini. She said to the Image:

> The launching of the novel was a major media event in the U.S. After all, you must remember it had already proved a super hit in Britain. They invited me to New York for the release. There was much fanfare. He sent me an email of congratulations.... Apologized that he couldn't get leave to attend (273).

The clarity, insight and genius of the novel now laughed at Manjula's vain glory and reputation. The Image told her in a deciphering tone, "perhaps...she (Malini) did win in the end?" (283) Manjula's bubbled pride in visiting seven prestigious American universities, bank accounts, property and financial investments evaporated slowly. When she gesticulated to wipe out the Image by unplugging the cable connection the Image spoke on the plasma screen :

> I am Malini Nayak, the English novelist. Manjula Nayak, the Kannada short story writer, was decimated the moment she read my novel. She thus obliterated all difference of ink and blood and language between us and at one full stroke morphed into me (283-84).

Meanwhile every TV screen showed a different image of Manjula gesticulating:

> I shall continue with the name of Manjula Nayak.... However I am in truth Malini, my genius of a sister who loved my husband and knew Kannada and wrote in English (284).

With the declaration of images on different screens there was a defening cacophony. Manjula went out into the dark, the sets were switched off and the studio became dark and empty. The plot was added with technology and electronic media which performed the truth telling function in the play. Apart from the protagonist and her Image the audience saw Manjula's splintered persona on each blank television screen set in a row. In a dramatic turn each screen became an independent viewpoint.

The play is exceptional for its use of technology to explore the ideological and psychological dimensions of the characters present and absent. It is Karnad's one of the most recent plays on contemporary theme that presents the study of human psychology. In its Ranga Shankara production where Arundhati Raja played lead role in the English version. Arundhati Nag had played the role in the Kannada version. In the role playing of Manjula both the experienced and powerful actresses displayed their own style of interpreting the psyche of the character. While Raja's role playing as Manjula was about an ordinary woman of average intelligence Nag's role gave a psychological edge to the characterisation of Manjula. Manjula's character is arresting and competent enough, jealous, shrewd and full of deception. The ending of the play gives a complex look to Manjula, her dissolving Image on the large plasma screen and sudden emergence of the Image that speaks in the voice of Malini. In Ashok Pai rightly remarks on Karnad's interpretation the *Journal of the Indian Psychiatry Society*:

> As in the other plays of Karnad, here also the action of the play proceeds by juxtaposing two opposites—in this case two sisters, one highly successful, healthy and aggressive ; the other paralysed in the lower limbs and increasingly withdrawing into herself.... However gripping the storyline may be, the focus of the play is on a psychoanalytical probing of the human personality. The two sisters become reverse images—one supposedly 'normal', socially successful and healthy; the other half-paralyzed and introverted. But the play demonstrates how the images are exchangeable. In fact they are two aspects of the same personality. Can there be a totally integrated personality? Are human beings doomed to fragmentation and incompleteness? Such are the uncomfortable questions the play raises (Qtd. in Mukherjee 342).

The play is described as a tremendous success for its presentation of emotion and external facts through technology. It evokes the emotions which are presented and embodied in the images. Through the play the playwright presents the considerable success of technology that could speak to us and could become a tool to interpret ourselves. The play is dialogic in form but promotes monologic viewpoints. Technology is used as tools of criticism of life, psyche and emotion.

The play ends with the disconnection of cable making the studio dark that appears now the debris of a heap of broken images. The playwright presents an analysis of Manjula's life, emotion, feeling and splintered-self which remind us Eliot's presentation of modern man's condition in *The Waste Land*. It expresses what "we see much more drama around us than ever before... [and] more people are involved in the "business" of drama than ever before " (Karnad 1995: 363). The play presents the premises on Indian authors and readers and their perception on English and other Indian languages. Again he shifts his premises from language debate to genre debate.

A.B. Dharwadker rightly remarks: "Karnad could have chosen to portray a fellow playwright in *Broken Images*, but he is well aware that a play in English, however successful its author, cannot compete with a novel in English, because of the qualitative differences between novels and plays as literary artifacts" (xxx). Karnad deals with the central issue that does not involve drama at all but the radically unequal status of fiction written in two contemporary languages, Karnada and English.

Wedding Album (2009), Karnad's latest play, next to his *A Heap of Broken Images* (2005) is a landmark production in Indian theatre. While both the plays are brilliant productions on contemporay themes, *Wedding Album* presents the humdrum life of the members of a south Indian Saraswat brahmin family where the parents are worried for the marriage of their daughter and son in an arranged way. The playwright demonstrates the urban middle class family members' 'anxiety of Indianness' in search of a suitable expat boy for their daughter and a suitable girl for their son. The play is all set in a theosophy infected brahmin family in Dharwad. Karnad presents the situations in Nadkarnis' living room where a conflicting situation takes place due to the different ideologies of the parents and their young son and two daughters. The Nadkarni parents have a traditional mindset. They are democratic, cooperative and consensual in all matters but assert their ideological hegemony in cultural matters without being 'coercion'. They like to keep their native anthropological and theosophical culture pure and free from the horrors of postcolonial and postmodern hybridity. But their children are in a conflictual position who in their ideological dichotomy feel exoticised with the universal culture, its cross-fertilization and hybridization in the inbetweeness and mobility of their thoughts They do not bother with the rhetoric of blame of their parents, rather in "restrictive notions of cultural identity" (Bhabha 38) they feel their home unhomely. They define their cultural postion in new theoretical insight and argue in favour of transnational cutlural hybridity.

The locale of the play is all set in a theosophy-infected Saraswat brahmin family in Dharawad, a city in Karnataka. The situations which are dealt with directly relate to Australia and America. The Nadkarnis are well-educated and have an international outlook on human relationship. The Nadkarni parents try their best to preserve their caste and tradition unique and sacrosant from the effect of hybridity and multiculturalism. In contrast to this, their young children have a 'cultural amnesia' in their multicultural heteroglossia. This makes the Nadkarni parents think about the liminality of their identity in the society. The young Nadkarnis have their international outlook in human relationship through the intellectual explorations on television, Internet and other tech media. The play appears to be a family drama on parent-child relationship. The play presents middle class anxieties in pan-Indian urban life. It demonstrates the anxieties, worries, ambition, prospects of love, marriage and search for life in their middle class status.

The play was first produced by the Prime Thetre Company at the Tata Auditorium, National Centre for Performing Arts, Mumbai on 10 May, 2008. Soon after its production the play became popular in Indian metropolis for its presentation of Hindu middle class life. The play presents the silent secrets of a south Indian brahmin family and its family members for self-fulfilment. The playwright deals with the contemporary problems of a middle class family. The choice of theme gives a clear picture of the self and psyche of the family members. The contemporary problems dealt with in the play expose the glory and gravity of secrets in middle class life. The acceptance of its popularity for contemporary elements differs from Eve Ensler's *Vagina Monologues* and Mahesh Dattani's *Dance Like a Man*.

All the incidents in the play take place in the Foucauldian parents' bedroom and kitchen. The playwright consiciously avoids to mention the names of the Father and Mother. It might be due to his wilful attempt to present the pungent and stinging core of a family to which he had his private affiliation in a kind of sanitised affliction. Neelam Mansingh Chowdry rightly remarks on the jacket of the book, "The slow peeling off of the narrative in *Wedding Album* is like digging into someone's private cupboard, unearthing hidden wages, private affliction and subterranean desires. Danger lurks in each scene and the characters are all on edge, desperate and living in many emotional and sexual zones." Karnad has his penetrating intellectual exploration of reality in an Indian middle class family. It is expected that the wedding will bring the Nadkarni clan together in a display of solidarity and mutual concern. He focuses the anxieties and resentments among the family members who are long buried within the bosom of the family. In anxiety and tension the older generation feels defunct due to new techological turmoil but the younger generation is buffeted by aspirations to easy prosperity, notions of sexual freedom, and dreams and phantasms. For the wedding preparation the Nadkarnis generally prefer to an arranged marriage in the traditional way. In the context of the play the playwright presents marriage, culture, tradition and Hindu values which are affected by the postcolonial dynamics. Apart from the familial issues the playwright adds technological supports like phone, computer, Internet, plane, car, autorickshaw and mobile for the arrangement of the marriage. He presents the worries of the Nadkarni parents for the butts of expenses that they had incurred for the marriage of their first daughter Hema 15 years back. Now their worries double for the arrangement of their second daughter Vidula's marriage with an NRI in the US and for their son Rohit's recurrent rejection to their proposals with a plea to build up his future.

The theme of the play goes like this. Mr. Nadkarni, the father, a retired doctor, is in goverment service. During his service days he is transferred to different small cities like Hubli, Sirsi, Bagalkot and Belgaum in Karnataka due to which he has neglected his children. He seems to be very sincere and dutiful in profession. He narrates his background, "I grew up in poverty. My brother Ramdas and I—we struggled. We often had to share a plate of gruel between us.The only meal that day, quite often. We ran from house to house for free meals offered by relatives" (16). Appreciating Mrs. Nadkarni's wifely and motherly duties he reminds his children in an emotional burst:

> Let me tell you she is being unfair.... unfair to herself. If we are all happily gathered together here, if we have been such a loving family, the credit must go to your mother. You don't know what she has been through for the sake of the family. You don't know what she has had to put up with. In my job, I was transferred every six months. From one small town to another. Three children. My salary—there was never anything left for her after the household expenses. But she never asked for anything for herself. Lived on two saris—wearing one while the other one dried on the line. And yet we never acknowledged her sacrifices, her skill at management...(91).

The Nadkarnis are a small family. The eldest daughter Hema is married and her husband Chandrakant is working in Australia. Hema generally stays with her husband in Australia and visits her parents annually. But this time she has come along without her son Ketan for her younger sister Vidula's marriage with Ashwin Panje, the nephew of Govind Rao who is scheduled to come to India for his engagement. Vidula, a graduate in Geography, is twenty-two and a half, and has been working for a travel agency for six months. Every member of the family is jubilant and in anxiety about Vidula's marriage. The Nadkarni family becomes lively with the activities of the two sisters and their only brother Rohit who is in love with Isabel Pinto, a Christian girl on the staff of Prativa Khan with whom Rohit is making a teleserial. The Nadkarnis are worried about Vidula's as well as Rohit's marriage. Rohit is already thirty-two and is in love with a girl outside their religion and caste. Rohit is in search of a good job. He writes stories and scripts for teleplays. Ramdas, the brother of their father, is the Police Commissioner with whom all the family members are emotionally attached but he never appears in the scene.

The Nadkarnis are cosmopolitan, international and liberal in outlook. The children are more liberal than their parents in every respect. They are conscious of their community, caste, idealism and status. They think, "once Vodula's wedding's over, Rohit will be free—they will then have time to meet and chat at leisure" (32). They know that "marriage is a gamble"(27) and its inevitablity needs guarantee with its community's conditions. They believe "A wedding is essentially an excuse for shopping" (31). It is important for them because Ashwin is coming to India to settle his marriage with Vidula. Secondly, Gopal and Vatsala, the members of the Sirur family, are coming from Hyderabad to settle their daughter Tapasya's marriage with Rohit. Gopal Sirur is the brother-in-law of his father. They are accompanied by Mohan and Mira Hattangadis. In a complex plot the playwright presents Tapasya, the daughter of Rohit's father's sister, twice removed. Apart from Rohit's ambition to build up his future his intention not to marry his cousin Tapasya may be due to his pathologically vitriolic hatred. Tapasya is a postgraduate in sociology, a creative and a gifted singer of classical music, sensitive, modern and tradition loving. But Rohit is ambitious and Americanised. He runs after Isabel for which his sister Hema taunts him, "Why should you take up with a Christian girl? Aren't there nice girls in our community?"(42). While the Sirurs propose Tapasya's marriage with Rohit, he does not say 'yes' to their proposal. In her reaction Vidula tells him, "To have a girl waiting for you—her parents kneeling before you—begging and pleading... It really must make you feel grand.... Why didn't you tell them you were going around with Isabel? You could have told them you two were as good as engaged" (42). Rohit objects saying that no one should tell him about his personal life as he finds no difference between Christian and Hindu girls these days. He says, "Their blouses are open right down to their navels. Boys at least button up their collars properly"(43). He is not serious about his marriage nor is concerned with the Sirurs for their only daughter Tapasya's marriage. Like many educated young men of the twenty-first century, she is goaded by his ambition and prospect of a career. He forgets that Tapasya's father had financed his trip to Germany for training in software production.

The Sirurs pray to Rohit for his consent to their proposal. It seems that Gopal Sirur is in a state of emotional breakdown and touches Rohit's feet seeking alliance for Tapasya. Gopal is worried because his son Sharad is coming back from the States on a six-weeks holiday during which he likes to finish their daughter's marriage. He tells Rohit in an emotional tone, "think of her, she has come here under the impression that you have. She has come from Hyderabad sure that everything will go well today and she will be engaged to you..."(38). In diffidence he says:

> I don't care if I have a stroke for the sake of my daughter. To you, Rohit, it may seem a small matter. But we have told everyone in Hyderabad. Our relations have congratulated us on getting such an excellent son-in-law. Her classmates have actually thrown a party to celebrate the event. And now if we go back and say—can you imagine? She won't be able to show her face. She is our only child, Rohit. She is sensitive. Don't hurt her please, don't wound her. We have brought her up like a flower. Don't insult her. Don't please. I'll fall to your feet... (39).

Rohit is unfazed and nonplussed with the concern of Gopal Sirur, Mohan and Mira also are baffled at his attitude, as they have come all the way from Hubli. Rohit knows that the Saraswat brahmins are educated and artistic but not adventurous, and they hope for a good job, safe salary and opportunities. He prefers first to build up his career. Both the Sirurs and Hattangadis fail to convince and impress Rohit for his alliance with Tapasya.

Mr.Nadkarni apppears to be very much participatory in his family affairs but not very performative in Vidula's marriage. He is old, reserved and has a stoic personality. He has struggled throughout his life in a middle class status. He is conscious of his position as a doctor after his retirement and prefers less extravaganza. He knows "the lower middle class inside out" (58). He is very liberal in thinking for his children and their future. In contrast to him Mrs.Nadkarni is full of Austinian pride and prejudice in her middle class vanity and likes to celebrate Vidula's marriage at per with their neighbours. She always regrets that fifteen years back they had Hema's marriage without any pomp and glamour. She grumbles and complains before her husband for not giving anything to Hema at the time of her marriage. But this time she says very assertively, "A wedding means expenses—there is no getting away from that" (15). Complaining for a compliance she says, "I have attended wedding in our neighbours' families. Accepted their hospitality. Gorged myself at their wedding feasts. And now when it comes to my own daughter's wedding, you want me to pack the guests off with a betel leaf and nut" (16). Joining with her mother Hema complains that no one was interested in shopping during her marriage while they are busy now shopping for Vidula.

Hema's husband works as the Chief Commercial Officer in a bank in Australia. Every year Hema comes to her parents and the two sisters enjoy their time together. Like Hema's husband Vidula's prospective groom Ashwin also works in the States. The two sisters believe that "These days most multinationals, international banks, corporations they all have Indians in top positions" and "Indians are about to take over the entire commercial world" (17). They are of the impression that Indians have a greater role in the corporate and commercial world. Hema's marriage with Chandrakant was not a big wedding. For her marriage her parents had taken three months' time to secure a loan from the bank. Hema and her husband were "quite content with a small fire altar and seven steps round it" (15). He is now in a transferable job but she never refuses to go trailing after her husband like the white wives. Differentiating the white and Indian wives whose husbands are in corporate positions she says:

> ... the white wife refuses to go trailing after her husband. We Indian women, on the other hand, are obedient Sati Savitris, ever willing to follow in our husbands' footsteps. Look at me—Melbourne, Johannesberg, Singapore and now Sydney. Our men may get all the top jobs. But I am in no better position than Ma (17).

In Hema's words the playwright expresses the existential suffering of Indian wives whose husbands work in the multinational corporate sectors. Mrs. Nadkarni does not like that her second daughter Vidula should enjoy her life like Hema after marrying an NRI in America. She thinks that the world is changing fast today. The prospect for girls is better enough today than forty years back when she had married their father. Today educated Indian girls have enough opportunity even after their marriage. At the time of Vidula's leaving her parents for Bangalore after her marriage Mrs. Nadkarni tells about her worries and agonies in an emotion-jammed tone:

> My father wouldn't even let me finish college. And Hema arrived soon after. And then you all. I never had any time for you children. Just rush, rush. And I achieved nothing in my life. But I was hoping at least you girls would do something. So many opportunities in today's world. We couldn't even dream of such a world. But Hema did nothing with her intelligence and good looks. Has been content to be a housewife. You are capable of anything if you will only make up your mind.... I am told there are lots of openings in America. They say you can take courses in everything—painting, ceramics, pottery, music. Don't throw away your talents in just bearing children. God gave me such lovely children. But I could give them no guidance. We did nothing for you. Don't do the same thing with your life (90).

Vidula understands her mother's concern but fails to promise her to keep them. She knows what would be the condition of her parents after her and her sister's departure. Like many Indian girls perform their perpetual duties after their marriage Vidula desires to perform her role as a mother, wife and daughter. She fails to realise her mother's concern for Rohit when her father prefers him to join a company job at Bangalore; her mother prefers him to continue his work in Dharwad and stay with them.

All the three children of the Nadkarnis think about love and marriage differently. But they have a common impression that their parents are old fashioned. They are attracted more by the dazzles of modernity. They blame their father for not having a house with all modern amenities. They consider their father's decision not to resign from his service and not bearing the risk of joining as a partner with his collegue Doctor Shanbhag in private practice (now an established man in the society) is a great mistake in his life. They think their father's living with his reputation without money is meaningless. They blame their father for his lack of farsightedness. Mr. Nadkarni becomes the lonely person in the family. His wife misunderstands his incapability to be rich and affluent. Children blame him for his love for his brother Ramdas, and for sitting alone without bothering what happens around him. Post-colonial influences have not affected Mr. Nadkarni. He is almost alienated in his family. In his reply to them he gives the example of his friend, Phadnis:

> He (Phadnis) had three sons in the US. His kidneys packed up, he was on the death bed. So the first son took leave and came. Waited for a month. But Phadnis wouldn't die. So the son went back. Next time Phadnis was critical, the second son came and waited. Used up his holidays. But Phadnis wouldn't oblige. The third son apparently told his mother, 'If Father doesn't die now, I can't come back for two years. I have promised my wife and children a holiday in the Maldives next year' (78).

Mr. Nadkarni marks the deterioration of values in family life and parent-child relationship due to the influence of materialism, commodification of culture and influence of technology. He feels the loss of cultural values as well as moral values which cause a turmoil in life. The young are buffeted by aspirations to easy properity, notions of sexual freedom, dreams and phantasms, and 'distance' technology.

'Distance' technology almost becomes a character in the play. As a sign of modernity it assists to the material progress of the mankind but affects the morality of individuals. With the help of it multinational corporate working Indians live like Ashwin who works like a god on four hands—a mobile in one hand, a computer in another, a phone in the third, and airmail letters in the fourth.

Vidula sends him email, talks over the phone and sees his photograph on video. The Nadkarnis are happy that Ashwin and Vidula like each other. Similarly during her week-long stay with her parents Hema gets many emails from her husband in Australia. E-tech helps the two sisters to have their emotional contacts with their life partners. The Nadkarnis know the details about Ashwin who works as a legal consultant of a US badminton team. They are happy that he is travelling with the team to Malaysia. They are informed about his coming with the team to Chennai from where he will proceed to Dharwad to keep his commitment. The family is worried because time is short for this auspicious occasion. They have to print cards, invite the relatives, order the goldsmith for jewellery, do shopping and arrange the wedding hall. They are happy that the multimedia helps them to find a suitable boy for their daugher. But at the same they realise how it badly affects the Saraswat culture and Hindu tradition in its misuse.

Multimedia has its evil impact on the younger generation. In the name of their career prospect and material success they are attracted for its evil designs. In contemporary perspective many youths are getting attracted for its power to corrupt. The playwright as a great sentinel of values, ethics, culure and tradition does not seem to like the entry of the multimedia in an individual's private matters. He presents its evil impact on young girls like Vidula. Vidula visits the internet cafe with the plea of playing video games and listening to the sermons by Swami Ananga Nath. But this exhibits the waywardness of middle class young girls. This rightly reveals how net-tech corrupts the young girls. Vidula enters the dark room of the net cafe to chat with "a pining peacock" who talks with her sensuously, "I know the voice of my Indian peahen. I dream of you. I pine for you" (64). In a sensuous appeal Vidula tells lies to get pleasure, "I told you I am a kept woman. Kept by a trader. I am his concubine. Maintained by a man much older than me.... He is dying. He has had a heart attack. Last night. He is in the ICU. Could be dead by tomorrow. His family is bound to throw me out. So I had to find a new master. A younger man. He lives in the US". (64). She becomes happy when the voice tells her in excitement, "I'll strip you. Then I'll rape you." Responding to his reaction Vidula tells "I can't wait. I can't... That sounds divine! I am yours... Go ahead. I am yours. All yours"

(65). She caresses and fondles her sensual organs to masturbate her feminine energy. When two youths attack the cafe, accuse her of watching the porn films and call her "a disgrace to... ancient Indian culture" (69) and "Hindu women!", Vidula gets disturbed. They also threaten to take her photograph to publish it in papers. She shamelessly defends herself from these pseudo guardians of tradition: "I have paid for the computer time. I have paid to be left alone in this room. To work here without being disturbed.... I'll do what I like here. Who the hell one you to question me" (70). It is difficult to call Vidula immoral or amoral due to her Saraswat caste consciousness. Amrit Srinivasan rightly remarks in the "Foreword":

> Whether willingly submitting herself as Kuchla the Jezebel to the disembodied randy voice of Swami Ananga Nath the Bodyless, in a darkened Cyber Cafe, or transmuting her guilt at being found out into hysterical rage, screaming 'sexual harassment' to make her moral tormentors run away—she is resourceful enough to find herself a surrogate swami, a flesh and blood stranger to help her work her way through hopeless desire. The subjugation she seeks in her secret, erotic world can after all be served as well through man and marriage and to higher purpose (xi).

Defending herself she accuses the youths, "You have come here to rape me" (70). She threatens to inform about the matter to her uncle Ramdas, the Police Commissioner. She is relieved when the internet cafe attendant tells her that the two youths had come only for their *hafta*. Karnad presents the vanity of young girls in our contemporary middle class urban life. Their worries and anxieties in life, involvement and activities in city internet cafes are displayed in the play with a realistic touch.

The Nadkarni family appears to be like many middle class families in our contemporary urban society where love, affection, jealousy, suspicion and ego lurk as weaknesses among the family members. While the older generation has some values in life the younger generation run after money and materialism. Vatsala rightly remarks, "they are not like us twenty-five years ago" (32). In spite of their beauty and brain the Nadkarni girls do not do virtually any positive work for them. They are proud of their husbands' good earning and dominance in the corporate world. While Vidula goes to the internet cafe for deriving sensual pleasure over e-media, Hema in her husband's absence and in her parents' house derives the same pleasure by flirting with Vivan, the son of a neighbour of the Nadkarnis. She receives love letters from him and shares her books with him. Hema's flip-plop nature with this Hindu vigilante even after her marriage and becoming the mother of a son is not appreciated in any culture. It seems that Hema is not happy just with the email printouts from her husband in Australia rather she needs her body engagement for emotional satisfication. Rohit is already thirty-two but he defers his marriage for three years with an apology for an opportunity of a job. He knows Tapasya and her parents' sacrifice for him but runs after Isabel. He believes that the Saraswats are not adventurous people in undertaking the risk of private enterprises but becomes adventurous in running after Isabel, going beyond the barricades of his caste and religion. He confidently forgets his loyalty to the Sirurs. While the Nadkarni daughters spend most of their time in buying saris, jewellery and shopping Rohit moves in the imaginary world of making teleserials. He is busy in search of new plots from contemporary situations of life for his stories. He imagines and improvises the life stories of two elderly women: Pratibha Khan, a fellow artist in his team, a lady from Orissa; and Radhabai, his family cook.

Vidula, like many educated urban Indian young girls, dreams of marrying an NRI. She thinks that the West can provide everything. But soon she realises that it is like a Pandora's box that provides nó peace and bliss in marital life. The glamour, success and social connections, efficiency and planning are the sacred ideals in the West which have affeced the intensity of intimacy in man-woman relationship. When Ashwin meets her in a local restaurant she discovers that he is a believer of heredity and genetics, and an Indomaniac. She discovers his two great assets—his brain and charm with which he has influenced and prospered in the West. She is happy that he believes in innocence and purity in womanhood for which he has come to marry an Indian girl. She appreciates his quest for a spiritual odessey through marriage. She thinks how he has become bored and tired of living in God's own country, and in the land of opportunities. Ashwin has won friends, glamour, success, social connections, and has enjoyed plenitude. He thinks that the West has material progress but it is spiritually hollow. He realises the meaninglessness of material values and is terrified with its glitters. Now in his notion of sacred ideals he romanticises about his nostalgic past and tries to escape from this godless and amoral world. He appreciates the Indians who believe in innocence, ideas of purity and ancient values. He translates his mind before Vidula:

> I want to be honest with you. I am passing through a crisis... a spiritual crisis. I am boiling inside like a volcano. I want you to share my agonizing search of myself. It will require an intellectual effort to understand the real me. It may even require an emotional giving-up. If you agree to... you will have to share my inner turmoil.... I believe you will find it enriching (79-80).

Ashwin appreciates India's ancient civilisation and culture which are full of wisdom and insight. He desires to have his innermost communication with India's spiritual tradition by marrying an Indian girl. This may surprise or disappoint many of the Indian urban girls who nurture their secret desire to marry the NRI candidates but it expresses the self-imposed responsibility of the NRIs when he tells Vidula, "I would like you to be my partner in carrying the best of our spiritual tradition to the West and save the West" (82). His words sound metaphoric but they mean a lot to save the West from a spiritual holocaust.

Ashwin is repulsive of Western marriage and sex without love. He knows that there are many things in the West which provide the passport to material success but they never promise peace. Narrating the effect of globalization, hybridization and reterritorialization in the West he says that it is in a spiritual holocaust. The people in the West have comfort but they lead life in spiritual crisis. Revealing the failure in the West and about his success there he confesses that he was not a bright boy in the class but due to his wild expectations he has fulfilled his ambition in the land of opportunity. He regrets that due to the lack of emotional giving up he has an inner turmoil. He realises that the whole Western culture is empty of values and meaning. It glitters without glory. The Amerians are now in a soul-searching mission. They have terrifying experiences without values in life. They like to take India for their spiritual guidance. The Americans have become the worshippers of Mammon who muses them with God's plenty. He enjoys there the "cultural difference... (which) is not the acquisition or accumulation of additional cultural knowledge; it is the momentous, if momentary extinction of the recognizable object of culture in the disturbed artifice of its signification, at the edge of experience" (Bhabha 126). He says:

> The European Industrial Revolution began by rejecting religion in favour of material values. But today that legacy is strangling the West. They have no spiritual moorings left. They are adrift in a godless, amoral world.... The fact is, the white man is played out. The hardworking white immigrant is a thing of the past and today it's we who are keeping the machine ticking. And, of course, making our fortunes. We Indians are right there where the Jews once stood. We shall soon take over the economy. But by peaceful means. My American collegues keep telling me, 'You Indians. You are honest. Hardworking. Most of all, peace-loving. Not like others. A community that leaves the rest of the world to itself (80).

In his perception of the East and West he believes:

> Cultural difference must not be understood as the free play of polarities and pluralities in the homogeneous empty time of the national community.... The analytic of cultural difference intervenes to transform the scenario of articulation.... The aim of cultural difference is to rearticulate the sum of knowledge from the perspective of the signifying position of the minority that resists totalization... producing other spaces of subaltern signification (Bhabha 162).

Ashwin philosophises the history of two great civilizations of the West and East. He is proud of India's ancient culture and tradition which build up the efficiency and work ethics of the Indians on foreign lands. Comparing the two he thinks that the Europeans have only efficiency and planning but the Indians dare to dominate the world with their ethics and philosophy. He believes:

> All our ancient culture, our spiritualism, our heritage. Everything had been remoulded to fit the market demand. Behind all our spiritual abracadabra, we had hitched our star, and our hope, to global capitalism. Geeta yajnas, Yogic techniques, upanishadic sermons.... The darkness of our souls illuminated with neon lights and stroboscopes. India had become the Walmart of spirituality (81).

Ashwin believes that efficiency to succeed materially without spirituality breeds psycho-spiritual depression. Now desiring to "Begin at the beginning" (81) he prefers to preserve Indian culture by marrying an Indian girl who will favour him for wisdom, insight and guidance. Looking back at his country he desires to marry Vidula who would be the sacred ideal of womanhood in her role playing as a mother, wife and daughter. Beyond video and email contacts he makes an innermost communication with Vidula and promises her that he will be affable and sociable to her all through their life. He also expects that she will bear the great responsibility to play a major role in her life.

Sending the daughter away to her in-law's house after her marriage is a great moment for the parents. Vidula's departure from her parental house is marked for two reasons: the moment of leaving the great emotional past and preparing to leave the motherland for a new future. While her fellow girl friends marry and bear the risk of leaving the parental home, Vidula bears the double risks of leaving her parental home and her motherland. If the former is the diurnal the latter is a sacrifice for her new mission and in search of a new life. She fails to accompany her husband to the US for some legal problems in the passport office and stays in India for three months after her marriage. The Nadkarnis have some problems for the posting of her uncle Ramdas's name in Vidula's birth certificate. For the passport of Vidula her birth certificate needs to be corrected. While Vidula takes the matter as a shame Rohit takes it lightly saying, "This is India, you know. Not Australia. We have a solution for everything" (49). Mrs. Nadkarni proposes to correct it through an affidavit by her father. This makes the sisters to suspect it either as a clerical mistake or a deliberate act of their uncle. They even suspect their uncle's motif if "he had his eyes on Ma?" (51). The two sisters also dislike their father's praising their uncle's good look and honesty.

A Few days after her marriage Vidula moves to Bangalore before leaving for America. It becomes an emotional farewell to her. While the parents advise her to let them know about her relationship with Ashwin, Rohit and Hema advise her, "Leave him and come back if you feel like it... We live in a modern world. A divorce is okay. It's no shame" (86). Vidula promises them, "I will never divorce Ashwin"(86). It appears that Vidula, the expat wife of Ashwin, does not know cooking like many urban girls. She has 'given up eating fish' for the sake of her husband. This kind of comitment to join with her husband in the US is a symbolic affirmation that expresses her ascetic resolve in private self on the eve of her departure from India.

The wedding album is covered with the scenes of the photographs of negotiation, preparation, shopping, interviews, free communication, promises and prospects about a daughter's marriage. The wedding album's bright photographs cover the members of the Nadkarni family in their Dharwad house. The Nadkarnis are distinct with their Saraswat culture, the south Indian way of lifestyle, and the influence of modernity. In the play the playwright not only tells about them but presents them as are photographic images. With them some other characters who appear as part and parcel of their life and daily activities. The playwright deals with them very effectively and weaves them in the main plot. Rohit and Pratibha work on a teleserial in a software production office.

In the sub-plot, Pratibha and Radhabai play important roles. Pratibha, a modern, self-made Oriya woman has taken a hard, personal decision like marrying a Khan to being a successful producer of television serials. She rejects Vidula's story as a possible theme for a future episode not for her private reasons of carrying on the family name, but for the public reasons of fulfilling a social obligation towards the women of the community. While Rohit is directly associated with Pratibha, Radhabai the cook is associated with his family. Rohit decides to make Pratibha the centre of his story as he is impressed by her words:

> I am forty. I am from Orissa. I came to Bangalore for reasons of my own and built up my business. Three years ago, I married a man ten years my senior. A Muslim. I married him when the anti-Muslim riots were at their worst. Because he offered me affection and security (pause). There's nothing I don't know about harassment (61).

But he finds Radhabai's life story more appealing, impressive, excellent and melodramatic due to her husband's death and her adopted daughter's forced madness. Radhabai is their cook who has been working for the family for the last seven years. After their male cook Nagappa's service for thirty years in their family

Radhabai fills his position and lives with them like a family member, The difference is that Nagappa was a good cook and gentle a soul but Radhabai is quarrelsome, demanding and not so good in cooking non-veg except preparing some sour curry with sprouted moong. Although she has fifty years of cooking experience she does not know how to prepare a hot-and-sour pomfret, curry a favourite item of the Nadkarnis.

The secret sorrow of Radhabai's life makes Rohit feel pity for her. To him it appears melodramatic like a modern serial on the television. Rohit thinks Radhabai's life story will serve a proper build-up for his and Pratibha's serial. He is also impressed with Radhabai's life story when Vidula narrates it:

> They lived in a village. They were so poor that the daughter, Yamuna, came to Bangalore looking for job. And found a good one. Used to send a fair amount back home. Then Radhabai's husband died and she too came to Bangalore. Took up a job as a cook with a family in Malleswaram. The day after her arrival, a messenger truned up and escorted her to her daughter's house and what does she find? Her daughter is being maintained by a rich trader.... So the mother and daughter met. They continued to meet.But Radhabai wanted to keep her job,so she never mentioned her daughter to the family she worked for.
>
> This went on for a couple of years. Then suddenly there was no communication from the daughter. No phone calls. No messages. So Radhabai went to her daughter's house and—and she found a lock on the door. The house was deserted. The neighbours told her that the trader had suddenly died and the young woman living there had been thrown out by his family. She was gone... One day Radhabai was on the terrace, working, and she heard kids shouting and cackling in the street. She looked down and she saw... Yamuna. She was standing there in the street calling out to her mother. Her sari was in tatters. Her hair was loose and dirty. The kids were laughing and throwing stones at her. She was obviously out of her senses, calling out, Amma, Amma, asking passersby, where's my Amma's house and hurling abuses at her tormentors.... Radhabai called out. But her daughter couldn't hear her.... She ran down to the street. But by the time she reached there, the daughter had disappeared.... Radhabai never saw her daughter again (52-53).

Rohit's imagination for the plot of the story widnes as he finds Radhabai's daughter reaching the gate one day when "The kids throwing stones at her, Radhabai chases the kids away. And tries to take the daughter in.. But the daughter doesn't recognize her mother.... She raves... She pushes Radhhabai away"(58). Meanwhile it rains and there is a thunderstorm. Her daughter screams and runs away. Radhabai melts away and collapses on the mudweeping. Rohit considers it a superb episode.

Apart from this aspect of Radhabai's life Rohit has gathered some practical experiences of her whims, temperament and independent thinking. He thinks over Radhabai's new *avatara* when she quarrels with his mother:

> We must have been arch enemies in some past life, so I'm paying for it now.God broke this forehead of mine took away my husband. Even He has no pity on me. So I have got to live in your house and take whatever humiliations you pile on me (21)

Radhabai prefers to do her cooking without seeking anybody's advice. If any one of the family members advises her she takes it differently. She says although she is hired for the family chores she is not a slave to any one. With Mrs. Nadkarni's threatening to send her back to her brother's house she says, "I can't go from house to house asking for a job now, not at my age" (22). She prefers to stay in her house and starve to death. When the squabbling is over she again comes to reality and says, "Ma has been an angel for me. Given me a roof over my head. Sat by my bedside all night when I was ill"(22). On the one hand Radhabai is extremely short tempered, whimscal and haughty, but becomes reasonable, loyal and grateful when she is guided by her whims. With his impression on Radhabai's life and temperament Rohit plans to make he a living character of his serial.

Wedding Album presents a very funny, and unnerving theme in a very 'real'and'interesting' manner. The play is about religious, sectarian, secret, erotic experiences of life. Marriage is the central theme that draws the readers' attention but behind this there is:

> The constellation of sexual, conjugal, caste, class, and age-related behaviours and attitudes of selfishness and sacrifice, chastity and commerce, obedience and authority, all integral to modern Hindu marriage, forms *Wedding Album*'s central

> narrative thread. But it is in enabling us to see these cultural blind spots for what they really are and that too inspite of ourselves, that Karnad displays his wizardry as a playwright. Superficially, a safe, simple, entertaining, and very real account of a pending marriage in a midle-class Karnataka-based Saraswat family, the Nadkarnis, *Wedding Album* works as modern myth, whose condensed logic straddles both the real and the tech-stimulated world of today, to help us confront our own mixed-up amoral, craven, unhappy selves (Srinivasan viii-ix).

The play is about international understanding, global success, of the Indians, excruciating truth in women's emotional plain and self-endurance, and their domestic sacrifice. Although marriage and sexuality are synonymous, asceticism and austerity in the south Indian brahmin marriage is presented for approval. In the play the cyber cafe is used for future match-making, adolescent precocity and life searching; the kitchen has become a parody—a battleground for class supremacy and competing female psyche; and Rohit's software production office weaves the story of a woman with his penetrating intellectual exploration of our contemporary reality.

Karnad takes the risk of locating certain issues in the familiar and private pace of women—the kitchen, the courtyard, and the inner sleeping quarters which remain present in the play. At the same time he has presented the corporate and commmercial places, television prpoduction studio, the internet cafe, and the local restaurant. The birth registration, passport and visa office, the city street, market and airport, and the expat Hindu homes in Australia and the USA remain the vibrant spaces. The play presents the myth of middle class Hindu family which presents some of its cultural blind spots. Focusing on sexual, conjugal, caste, class, and age-related behaviour; and attitudes of selfishness and sacrifice, chastity and commerce, obedience and authority he makes them integral to modern Hindu marriage and important matters of social science in India today.

After working too long on the traditional Indian theatre Karnad has produced a few modern avant-garde plays in experimental theatre. Although his plays are chiefly based on the archetypes of history, myth and folklore he deals with contemporary themes in *A Heap of Broken Images* and *Wedding*

Album. These plays have the brilliant use of technology that presents the problematics of characterization and the skill of the performers in their existential situation. The plays continually interrelate performance and entertainment. While in his traditional plays he presents more about social background, culture, belief, politics and tradition, his plays on contemporary themes deal with hybridity of culture, ideology, universalism, and influence of technology and globalization. In both the plays Karnad has made a shift from traditional world to the world of technology. His traditional plays only deal with the matters related to the past but his plays on contemporary themes deal with certain communicational, representational, fictional, linguistic and structural principles.

A Heap of Broken Images has a riveting plot set in the deployment of technology and electronic media which are used as a truth-telling apparatus for the exploration of ideological and psychological dimensions of the individual. It reveals an individual's overpowering ambition and greed, selfish interest, vulgarized milieu and sketching of human mind. Language controversy in the protagonist's creative talent combines with the innermost sentiment of her conjugal life. The play also deals with the protagonist's impression on her crippled and introspective sister. The non-participatory audience have many questions in their silence which the protagonist replies in her monologue. The protagonist interacts with her image on the plasma screen. The interaction leads her to an emotional outburst which she has shared with her sister in love and committed in the form of a crime. The Image is her inner self and conscience that compels her outerself to surrender before it. Her revealation of truth may be a *prayashchitta* for her cardinal sin in her authorial self but it reveals her *pravriti* in human nature. Protagonist's *pravriti, ashakti* and *prayashchitta* are expressed in her perception, inference, defusion, dream and memory. Memories of her dead sister now stifle her with conflicting emotions, impulses and desires. *Wedding Album* presents the pungent and stinging core of a family in which Karnad has peeled off individual's hidden urges, private afflictions and subterranean desires. The play is a classic portrayal of contemporary middle class Hindu family where the parents and children are the victims of their own ideologies. Materialism and its dazzles affect the life of the individuals in their middleclass milieu. Theosophical culture and horrors of hybridity are constantly in conflict. The central narrative thread of the play combines the sexual, conjugal, caste, class and age-related behaviours and attitudes. Materialism, marriage, asceticism and austerity in South Indian Saraswat family culture is projected in pan-Indian perspective. Analysing the family values and individual values Karnad presents how modern man in general and the Indians in particular have anxieties in search of pleasures without any soul-searching purpose in life. In the archetypal framework of technology and portrayal of culture-infected society he presents contemporary reality in his dramatic aesthetics.

Works Cited

Bhabha, Homi. *The Location of Culture*. London: Routledge, 1994.

Dass, Veena Noble. "Psychology of Social Development: A Study of *Naga-Mandala* and *Tale-Danda*". *The Plays of Girish Karnad: Critical Perspectives*. Ed. Jaydipsinh Dodiya. New Delhi: Prestige Books, 1999.

Dharwadker, Aparna Bhargava. "Introduction". *Collected Plays*(vol. II). New Delhi: OUP,2005.

Karnad, Girish. "Interview with Kirtinath Kurtkoti". *Contempory Indian Theatre*. New Delhi: Sangeet Natak Akademi, 1989.

______________ . "In search of New Theatre". *Contemporary India*. Ed. Carla M. Borden. Delhi: Oxfond University Press, 1989.

______________ . "Performance, Meaning, and the Materials of Modern Indian Theatre". Interview with Aparna Bhargava Dharwadker. *New Theatre Quarterly*. 44 (1995).

______________ . *"Broken Images"*. *Collected Plays*(vol.II) New Delhi: Oxford University Press.2005. (All textual references are made to this edition)

______________ . "In his own Voice: A Conversation with Girish Karnad". *Girish Karnad's Plays: Performance and Critical Perspectives*. Ed. Tutun Mukherjee. New Delhi: Pencraft International, 2008.

Wedding Album. New Delhi: OUP, 2009. (All textual references are made to his edition)

Loomba, Ania. *Colonialism / Postcolonialism*. London and New York' Routledge, 1998.

Mukherjee, Tutun. "Persistence of Classical Categories in Modern Indian Drama: Girish Karnad's *Hayavadana*". *Literature and Popular Culture*. Eds. R.S. Sharma et. al. Hyderabad: Cauvery, 1990.

______________ . "The Splintered self : *A Heap of Broken Images* at Rangashankara". *Girish Karnad's Plays: Performance and Critical Perspectives*. Ed. Tutun Mukherjee. New Delhi: Percraft International, 2008.

Muller, John P. and William J. Richardson. *Lacan and Language: A Reader's Guide to Ecrits*. New York: International University Press, 1982.

Murty, U.R. Anantha, Prasanna, Girish Karnad. "Girish Karnad, The Playwright: A Discussion". *Indian Literature*. (No 169) 38:5, (September-October), 1995.

Rajeswaran, Sridhar. "The words of a Dead man are Modified in the Guts of the Living: Do Touchstones Valorise Girish Karnad's Writing?" *The Journal of Indian Writing in English*. 31:2 (July) 2003.

Ramanujan, A.K. "Two Realms of Kannada Folklore". *Another Harmony*. Eds. Stuart H. Blackburn and A.K. Ramanujan. Berkeley: University of California press, 1987.

______________ . "Telling Tales". *Daedalus*. Fall 1989.

______________ . "Introduction " to his *Folktales from India*. New Delhi: Viking,1993.

Tiwari, Shubha. *Contemporary Indian Dramatists*. New Delhi: Atlantic Publishers and Distributors, 2007.

6 Conclusion

Girish Karnad's contribution to Indian English drama is incredible. He enunciates his ideas and source materials from myths, legends, folklores and history and presents them in his plays with higher ideals and philosophy. His plays are research oriented. In them he 'reworks' and 'reinterprets' the archetyes with aesthethetics in his dramaturgical presentation. His protagonists are the human characters projected as primordial images in Indian thought and psyche. Through them he presents their human experience which has been somehow genetically coded and transferred to successive generations. The situations and the incidents he narrates in his plays are often startling but accepted unconditionally. While analysing his plays one achieves the highest aesthetic experience and concrete knowledge about human life. There is both beauty and taste in life as the philosophies of his plays. The philosophy of his plays not only deals with the fundamental aspect of *rasa* but something higher in responses unconditionally. Analysing history, myth and folklore as the chief ingredients of his plays he extracts a unique taste of delicacy and natural beauty for the audience.

While the Indian aesthetic theorists Anandvardhana and Abhinavagupta present beauty as a philosophy in the understanding and evaluation of poetry, Karnad makes a philosophical study of the certain state of mind of his protagonists with the analysis of logical and ideological questions, concepts and arguments. For Karnad drama is not mere entertainment but a deeper study of human behaviour, social consciousness and psychological effect which are found in other fine arts. It is said that there is no *rasa* outside *natya,* and common spectators derive *rasanubhuti* (experience of literary flavours) from it. A common man with ordinary sight develops his insight in Karnad's transpersonalisation of human emotions which is called *Sadharnikarana* in the objective representation of human emotions.

The theory of aesthetics in Karnad's plays is understood in *sanaketitartha* (universal acceptance of the meaning). Through *anubhavas* (universalised responses) and *vyavhicaribhavas* (universal moods and feelings) the spectator ties and associates himself with the sordid private lives of the characters. In the emotional plane through sorrow, love, fear and disgust the spectator combines himself to the collective human existence. Karnad's plays arouse latent emotion of aesthetic experience and display them in unconscious mental forces and anxieties. In the presentation of human psyche and emotion he incorporates *sthayibhava* (permanent emotion) in the display of potential traumas, taming of anxiety and universal validity of human emotions. Apart from this the archetypes of his plays establish the aesthetics that deals with a broad field of knowledge and inquiry. In the mapping of human face and body, attitude and emotion, soul and psyche he projects:

> The concers of contemporary aesthetics (which) include such diverse problems as the name of style and its aesthetic significance; the relation of aesthetic judgment to culture; the viability of a history of art; the relevance of Freudian psychology and other forms of psychological study to criticism; and the place of aesthetic judgment in practical reasoning in the conduct of everyday affairs (*The New Encyclopaedia Britannica*. I:123)

Karnad is deeply rooted in Indian culture and tradition and his dramatic genius is equipped with creative imagination and explores the treaded and untreaded floors of human psyche. In his choice of theme, mingling of contemporary politics and history, ancient myths and contemporary reality, genre of folklore and enunciation of his ideas he tries to rejuvenate the contemporary life in his dramatic genius and creative imagination. In the analytical presentation of myth, folklore and history and in the intellectual experience of stage and stagecraft he makes the subject matters as the powerful vehicle for his dramatic expression.

The past is alway vibrant for Karnad. In his dramatic imagination he uses the past as a kinetic system of expression. He analyses the past in his dramaturgical presentation and projects his critical insight through 'a theatrical approach'. The bulk of his thematic corpus is consciously redrawn and reinterpreted in individual's contemporary realities with reasonable hypothesis. In his plays myth relates to the unconsciousness, follklore reletes to the traditional world of Indian belief, history relates to the consciousness of the audience, and contemporaneity relates to the pan-Indian socio-cultural issues and the effect of globlization on it.

Assessment of times is an important factor in Karnad's plays. The past plays a dominant role in his imagination. Dramatising the issues, incidents and events in the archetypes of myth, folklore and history he not only nurtures his nostalgia for it but values it much. For him present appears to be boring, disgusting, and amnesic, and the past appears lively. He behieves that the past is desirable and possibly necessary for motivation to confront the challenges in the present and shape the future.

In Karnad's perception the past needs attention because it has manoeuvrable effect in the context of affecting the future. In the dramatisation of the past he analyses the characters, events and incidents in contemporary perspective. Visualising the past in contemporary context he makes it a valuable source to understand individual's suffering. He never rewrites history but reinterprets it in fictional terms. He reinterprets the life and reign of the past rulers in myth and history and the rich tradition and cultural heritage of India. His plays on Indian myths are the thesis plays which carnivalise the glorious past and rich cultural heritage of India. In them he projects higher ideals and communicates the classical tradition and culture of India. But in some of his plays he communicates the sub-culture in the description of the world where human and non-human, the ordinary and the extraordinary, the normative and the transgressive merge. His plays on folk elements are framed in a mechanical conception. His characters in myth and folklore are superior to the characters in history as they deal with the cultures, truth, universality, ethics, aphorism, rites and with the carnivalisation of rituals.

I

Myth is the centripetal force of the unconscious human mind that emerges from the many sided force and becomes the property of *kavya pratibha* (poetic imagination) for a creative writer. It operates more powerfully and evocatively than the power of language itself. Myths spellbind the readers with mystifying effects and many new options and ideas. Myths affect more powerfully through sensitive language. The words used in myths create several meanings and all the meanings seem relevant in the archetypes of myths and psyche of the readers in their suggestive forms. They play important roles as religious and cultural force of society. They widen the artistic and imaginative range of the writer and reader through symbols and suggestive images.

India is a land of myths. Mythical stories are described in *puranas* to create awareness among the common people so that they may understand the subtlety of the *Vedas*. In order to educate the people, implement them in practices and propound certain religious doctrines, mythical stories were created. Myths generally deal with the permanent and great problems which the human beings face in the matters of love, war, sin, courage, authority, feelings and ambition. Although in myths certain facts are exaggerated the purpose of narrating the things to cultivate high standard in life and society remain universally constant.

Indian mythology is a dynamic force that informs and educates the Indians about their history, culture and inner consciousness through experiences. This myriad naturedness and multilayered perspectives of myth is worked out well in the veteran dramatists like Karnad. His genius and craftmanship have transformed myths through many levels of imterpretation and treatment. He lifts up the ancient cultural myths and adapts them to the new socio-cultural reality in the pan-Indian experience. In his dramatic presentation myths like folklores serve magic and miracles as integral components which form the backbone of the native belief-system. In dramatization of myths he presents its significant role in the correction of social and cultural aberration, be it apparent or latent, physical or psychic. In the archetypes of Indian myths what he accomplishes is mythic reterritorialization, reclaiming of ethnic roots and assertion of identity. His tratment of myth is based on the aesthetics of understanding beauty of life and its philosophy. In his plays he uses myths as a viable media to understand and analyse psychology, and draw a judgment or practical reasoning on the everyday affairs of life.

Karnad's approach to myth is a commentary on everday aspect of our life. In the archetypes of myths he rebuilds the "synthetic power of the mythopoetic imagination which can unify even seemingly inconceivable elements and positions" (Dorairaj 71) and justifies his cause to India's rich cultural tradition. The most facinating aspect of his dealing with myths is his self-reflexivity that serves as subconscious signals which lead on to another myth in turn and act as a conduit illuminating the third one.

Myth is the recurrent theme in Girish Karnad's *Yayati, The Fire and the Rain* and *Bali: The Sacrifice.* In these plays Karnad not only uses myths as the narratives but uses them in contemporary reality exploring new meanings and oportunities for individual's philosophical reflexivity. *Yayati* is the product of his juvenilia based on the conflict between the choice for idealism and parochial considerations. Dramatising the mythical content of Chandravamshi King Yayati's exchanging of his untime decrepitude with his youngest son Pooru in the *Mahabharata* he highlights Yayati's conflict between personal expectations and public aspirations. About the myth he says that this "enabled me to articulate for myself a set of values that I had been unable to arrive at rationally" (*Three Plays* 3).

The psychological isolation of Karnad during his life abroad for further studies had brought him a stifling and claustrophobic realization in life. With the imagination of this realization in the archetype of Yayati's myth he presents the moral transgression of Yayati in fear of evading punishment. Yayati's cohabitation with his wife Devayani's slave Sharmishtha, the Asura princess invites a challenge to his moral integrity and royal authority. This enrages Shukracharya, the father of Devayani, who curses Yayati to enjoy senility prematurely. Yayati's fear and flair for life make him 'a self-centred epicurean' who exploits his youngest son Pooru's extreme devotion and loyalty and tries to evade the truth. Karnad portrays Yayati's psychological cannibalism that he validates in his patriarchal authority, filial relation and moral transgression. In his royal position the king never bears responsibility for his own actions and approaches Pooru to exchange his youth with his old age. Pooru's sacrifice may be due to his extreme devotion and loyalty or due to his unwonthiness of his birth and self-hating overweight of dynnastic tradition but Karnad presents it as a supreme sacrifice.

In the archetype of myth Karnad adapts the persuasive philosophy of Existentialism. Yayati's pleading before Pooru for his youth bears the testimony of modern man's selfishness and desire for living. Again in the fictional presentation of Pooru's wife Chitralekha he gives an ethical and dialectical weight to the woman character quite different from Sharmishtha and Devayani. Without Pooru's youth Chitralekha is a 'corpse, a lunatic, a fallen woman'. As a young woman with her passion for sensuality she indicates Yayati to perform incestuous affairs with her with the logic of accepting his son's youth. Chitralekha's failure to convince Yayati to fulfil her desire and failure to face the eventualities of life due to Pooru's premature old age create a psychic revulsion. This compels her to commit suicide. While Pooru has the supreme sacrifice for his father Chitralekha has sacrificed her life in a perversion. On the other hand, due to the burden of his culture Yayati's feels guilty, returns his youth to Pooru in repentence and withdraws himself from the mundane pleasures of life, and goes into the forest for penitence. Although issue of responsibility is central to the play Karnad examines the moments of crisis in contemporary realities like friendship, father-son relationship, mistress-maid conflict over their passion and pleasure, class-caste-race conflict, individula's behavioural traits, woman's volatile emotions, man's craving for *sanjeevani vidya*, a son's supreme sacrifice and father's desire for senuality.

The Fire and the Rain is the "reenactment of puranic myth from the *Mahabharata*—of Indra's destruction of his brother out of jealous fury" (Maya 69) in the story of Yavakri from Chapters 135-8 of the 'Vana Parva'. In the performance of the myth Karnad amplifies and alters the obscure myth for a multi-layered reflection on cultural codes, modes of representation and forms of attachment with a caution about the misapplication of powers that the human beings receive from the gods after great penance. Karnad presents how human beings beyoud *artha* and *lova* get involved in mortal feud for knowledge, and moral torpitude in the search of superiority and power.

In the play Karnad reimagines the world of Hindu antiquity and constructs a tangential story of passion, loss and sacrifice in the contexts of Vedic ritual, spiritual discipline, social and ethical differences between human agents. In the good understanding of Raibhya and Bharadwaja in a priestly family their sons have spoilt their relationship in a feud for knowledge, superiority and power. Raibhya's sons Paravasu and Arvasu gain position in society but their cousin Yavakri is engaged in acquiring knowledge for ten years without proper learning. Yavakri is vengeful because his father is neglected and not invited to the king's fire sacrifice as the chief priest where his cousin Paravasu acts as the chief priest. Secondly paravasu has married Vishakha with whom Yavakri had his youthful love. Time is the great factor that plays an important role in the play. Knowledge does not help Yavakri as it is overpowered by passion.

Soon after his arrival from *tapasya* he molests Vishakha to satisfy his senses and to take revenge on Raibhya's family. Yavakri's molesting to Vishakha may be due to his previous love for her or a revenge for the insults inflicted on his father but in return Raibhya creates a demon, a spirit in form who destroys Yavakri. This makes Bharadwaja remorseful with his son's death. He curses Raibhya to suffer death in the hands of his own son and then kills himself in remorse. Paravasu's return from the King's fire sacrifice for his sensual gratification with Vishakha breaks the sanctity of the fire sacrifice. He mistakes his father as a wild animal due to his wearing of the deerskin and accidentally kills him. Although Paravasu orders Arvasu to perform his father's penitential ceremony he accuses him of patricide when Arvasu returns to the fire sacrifice. All the lead characters in the play are involved in the practice of evil and sin. There is the cycle of evil in the play. Virtue wins in the play. But it is too late. The death of virtuous ones make it a tradegy.

Yavakri's *tapasys* for knowledge without an insight into the human nature is a 'self-immolation'. Paravasu's patricide and betrayal to his younger brother Paravasu is a denunciation of human values, and Arvasu's performing his father's penitential rite and love for the low caste girl Nittilai is a 'self-effacement' and 'self-mortification'. For Yavakri's passion in his words, "I want knowledge so I can be vicious, destructive!"(23) P. Jayalakshmi rightly remarks, "The nature and purpose of knowledge attained by men like Raibhya, Paravasu and Yavakri leads neither to disciplined life dedicated to common good nor toward the Absolute Brahman... as they stand as instance of life and energy wasted in pursuit of personal gain" (Mukherjee 257). Gender and caste become the dominant factors. Vishakha is surrounded by learned men but leads the life of an oppressed woman. She is a woman abandoned twice by her youthful lover Yavakri for the sake of knowledge before her marriage and her busband Paravasu for the fire sacrifice. Nittilai is killed by her own tribe and family men for her intercaste and interreligious affiliation in filial bonds with Arvasu. Both the women characters have their emotional repression. Karnad has made them as literary constructs rather than colllective consciousness of women.

In the play, fire sacrifice is a propitiatory ritual intended to end society's suffering by bringing rain. It is symbolic for atonement but for the audiences it is pervasive and generates a sense of loss as "Paravasu... offers up Vishakha's life, first to his sensual appetite and then to his lust for fame, while Vishakha unwillingly sacrifices Yavakri to her very love for him" (Dharwadker xx). The play has a poetic and dramatic composition in the display of complicated human relationship. It presents a fine analysis of human psyche in the depiction of jealousy of man against man, father against son, brother against brother, wife against husband, and high caste against low caste. In the deeper level the play presents man against God, freedom against bondage, rituals against sacrifices, hate against love, attraction against repulsion, illusion against reality, passion against knowledge, ignorance and falsehood against truth, arrogance against generosity and victory of truth against the viciousness of life. The play has the structural link with the original myth of the *Mahabharata,* and displays the Indian ethos and modern man's apathy towards complicated human relationships.

Bali: The Sacrifice is the English version of Girish Karnad reworked on his Kannada play *Hittina Hunja*. The play has specific premodern source from the thirteenth century Kannada epic, *Yashodhara Charite,* which can in turn be traced back to eleventh and ninth century Sankrit epics. The novelty and strength of *Bali* lies in the unconventionality of its four characters—Queen Mother, Queen, King, and the Mahout. The two male characters are perfect antithesis and hierarchical reversals. The King is cultivated, sentitive and valiant but impotent; and the Mahout is crude, amoral, cowardly, but potent. The radical disparities between the royal couple and the Mahout present the class structure of ancient Indian society that underscores an egalitarian message about the union of a queen and her servant. The playwright presents the conflicting self of the King after his marriage who is unable to forget his kshatriya antecedents in his royal culture and respect for his mother nor wilfully suspends the practice of non-violence in his wife's religion. The Queen remains barren for fifteen years even after her marraige and this makes her psychologically vulnerable to infidelity. She is enescapably seduced by the Mahout's song and seeks for an anonymous coupling with him that violates the boundaries of caste and class. When she is challenged for her adultery and sensuality she has a 'deep spiritual rift' and 'complex ethical twist' that highlights the possibilities of life in a solipsistic world.

The Queen's illicit involvement with the Mahout for completenss by becoming a mother and Queen Mother's idea of *bali* by offering sacrifice to propitiate her family deities "assimilate the sexual issues to a historically nuanced meditation on the nature and psychology of violence" (Dharwadker xxxv). In her existential dilemma the Queen surrenders to the pressures of social conformity, breaks the conventional family roles and in a guilt consciousness accepts violence against her faith for the purgation of her soul. The Queen Mother's sacrifice of the cock of dough to propitiate her family gods in order to liberate her family from sin and degeneration is a symbolic performance that carries the concept of thought crime which promotes crime in action. The concept of violence in thought and action are obviously realistic and ritually celebrated. But in the dramaturgical presentation the acient myth becomes a magic when the cock of dough crows like a real cock heightening the power of belief systems and their clash in beliefs. In reality a cock crows outside and the Queen pats the dough like a live baby. As the King squashes it the Queen in anger and hatred toward her plunges the sword in her. The *bali* is planned to be harmless and it is a facile sacrifice to purgate the Queen's sin in her sexual gratification for procreation. The King has his Nietzschean suffering for his marraige with the Queen inspite of fundamental incompatibility in faith and confrontation between orthodoxy and heterodoxy. Violence is the central debatable topic in Hinduism, Jainism and Buddhism. In the play Karnad presents this myth of the cock of dough for the philosophical exploration of-love, jealousy, desire, betrayal and violence between man and woman who are bound by the ties of blood and marriage, or encounter each other in the perfect freedom of anonymity.

The play presents the problems like a kshatriya King's impotency, forsaking of his faith and embracing of his wife's faith, his dilemma about the right path; the Queen breaking the conventional feminine roles forgetting the barriers of royal decorum, accaptance of symbolic sacrifice for atonement, imagination with the thought that the sacrifice of cock of dough can lead her to death; the Queen Mother's belief in salvation through the condemnable actions of brutality, violence and bloodshed; and aesthetic beauty of Mahout's song in spite of his crudeness and ugliness. In the archetype of myth the playwright presents the complex issues of social conflict, sublimal pressure and violence which provoke physical, emotional and psychological repercussions of the characters. Religious conversions and faith change are the recurrent issues in Indian sociology. Karnad uses this in the archetype of myth to negotiate the acepted idealogical frames which have more functional relevance today.

In the archetypes of myth Karnad presents the aesthetics of life. Choosing the plots for his plays he has frequented to the "world of Indian myths, including the epics and *puranas*" (Dhanavel 2000:57). For a cosmopolitan commitment myth has nailed him to his past. In *Yayati, The Fire and the Rain* and *Bali: The Sacrifice* he has amplified and altered the obscured myths in his thematic engagement and presents them in multilayered socio-cultural dimensions and modes of representation. His treatment of mythical themes directly deal with the social and philosophical aspects of life. In the reworking of myths he has analysed casteism, asceticism, communalism, difference between sacred and secular, rigours of rituals and parochialism in religious concepts. For his tracing of the line between the laudable values and their actual implementation in the context of his plays Karnad hints at a positivist and inclusivist possibility of all ideologies. Analysing his vision on myth Sumita Roy remarks:

> The myth which he uses as the skeleton of his play abounds in numerous interesting possibilities and Karnad successfully uses them to raise relevant questions about the need to negotiate the accepted ideological frames being adhered to at present in order to arrive at a set of principles which have more functional relevance (Mukherjee 293).

Myth has enabled him to articulate a set of values in individual's psychological cannibalism, anxieties, senselessness of punishment, magical possibilities, claustrophobic atmosphere, alienated self, sensuality, quest for knowledge, jealousy, zeal for revenge and religious parochialism which project new possibilities and cosmopolitan commitment in twenty-first century.

II

Karnad takes refuge in the past to reimagine the present. The Past is not dead for him rather it is alive to activate the present in his dramatic imagination. After myth he reinterprets folktales and presents them in dramatic performances keeping the contemporary social and cultural issues in his mind. In the redrawal of folktales in dramatric presentations he draws the absurdity of life with individuals' elemental passions and conflicts. His understanding of myths and folktales are highly philosophical and psychological. In myths and folktales he uses his positive concept to assess the class and caste consciousness, individual's spatial condition, contemporary life, human predicament and evil practices in the names of custom and culture in our society. His folk narratives are the cultural constructs to shape the individual in accordane with the tradition. It appears that Karnad's folk plays are experimental on individual's existential reality. His handling of the folk sources in his plots makes it clear that his interpretation of the ancient Indian stories not only differs substantially from the originals but also indicates his bold attempt at investigating old legends with new meanings, which have the urgent relevance to the present day thinking about men and his world.

Folk elements in Karnad's plays provide possibilities for resistance and reassessment of ruling ideologies through multiple methods of engagement ranging from methodology, folk forms and old stories reclaiming the aesthetics of performance. His folk plays are a part of Indian modern theatre in which he has characterized the individuals and their spiritual and material essentialisms in nationalist discourse. His plays on folk elements have thematic richness, socio-cultural implication and "frameworks of false essentialism" (Chatterjee 134). All his folk plays present a psychoanalytical approach to understand our critical problems. *Hayavadana* is based on one of the stories of *Vetala Panchavimsati* which forms part of Kshemendra's the *Brihat Katha Manjari* and Somadeva's *Katha Saritasagara*. While each of these stories posesses a riddle at the end with Vetala's challenge to the King Vikram to solve Karnad shapes them in the theme of incompleteness with a modern source from Thomas Mann's story 'The Story of the Transposed Heads'. Although King Vikrama and Vetala in the main story are a symbolic significance they suggest individual's education in self-knowledge and in a battle of wits. The stories have symbolic interpretation of mutual relations of two couples and they serve as brain teasers. In the story of the play Karnad tries to pose existential problem of the 'Being' and the metaphysical anguish in human condition. Combining the plot of the transposed heads with the story of *Hayavadana* he unites the flesh and spirit in human life with the external sexual-religious urges.

The play presents as many as five examples of fractured personality suffering from want of integration. It is based on the story of a woman's tavelling with her husband and his friend who in mutual suspicion, doubts and fustration sacrifice themselves before a deity in the forest. The woman finds their decapitated bodies in the temple and prays the deity, to get the boon to bring them back to life. But with the deity's boon she switches their heads alternatively by mistake and in haste. As this results the problem of 'true' identity of her husband and friend in an ambiguous solution she takes the side of the body with her husband's head. She justifies her decision as head is the only organ that rules the other limbs of the body. With the coming out of the hybrid of body and head Padmini in her willing suspension and self-willed amnesia forgets the accidental transposition of the heads and bodies and acquaints herself with the ideal body and head. "The new bodies of the two men change inexorably until they are compatible with the heads once again; but the original bodies also exert their own subversive power, and change the heads indefinably" (Dharwadker xxvi). Mann's logic propounds that the head should determine the limb and body should fit the head.

While in the main plot it satisfies Devadatta and Padmini neglecting Kapila's cause in the sub-plot, the horseman deepens the significance of the main plot of incompleteness. In the sub-plot horseman's search for completeness ends comically with his becoming a complete horse; the animal body triumphs over what is considered the best in man, the human head. Padmini's child biologically belongs to Devadatta's head and Kapila's body; and it exhibits the qualities of Kapila in its violence and unintelligible activities. The changes which accompany the transpositions are not only physical and superficial but also instrumental for the solution that is sought in the individuals' psyche. The problem created out of the dualism in human condition presents the human tragedy in imperfection of the divine, the elephant-headed and potbellied Ganesha and the human Hayavadana in the hybrid form who is painfully suspended between the animal and the human world. Apart from the presentation of animal and human worlds in the play the playwright presents the divine world that upholds traditional values, the means of questioning the values and various conventions like the chorus, the masks, the seemingly unrelated comic episodes, the mixing of human and non-human worlds.

Hayavadana is a play with bold experiment in Indian dramatic technique and casts several features of folk drama. The playwright employs the technique of singing benedictory verses and offering worship to god Ganesha by the narrator figure called Bhagavata who is an *avatar* of the Sutradhara of ancient Sanskrit drama. Experimenting the theme of completeness in the ambiguous human condition of incompleteness Karnad abundantly interprets the ancient Indian story. His handling of sources not only differs substantially from his originals but also indicates a bold attempt at investing an old legend with new meaning which has an urgent relevance to present day thinking about men and his world.

The play is a reflexive rehearsal on the question of identity in philosophical reflection. The subject matter is a scrutiny of real persona, cultural contexts, woman in the psychosexual relations, marriage and fulfilment of her amoral desire within the constraints of patriarchy, feminine behaviour, interchangeability of male partners, woman's fidelity, notions of male proprietorship, romanticizing of maternal role and narrative stress on magic. The conventional folk structure of the play-within-a play is in a reflexive format that defines the conventions of folk performance to ironic scrutiny. While the main plot revolves around three major characters—Devadatta, Kapila and

Padmini—the sub-plot deepens with the significance of incompleteness in Hayavadana's search for completeness in the main plot, and with Padmini's child that biologically belongs to Devadatta's head and Kapila's body. Each character presents not only a complex psychological entity but an ethical archetype. Padmini has a Freudian slip of attching the wrong heads. The primary significance of the play stands on the identity of a person and on the dichotomy of head and body. Analysing the thinking part and displaying part on the question of identity crisis Karnad presents individual's inner and exterior in the contexts of tradition and modernity. The play displays individual's complex psyche in mythical and ethical archetypes. The folk elements in the play serve philosophy and educative values and they not only teach the contemporary audience but also create a mind bugling effect due to shape shifting in the ambiguous nature of human personality.

Naga-Mandala is a highly evocative play based on the story of a King Cobra and a newly married woman oppressed in the patriarchal system. The main story of the play is encapsulated within the metanarrative of a male story teller and his artistic anxieties. The play combines an imaginative expression of the ideas on community life and amalgamation of human, abstract and magical elements creating a synthesis of theme. It is charged with philosophy and fancy in feminine simplicity, innocence and powerlessness in the secure world of childhood and parental love. It presents the matrimonial world where her ill-tempered, tyrannical and two-dimensional husband is responsible for her psychic collapse. Naga, the King Cobra in folk belief, has a dramatic appearance. Naga has a humanised form in the play. In folk impression the *naga* is the phallic symbol of fertility often believed as a handsome man or half-man and half-snake, the top half being the torso of a man, the lower half a coiled snake and mixing the human and non-human. In pan-Indian belief the *naga* stands as a spiritual metaphor for women's fertility. In south India it is worshipped with rituals and cult practices. The *naga* is believed as the organic potential of male sensuousness that leads to the flowering of female sexuality and fruition in pregnancy and child birth. The metamorphosis of the male and the sanctification of the female are presented in the *naga* myth. Rani is the metaphor for the situation of a young girl who finds her husband Appanna in two unconnected roles—a stranger during the day and a lover at night. Rani and Appanna become strangers to each other as Appanna treats her with contempt, aggression and mistrust. Sympathising with Rani's fears, anxieties and psychological problems, Appanna's exploitation and double standard in the functioning of the male responsibilities of the institution of marriage Naga comes to her rescue. In the dramatized / fictionalized presentation of Naga myth in the sub-text and Rani-Appanna in the main plot the playwright gives an aesthetic presentation of the Naga cult that promotes the ritualistic worship of the snake.

The play evokes the critical faculties of the audiences to understand the injustice of the patriarchal moral code, the surface of mental or spiritual reality, a young wife's faithfulness and her husband's faithlessness and callous attitude. In the dramatization of the snake story the playwright presents the predicament of a woman who is neither able to abandon the reality nor capable to severe her loyalty. If Rani is the symbol of woman's eternal endurance of all male specified oppressions, Appanna is an irony strangely symbolise 'fidelity' in his extramarital relationship. Naga as Appanna visits Rani in the night and fulfils her feminine desires. Rani's acceptance of harassment and pains inflicted on her by Appanna during the day time subsequently turns her into deification that further transforms her husband. Kurudavva's magic root and Rani's throwing of its potion on the ant-hill are incidental cases but it manipulates the psychic reaction of her husband. The use of magic in the folk belief transforms the cold, aggressive and indifferent husband into a subdued, tamed one and they accept the judgement for the interst of their family and community. Both accept the social pressure and put aside the personal feelings about selfhood, fantasies and dreams about love and freedom. The oppressed gets liberated miraculously with the mercy of Naga and this transforms the oppressor into benefactor. In dramatization of the snake-lover's story Karnad narrates beautifully about the socialization process of both man and woman, woman's tranition from adolescence to adult roles, different psychological stages and cultural relationship in a traditional society. This probes into the female and male growth into selfhood and their mature adjustment with the social roles appointed for them in a traditional society. In the end Rani comes triumphant after the snake ordeal, gains respect, social responsibility, love from her aggressive and indifferent husband although he is not fully convinced. The play presents the male assumption of keeping full control over the female body, sexuality and virtue through the institution of family and values like chastity. It provides an understanding into the complex nature of human relations and presents woman's way of adjusting into their difficult social roles.

As a morality play *Naga-Mandala* transcends the destructive forces and channels them as constructive froces for the well-being of an all encompassing animate and inanimate world. Magic is transformed into miracle when the village elders proclaim Rani as a symbol of divinity for the manifestation of her supernatural sign. Although "The morale of the play seems to be that it does not propagate the social liberation theory of the hourglass in which the historical unit of time—in critical and social context—the oppressor becomes the oppressed and the oppressed becomes the oppressor" (George 215). Rani's supernatural sign shapes wisdom codes and wisdom codes becomes moral codes. Moral codes are often combined with the tradition and aesthetics of culture which is based on the subjective experience of the individuals and in their belief system. This wisdom codes become the basis and criteria for folk judgement which though appears irrational in perception it intends to provide us aesthetic consumption. The snake lover's magical visits to Rani in the form of Appanna after enjoying the love potion of magic roots are determined by the familar folk logic that beauty and innocence must triumph without the overt violation of moral norms. Rani's happiness for her pregnancy is hypothised as hypocritical in her feminine role but the snake ordeal makes her "a goddess incarnate". In the patriarchal system masculine controls the feminine in woman's different roles as a daughter, wife, woman, mother-to-be. Karnad defends a woman against the commodification of woman's body in male dominated society. In the vulgar display of the hegemonic structure of patriarchal power man treats woman as a disposable object. Chastity is a male construct experimented in woman's spatiality and in male philosophy of motherhood but it is deliberately overlooked in his extramarital relation, oppression and violence against woman. Sex beyond marriage is a morbid concept, a sin and earns a social stigma worse than death. The play presents male chauvinism and patriarchal culture that deflates the concept of chastity, gender distinctions religious fanaticism, and superstition in traditional belief. It probes into the female and male growth of self and their nature of adjustment in their social roles appointed for them in a traditional society.

Flowers: *A Dramatic Monologue* gives a phallic projectile of the Shivalinga that confirms the power of a priest's worship with spiritual and aesthetic intensity in a ritualistic practice. The playwright highlights spontaneous as well as self-generated devotion, and aesthetic sensibility of the priest in worshipping and beautifying the *lingam*. Although the play is a monologue in its technique it is a "mixed genre : a prose piece or a radio play, a single narrator, the absent unidentified listener, the conflict which the psyche and outside it, the work eludes a defined identity" (Jain 346). In *Hayavadana* and *Naga-Mandala* Karnad highlights the differences of ideologies and philosophies through the performances of folk elements but in *Flowers* his dramatic archetype is based on the core event of the Shivalinga that sprouts hair. It recasts the folk legend of Veeranna of Chitradurga region in Karnataka as a conflict between religious devotion and erotic love, undergirded by the priest's guilt at his daily betrayal of his wife. The priest betrays his wife and devotion for the lingam, and manipulates the sanctity of the temple by decorating the smooth and slippery sunrface of the *lingam* and body contours of his courtesan-mistress Ranganayaki with the same flowers. In the presentation of a triangulated desire between a man and two women, the authoritarian power of the Chieftain and devotion for the *lingam,* the priest becomes a torn self. The priest's home is a place where his wife, two children and aged parents live. In a joint family system he is denied his privacy in love-making for which he furtively indulges himself in it with the courtesan. His worshipping the *lingam* for spiritual bliss in personal philosophy differs from the worshipping of courtesan's body for sensual pleasure. The courtesan's intrusion in the priest's spiritual life affects his ritulistic performances in worshipping the *lingam*.

The mundane affects the spiritual, and the spiritual revitalizes the mundane. In Hindu traditional belief the sensual appears integral to the spiritual. The sensual vitalizes the spiritual in the priest's desperate search for peace, bliss and security when the

Chieftain finds a hair in the *prasad* and challenges the priest's explanation that the lingam can have a hair for his devotee. Being dragged between the 'sacred' and the 'profane' the priest violates the sacred and surrenders to the profane. When his duality is doubted by the Chieftain he returns to the *lingam* in an absolute surrender, a vital spiritual force in folk belief. Denouncing the wrongs done in his life he returns to the lingam for his safety and spiritual satisfaction. Narrating his existential situation he says, "I felt better. It brought back the warm security of the being in the company of an old friend" (252). In faith and faithlessness he falters wordening whether God could help him or punish him. With the arrival of the Chieftain the priest offers his final payer before the lingam in the darkness of the inner sanctum of the temple. The miracle generates faith and absolute faith generates magic. This makes the priest find a long and thick hair that comes cascading from the *lingam*. The Chieftain inspects the hair of the *lingam* by plucking it with the help of one of his brahmin courtiers. The Chieftain is convinced with the priest's devotion for the *lingam*. The priest's devotion and return from the sensual world to the spiritual world revitalizes his faith in the *lingam*.

Faith in God establishes the strength in the psyche of the folk community. It serves as a magic for them. In faith they enjoy divine mystery and symbolism. Faithlessness decapacitates them from the throes of life. The priest's thought of desecration to the sanctity of the *lingam*, and cruelty to two women make him feel guilty. His temporal and spatial suffering, religious and spiritual belief, dissatisfaction and devotion, life in priesthood and sainthood, realization of human desecration and divine discretion, human inhibition and divine intervention, archetypal image of lingam and aesthetic of self's surrendering to the Almighty, struggle through consciousness and conscience make him realise the *atman*. The ending of the monologue presents the differences between the imagination and representation, sensual and celestial, pure and polluted, sacred and profane, public humiliation and personal salvation, and pleasure and penance in individual's mundane reality and everyday spatiality.

Karnad has effectively used the folktales as archetypes in *Hayavadara, Naga-Mandala* and *Flower: A Dramatic Monologue*. It appears that he has attempted to subvert the hegemonic discourses and dominant ideologies as prescibed in the Indian folktales. Expressing his trust in the tradition he treads to assess and evaluate it in contemparary perspective. In *Hayavadana* he hypothises that head is superior to body and explores a wide range of cultural politics which is fundamentally concerned with the legitimisation of social relations of inquality and struggle to transform them. Throughout the play the playwright works through various hierarchial oppositions such as man/woman, upper caste/lower caste, the eltie/ the folk, and human/non-human which are subsumed under head/body opposition, and repudiates the notion that the components are indentified with head, soul, spirit and reason are superior, and the second components like instinct, materiality and sexuality are inferior.

Reworking with the ancient floktales in contemporary perspective Karned follows the techinique to weave the stories within stories, running parallel, merging, spiralling, and circulating in an internal rhythm. Discovering the traditional world of folktales he expresses his motif to address the most contentious issues like caste, gender and other social differences in our contemporary life. *Naga-Mandala* presents the love between a woman and a *naga*. In the fictional imagination of Naga's love for a woman the play is purposefully set to oppose the totalitarian and hegemonic concept of patriarchy that sets rules for a woman who lives in oppressive family system. The story of love-making between human and non-human in the magic of Naga's shape-changing is found in folktales. In the folktales, the motif of journey through moultiple protective and dangerous layers to get at the secret is used in the plays to convey an entangled and compounded sense of secrecy, mystery, power and horror that mark a woman's struggle at multiple levels against deeply-entrenched patriarchy. In the interplay between reality and fantasy one can only be explained as revelatory of the incomprehensible, elusive and mysterious nature of love and lovers' ways akin to supernatural occurances like Naga's changing into human Appanna in its wild sexuality. *Flowers* is his first folk play written in English differs from his previous folk themes. It presents a priest's devotion to the Shiva Lingam in his spiritual quest and has sensual passion for the courtesan Chandravati. The Chieftain's question to the priest, "Does God have long hair"? invades his peace and evokes his fear of self destruction. Karnad's portrayal of the priest's sexual awakening in the home of courtesan Ranganayaki turns his world of ossified routine upside down and confirms his power of worship in self-assessment and spiritual effectiveness.

III

History appeals to the modern sensibilities in Karnad's plays. He uses it more in a canonical way. In many ways it seems that his historical plays are intended as political critiques of the post-independence era. In the context of history Karnad explores many social issues relating to class, caste and contemporary realities. Choosing a few idealistic kings of Indian history he reconstructs them in contemporary socio-political environment. Transcending all barriers interpretations in history he presents his historical protagonists as secular humanists and how their idealism and commitments to Indian culture, tradition and pluralistic values are still relevant to the Indians in the twenty-first century. He depicts the kings and warriors of history appreciates their idealism and love for their subjects and country without becoming blind to their faults. His historical protagonists are not free from human errors. He presents their disillusionment, despair and failure due to alienation and treachery in interpersonal relationship and power of corrupt practices by their own men. His protagonists in historical plays are the victims of their own self's 'split' psyche. While internally they become premature utopias and this invites their fall externally they fall victims to treachery and betrayal in interpersonal relationship.

For Karnad history is the vehicle for dramatic expressions. Dealing with the pre-modern and modern Indian history he redraws the historical personalities, their life and administrnation, dreams and visions, social and political crisis and time past in time present. History is projected in contemporary discourse and socio-political dynamics. Karnad interprets history in present continuous and visions its warnings for the future. To him it appears that "the realm of history is where past and future, no longer and not yet, come together in a single moment. What we usually call the present in drama is self-appraisal; from the past is born the future which struggles free of the old and of all that stands in opposition" (Lukacs 426-27). In *Tale-danda, Tughlaq* and *The Dreams of Tipu Sultan* (not in order of publications but in order of the historical incidents present in them) Karnad makes an attempt to project the historical personalities in contemporary terms. Although his historical personalities are fictional creations in definite geopraphical, political and cultured contexts he combines 'truth' and fiction in them and in the interdependence of the two.

Tale-danda is a solid issue-oriented 'performative' text. It presents the socio-cultural and political issues of Kalyan in twelfth century Karnataka. Basavanna, the revolutionary saint-poet of Kalyan, was the chief source of inspiration for the play. Presenting the, life and career of Basavanna during King Bijjala's reign Karnad imagines how caste and religious conflict affects the Indian life. With the ideas from the regional history of Karnataka Karnad was buffetted with the ideas from the turmoil over the Mandal-Mandir issues in India in the early part of the 1990s. He observed how the twelfth century incident reverberated in the late twentieth century with the polarization of Indian society on the basis of caste and religious conflicts. Karnad behieves that history enables how to confront the challenges in the present. But he is shocked that history has taught us something that is nothing by moving the nation to a dangerous direction and repetitions of history in nation's fate has become tragic caricatures at different times. In the animosity of the caste Hindus, socio-economic change and 'soul searching' and 'soul conversion' of the low castes Karnad projects the effects of Mandalization in the pan-Indian situation. With his concern for the contemporary socio-political and religious movement he dramatises Basavanna's zeal for reformation and unawareness of his limitations, and Bijjalas's idealistic expression and sublimity. The *sharanas* who hope for the emergence of new environment for their leader and ruler's egalitarian ethos are finally destined to grope in a disaster. Karnad presents the consequences of religious fanaticism, popular support for violence and bloodshed in the name of caste and religion in the conftict between the brahmins and *sharanas* in king Bijjala's empire.

Basavanna was a spiritual leader and social reformer. He had a remarkable group of followers who courageously attempted for social reformation. These followers were chiefly low-castes and called as sharanas. In their action the sharanas tried their best for the upliftment of their socio-economic condition and spiritual search, and preached a new philosophy to motivate the thought of the low castes. But this displeased the conservative brahmins who were highly conscious of their caste and creed. Karnad was impressed by Basavanna's egalitarian and secular thinking. In the Mandalization of Indian politics Karnad believes that Indian politicians do caste politics without any egalitarian concept. Playing the caste card in politics they lead the nation to a civilizational darkness. Keeping the brahmin-sharana conflict and real-politik of 1989 in mind he presents caste as a recurrent issue that breeds contempt and controversy in India's political discourse. Apart from caste ghettos, rejection of idol worship, performing of rituals, superstitions, profiteering and other obscurantist ideas, "Karnad attempts neither to eulogize Bijjala nor sketch a unilateral history of the time. His unwavering focus is on the turbulence within society that is exploited by political opportunisits to unleash bloody massacre and repression" (Karishnamurthy 232). If Basavanna's imagination of casteless society is in the plasma of Gandhian ethos Karnad portrays the Indian political leaders in the embryeo of Sovideva. Basavanna's dream is "Thus Gandhi's dream of demolishing the stratification of Hindu society on caste grounds (which) was repeatedly shattered. Gandhi's dream was the kind of dream that Basavanna had once dreamt" (ibid. 231). The spread of violence in the name of caste and religion has become the last possible art in politics today. The corrupt politicians accept this ideology and shatter the Gandhian dream of an imagined nation. Karnad presents how caste politics overthrows the idealism of Basavanna and pragmatism of Bijjala with the help of cruelty and violence. Caste politics destroys the spirit of secularism in democracy. The dreams of the sharanas were shattered. In a brilliant analysis of caste and religious politics Karnad apprehends the fruition of Indian democracy. Expressing his interest in twelfth ceutury Kannada history and India's socio-political dynamics during 'Mandir' and 'Mandal' movement Karnad presents how his country is gripped by a dangerous caste and religious politics.

Tughlaq is Karnad's first major post-independence play based on his 'marvellous' discovery of the fourteenth-century emperor, Muhammad bin Tughlaq of Delhi Sultanate, who had brought a decisive end to the 'golden age' of classical Hinduism and introduced Islam as a dominant political and cultural force in the subcontinent. The play presents an important phase of 'Islamic imperialism' in India in the historical reenactment of Mughal emperor Tughlaq. The play is about the history of Tughlaq's spectacular failure. The playwright not only portrays the physical and emotional planes of Tughlaq as a typical 'oriental despot' but highlights his religious, political, social, psychological and inter-personal concerns. Drawing his impression on Tughlaq's twenty-years of reign in medieval Indian history from the sources of historians like Zia-ud-din Barani and British historians like James Mill and Vincent Simth Karnad portrays this most idealistic and intelligent emperor and his ojective views with a striking parallel to the first two decades of Jawaharlal Nehru's idealistic and troubled leadership. In Karnad's view Nehru appeared remarkably like Tughlaq in his propensity for failure despite his extraordinary intellect. In the play he dramatises Tughlaq as a parallel between the pre-modern and contemporary Indian political and cultural experiences, and reenacts in him post-independent India's crisis of secular nationhood. Tughlaq and his administrative experiments are a satire on Nehru and his favourite dream-plans. Tughlaq is an anachronism to Nehru. Nehru's long-term plans and solutions were too mercurial like that of Tughlaq. The authoritarian and opportunistic political style of administration of Nehru and Tughlaq were nearly same. The objectives and the policies of the two leaders which they carried out were like bundles of conflicting contradictions. Both the leaders inhabited a world of their own not cognizant of reality as they were induced too much with idealism and hence turned out to be failures or predatory and hence fatal to the society.

Tughlaq is the ironic portrayal of Nehru's loss of political innocence in 1960s. In Tughlaq's power dynamics cruelty and tyranny play an important role. At the same time Karnad gives a prophetic commentary on Tughlaq's idealogy of secularism and the forces which subvert his ideology. Tughlaq was a brilliant emperor but he is regarded as one of the biggest failures. He introduced policies without foresight and for the result he earned the nickname 'Mahammed the Mad'. He was secular in outlook and dynamic in administration but his secular vision and welfare attitude were dispelled by his dirty politics in murdering his father and friends. His desire to do good and be good proved him incongruous and villainous. He neither became able to protect and govern his people nor did he derive happiness at the emotional level because his society was deteriorated morally and materially. The psyche of Tughlaq is marked with contradiction when the benevolent emperor and ruthless ruler says:

> Come my people, I am waiting for you. Confinde in me your worries. Let me share your joys. Let's laugh and cry together and then, let's pray. Let's pray till our bodies melt and flow and our blood turns into air. History is ours to play with—ours now! (10).

> God, God in Heaven, please help me. Please don't let go of my hand. My skin drips with blood and I don't know how much of it is mine and how much of others. I started in your path. Lord why am I wandering naked in this desert now? I started in search of you. Why am I become a pig rolling in this gory mud? Raise me. Clean me. Cover me with your Infinite Mercy. I can only clutch at the hem of your cloak with my bloody fingers and plead. I can only beg—have pity on me (67).

In the guise of a saviour Tughlaq commits murders, causes upheavals, upsets the economy, transfers the capital in an immature decision and violates the moral codes like a monster. The play projects contemporary Indians' disillusionment in the politics of independent India. For cynicism and gradual erosion of ethics in the realpolitik.

Our interpretation of the play is one in which the politics of the entire situation are all-important and the violence of the second half of the play evident. It is for this purpose that all the murders merely mentioned in the script are presented on the stage, "... that it has relevence to us today. The play now no longer remains merely the tragic history of a medieval monarch, but grows to larger proportions with Tughlaq himself becoming a sysmbol of our times" (Jacob105-106).

The audience of diferent generations in digfferent socio-political conditions may look at the history presented in the play through the lens of contemporaneity. Dramatising a historically important era Karnad makes the audience acutely conscious to tread upon the mysterious inner chambers of power politics and the public areas of those affected by it. Karnad reminds us that when genuine idealism fails the practice of power politics, humiliation and political enslavement start, and it widens the gulf between the ruler and the ruled.

On the celebration of fifty years of India's independence in 1996 Karnad imagined some circumstances afresh on the destruction of Vijayanagar empire in the history of southern India. He thought of the British imperialism in its crucial early stages of military expansion and the British conflict with Tipu Sultan. He wanted to give a historical reconstruction by portraying his life. *The Dreams of Tipu Sultan* is his latest historical play. It is highly politically perceptive and modelled in many respects with Karnad's *Tughlaq* and *Tale-danda*. The play is based on a rare blend of dreams, thought processes and action of Tipu who was popularly called the Tiger of Mysore. Tipu was a visionary. He had the dream of a republic that came true about one hundred and fifty years later when India ushered itself into a new era on 26 January 1950. Karnad presents Tipu's life, conviction, alienation and death which constitute too large an event to comfortably fit into the pages of history. Karnad projects him much ahead of India's contemporary rulers for his single handedly fighting against the English, passion for an independent state, secular sensibility, love for science and technology and policies for trade and commerce. The playwright presents his farsightedness with some accuracy and hypotheses. The British designs, Tipu's uncompromising pride and spirit of nationalism, treachery and deceit of his own nobles that invited his fall are presented with all historicity. The factors responsible to cause his tragic death and the fall of his Seringapattam Fort are presented in the play. Karnad focuses on Tipu's fascinating sides of vulnerabilities and vicissitudes that made him a legendary figure.

In the portrayal of Tipu's character "Karnad interlineates 'textualized' history and legend, lore and memory because all these modes of transmission are germane to the story of Tipu. The ruler's fabled persona as the Tiger of Mysore thus figures prominently in action, both as oral legend and as a military reality..." (Dharwadker xxiv). Analysing the dreams of this great hero Karnad frames the plot of the play with archetypal presentatin of historical realism and some of the aspects of Indo-Bristish relationship, political perceptiveness and his desire to garb India with modernity. Unravelling the facts in history he delves deep into Tipu's personal life and how he spent forty-nine years on horse back and fought unto death to prevent the British take over of the southern states. He would not have lost if he had not been betrayed by his own people. Betrayal in politics may give chance to a leader to rise in power but it is a cardinal sin that invites the fall of nation or civilization. In the portrayal of Tipu's impression on betrayal of his trusted officers he tells regretably before his fall:

> When our fort was besieged by Cornwallis. I know several of my officers had already started secret negotiations with him. I even knew who they were....Yet I couldn't expose them without bringing the whole edifice down. I had to keep saying they were the true pillars of my kingdom, that I depended on their loyalty to me and my family—and hope for the best. Hope that when the moment came, they wouldn't stab me in the back. But the English fight for something called England.... It's not a religion that sustains them, nor a land that feeds them. They wouldn't be here if it did. It's just a dream. for which they are willing to kill and die.... They have couquered our land, plundered its riches. And now they've started taking away our children (52).

He becomes prophetic and warns his Maratha counterpart, "Make sure it's not your children next time" (55). In the crucial quadrangulation between Wellesley, the Nizam (though absent in the play) of Hyderabad, Nana Phadnavis and Tipu himself, Tipu realizes England's territorial ambitions, undependability in his friendship with the Nizam, and the hawkish and selfish nature of Maratha ruler who are all ready to rob his land. Yet in courage, policy making and military reality he appears as the Mechiavellian schemer by appeasing the Marathas and the Nizam, and engages the French against the British. When hostile Marathas and the Nizam do not acknowledge his sacrifice and intention as a defeated soldier he enters into humiliating treaties with the English. Tipu's peace treaties are very painfully drawn with powerful elegiac quality in some of the scenes of the play. Each of his four dreams is a political allegory of his reign. His understanding of political economy, excitement over the 'new ideas' of Europe, interest in commerce and desire to modernise the army project express his visionary skill. In a highly selective and reflexive way the playwright presents Tipu's political career as a fabled and legendary ruler, a 'proto-nationalist' and modernising impulses with which he resisted the Englishman's colonialist mission till his death. Although Tipu's mind, vision, policy and impulses could not enlighten his contemporaries they enlighten the rulers, policy makers and administrators of today. His compromise with the uncompromisables was for the cause of his subjects. This shows his magnanimity, skill of adminstration, military preparedness and idea of secularism. When he gives his sons as security to the British for the cause of his empire this becomes a moral lesson to the present day politicians and rulers who wilfully vandalize the values in politics, and manipulate the seeds of patriotism in their selfishness, intriguing and double speak nature.

The play not only presents Tipu's fighting for the dignity of the Indian conscience but also how he continued his struggle to free India from the fears of facing the enemy. Remembering his spirit, fearlessness and tenacity Lord Cornwallis had rightly remarked, "How amazing is the spirit of this king" (Forrest 337). For his nature, ambition and vision he is rightly viewed by the historians as the ferocious tiger who guarded his fort nearly for fifty years. As a legendary ruler he had a probing and illuminated mind, excited scientific curiosity, and sensitiveness of a friendly king which are presented in the dramaturgical production of his survival tricks.

Karnad presents history with modern sensibilities. He projects the ideals, philosophies and policies of his protagonists in history in a canonical way. He makes history as an instrument to cultivate the present. All his historical plays are intended as political critiques. Aparna Bhargava Dharwadker rightly remarks:

> The history plays draw extensively on printed sources, combine real life individuals with fictional characters, and recreate particular places at particular moments in time. More than any of his contemporaries, Karnad therefore possesses a dramatic imagination that ranges widely in time and space, and allows him to 'speak through' a remarkable diverse cast of characters (xi).

It appears that his looking at history bears political overtones. All the three protagonists are secular humanists and they have deep commitment to the Indian culture, tradition and India's pluralistic values. Karnad does not desire to see history as a narration about the deads but a living lesson for the contemporary leaders and rulers who deliberately become blind at their faults. He presents them as brilliant visionaries and premature utopias who become the victims of power politics and corrupt human relationship. In *Tale-danda* he weaves Basavanna's idealism and Bijjala's pragmatism in concept of Gandhian ideology for a social resurrection.

In *Tughlaq* he presents the macabre end of Nehru and his daughter Indira Gandhi's political dynasty in protagonist's madness for authority and total power which invite his discomfiture and susceptibleness to tragic lapses. As "an unattainable utopia" (Gupta 47) Tughlaq commits indiscriminate cruelty "with the best intentions, excellent ideas, but no balance or patience, no sense of proportion" that became a "transcendent failure" (Lane-Poole 125). His "Perversion of judgment... leaves us in doubt whether he was not affected by some degree of insanity" (Elphinstone 59) or due to the absence of any civilizing infhuence on him.

In *The Dreams of Tipu Sultan* Karnad presents many factual incidents of Tipu's life which focus on his plans, tense progression and impression on Indian rulers as thoughtless. Being the "Pegasus of his dreams" (Sudhir 316) Tipu nurtures his plans and visions but he is neutralised in the secret plans of his trusted lieutenants. As a visionary like Tughlaq and with the emancipatory vision of Basavanna he stands as a contrast and a rare personality in history who dares to yoke ethics with economics, politics with patriotism, dream with reality, and peace with progress. If Bijjala falls victim to his aspiration, Tughlaq appears as a hegemonic orientalist and "one of the wonders of the age" (Elphinstone 59) for his great mistakes in the crisis of governability Tipu, the most idealistic, romantic and visionary king has his 'tryst with destiny' for his highly polemical knowledge, and disillusionment and disenchantment in his mercurial, manipulative and conspiratorial subordinates. All the protagonists in some ways and at different degrees are fallen and forgotten patriots in Indian history. Karnad projects them with some fresh understanding with differnces without diluting history.

IV

The meaning of contemporaneity is in a flux. It refers relatively to the past and to the future and rivets in the present. Like 'time' in Eliot's echo Karnad has used 'contemporaneity' in the past, the present and the future. The meaning and purpose of time set in the past, projects the possibilites in the present and refers to the prospects in the future. While all his major plays deal with the time factor in the past in his reworking with myths, folklores and history he recontextualises it in the present day life of the Indians. Myth, folktales and history deal with the facts and incidents in the past but Karnad reworks them in contemporary contexts. Since technology, electronic media and e-tech play a vital role in twenty-first century he makes them almost the characters in his most recent plays.

Karnad not only presents them as man made instruments but also makes them truth-telling apparatus which play greater role in individual's private and public life, inner psychology and belief. *A Heap of Broken Images* and *Wedding Album* are his most recent plays on present day situations in which technology plays an important role. In dramatization of the Indian middleclass family life he presents how Western influence through technology, industrialization and globalization has affected traditional Indian life. With the postcolonial effect and impact of globalization Indian psyche slowly sways away from tradition, cultural values, normative ethics and steadily becomes tech-addicted for money, matter, prosperity and plenitude. In new thinking tradition is believed old and obsolete, irrational and superstitious; and remade with hybridity, multiculturalism, globalization, resistance, struggle for existence in Darwinian sense, challenge to capitalist idealism and neo-colonialism. These plays appear to be the critiques of contemporary realities and present the definition of life in changing socio-cultural dynamics of life in the twenty-first century.

A Heap of Broken Images and *Wedding Album* can be included in modern theatre for their theme and technique. Presenting the middle class Indian life in metropolitan cities he dramatises how the members of middle class families talk, beheave and lead their life like the English people and try to gain access in trade and administration and establish their prominence in the international scenario. In dramatization of contemporary realities Karnad presents their existential problems, struggle for survival, and modern day principles which are void of spirituality due to the effect of materialistic life, corruption in high places, influence of science and technology, loss of moral values in family and social life, and gradual collapse of certain norms and values in society. While the older generation has cultural austerity the younger generation suffers from a cultural amnesia in urban setting, technology adjusted family life, materialistic culture, east-west conflict and impact of macro-economy. In both the plays Karnad has presented his characters who suffer from physical and psychological exile due to their desire to control the global economy. Presenting them as outsiders within and insiders without he reveals incongruity in parent-child relationship, and spiritual essence and material essentialism. Both the plays deal with postcolonial elements like individual's psychological and physical exile, parents' liberal doctrine, children's dis(loyality) to their parents for their idealistic supremacy which challenge parent-child intimacy. Parents are portrayed as preservers of culture but their children become the culture vultures in their notion of self-determination and desire for autonomy. Presenting the Indian family life and society in a flux Karnad focuses on the incongruous process of adjustment, interpretation, incorporation and dilution of values, morals and interests in tradtion. The young children in their oppositional ideologies believe that their parents are myopically liberal in their global trajectory and cultural uprootedness.

Broken Images presents a debate on the language conundrums in India that has grown steadily edgier since independence. Politics of language is a postcolonial issue. It highlights the subalternism of native languages and imperialism of foreign language, i.e., English that dominates in the psyche of the Indian intellectuals, their thought process and energises their interest to compete and coordinate in the global market. Through the protagonist Karnad expresses his authorial voice against a creative writer's dishonesty, desperation, cowardliness and opportunism. In the self of a bilingual author he propounds that writing in English other than mother tongue is not the violation of authorial ethics. An author's swaying away from mother-tongue to other tongue is not a betrayal rather it is an attempt for new identity. When Manjula's pseudo-authorial self asserts her logic in bilingual creativity her Image on the plasma screen interogates her inner self whether she is materially lured for English. In language dichotomy she does not believe that writing in English is a tenacity in her creative self nor a deliberate attempt to establish identity suppressing her mother tongue in an act of inferiorization. However for her coalescing with the mother tongue and being contaminated by the foreign tongue she is believed for establishing the identity without integrity by the non-participating auaience.

The play dramatises the logics on integrity and corruption, wholeness and fragmentation, rootedness and rootlessness, decolonization and recolonization. The protagonist's arguments before her Image can be hypothised differently for her sudden transition from mother tongue to foreign tongue that steadily leads her to an emotional breakdown. After the language conundrums the non-participatory audience observe how she is haunted by the spirit of her dead sister. Replying to the investigative questions of her Image on the plasma screen she gets dissolved and her false vanities vapourise. In a sudden burst she discloses the secret of her success that goes to her dead sister who in reality had drafted the masterpiece.

Manjula admits that she has earned name, fame, money and fortune for her novel that was really written by Malini, her younger sister. She breaks down emotionally before the public when the Image delves deep into her psyche. She reveals how she has committed the crime of plagiarism being overpowered by ambition, greed, selfishness, quest for identity and vulgarized milieu of her family.

Electronic media is almost a character in the play. The plasma screen on the stage has become a truth-telling apparatus that explores the psychological dimension of the protagonist steadily peeling off her hidden urges, private afflictions and subterranean desires. The protagonist's Image on the plasma screen is a mediated metaphor that intelligently extracts the truths from her mind. In stage production the plwywright presents the aesthetics of electronic technology that frames the probing questions to study the human mind. The plasma screen that acts like a polygraph justifies as a persona by slowly fragmenting and splintering the false identity and the ego of the protagonist.

Wedding Album is Karnad's latest play gives a photographic presentation of the members of a middle class family and their preparation for the marriage of their grown up son and daughter and worries for suitable candidates. In the play the playwright presents the 'anxiety of Indianness' of the parents in a middle class south Indian Saraswat brahmin family for the marriage of their son and daughter. Encompassing their psychology, Indian sociology, philosophical and religious beliefs, social and scientific transformations the parents believe that "An Indian, then, is a person who owns up the entire Indian heritage and not merely a portion of it. This integral cultural awareness is an indispensable feature of Indianness" (Gokak 24).

The play reveals the ins and outs of a middle class family members who have international outlook for marriage, job sector and establishing relationship. The Nadkarnis are generally traditional in their way of living and outlook. As in *Broken Images* electronic media plays an important role in *Wedding Album* the thinking, perception and style of living of younger generation is greatly affected by tech-medias. The Nadkarnis are tradition-lovers. They like to preserve it in their continental travels. In their middle class status they crave for money, wealth and prosperity. The parental authority does not like to allow their young children to enjoy sexual freedom in marriage going beyond the boundary of caste and culture. While the young Nadkarni girl Vidula visits the net cafe to chat with her 'pining peacock' for her emotional satisfaction her elder sister Hema, though married, prefers to stay at her parents' home and flirts with their neighbour's son as her husband works for a multinational company and stays out in Australia. Their son Rohit is quite late for marriage and flirts with a Chistrian girl. He says that he will not marry unless and until he becomes financially sound. The parents are liberal minded but they do not like to see any cultural holocaust in the name of marriage. The culture-infected Nadkarnis have modern outlook and choice for prospective grooms from corporate sectors but they do not prefer inter-religious marriage for their son. They prefer to see tradition and talent go side by side but they do not like to see talent to tread upon tradition. They prefer ethnic purity in postcolonial perspective. In marriage, austerity of caste and culture is prefered but they do not like their caste diluted with the impact of globalization and e-tech. Through the wedding of their son and daughter they like to see marriage as a kind of mission and spiritual odessey. The play focuses on some of the cultural blind spots in love, marriage and sexuality of younger generation; and asceticism and austerity in the older generation.

Mapping the emotional and sexual zones of the younger ones Karnad projects his intellectual exploration of irreverent, subversive and radical facts of a middle-class family as never seen before.

V

Karnad's plays are highly evocative and perceptive on myths, legends, folktales and histories. In adaptation of episodes from myths, specific folklores, history and contemporary reality he analyses social, political and cultural scenario, Indian habits and beliefs, totalitarian and hegemonic tendency of caste structures, tendency of priestly class, Hindu customs, irony of fate, law of Karma, individual's inconsistencies and hypocrisy, existential position, self-sacrificing nature, belief in *karma* and rebirth, desire for completeness and application of technical device in the use of masks and electronic apparatus and other tech medias. All his plays are invariably set in Indian geographical setting with the subject matters drawn from racial, linguistic, casteist, traditional, conventional, psychological, sociological, legendary and literary fields. Through socially and politically charged ideas, revolutionary zeal and literary allusions he has presented eternal philosophical questions on cognitive, behavioural and particular India milieu. His subject matters always deal with Indian tradition, culture, politics, Indian way of thinking and human nature in a profound and with universal overtones. In dealing with the subject matter Karnad prefers wisdom, projects individual's inner thoughts, happiness and belief psychologically and critically like Vastsyayana and Kalidasa. His subject matter is broadly contemporary and profoundly universal with Indian flavour.

Apart from the Indian setting, culture, philosophical and religious beliefs, historical incidents, sociological and anthropological survey with the enunication of contemporary realism Karnad's plays appear to be monumental creations with rich and vibrant, multilayered suggestive and ambivalent meanings. A holistic approach to Karnad's plays evokes response to his naturalistic theatre. A holistic approach to Karnad's plays evokes response to his naturalistic theatre which strictly define and constitute our contemporary time. With society's socio-political dimensions he weaves individual's psychology with mind-body dualism, hypocritical attitudes of our past rulers; and caste, class and gender dichotomies. Karnad consistently banks upon the traditional Indian dramatic forms and conventions. All his plays are "literary excavations of the Indian collective past—the racial, the primitivistic, the mythical, the legendary and the historical" (Dhanavel 105-106). His plays are very potential for suggesting meaning, evocative power, infinite possibilities as "perennial" (Chakravartee 49) source of life's possibilities in individual's irony of fate, law of *karma*, relationship, inconsistency, hypocrisy, self-sacrificing nature, desire for completeness, existential position which are Indian in characteristics but profoundly universal. Karnad as a champion of tradition culture, values in politics and modernity performs some social function in his dramatic enterprise with universalistic, allegorical and ritualized performances. In the thematic configuration of his plays he has adaptations and applications of his critical perspectives in the textures of his plays. Application of techinical device with the use of masks and electronic apparatus are important to reveal the inner and outer self of the individuals.

Like all great literary works Karnad's plays can be considered as 'contemporary classics'. In the mythical, folklorish and historical archetypes Karnad presents individual's existential dilemmas, search for essence, fantasy and illusion, conservation of culture and contemporaneity, passion and possibility, horizon of thought and holistic approach to life. Through characterization he analyses cultural specificities, individual's transition from past to contemporary reality, and transformation of body and psyche in India's socio-cultural-historical milieu. In the theatrical presentation of his plays Karnad provides both traditional and technical aesthetics which can be evaluated differently from time to time and from place to place.

Works Cited

Chakravartee, Moutushi. "Moutushi Chakravartee talks to Girish Karnad". *Tenor-7* (September), 1991: 46-50.

Chatterjee, Partha. *The Nation and its Fragments*. Princeton: Princeton University Press, 1993.

Dhanavel, P. *The Indian Imagination of Girish Karnad*. New Delhi: Prestige Books, 2000.

Dharwadker, A.B. "Introduction" to Girish Karnad's *Collected Plays* (Vol. II) New Delhi: OUP, 2005.

Dharwadker, A.B. "Introduction" to Girish Karnad's *Collected Plays* (Vol. I). New Delhi: O.U.P. 2005.

Dorairaj, Joseph. *Myth and Literature*. FRRC: Palayankottai, 2003.

Elphinstone, Mount Stuart. *The History of India*. (Vol. I) London: Murray, 1841.

Forrest, Denys. *Tiger of Mysore*: *The Life and Death of Tipu Sultan*. Delhi: Allied Publishers, 1970.

George, Jose. "*Nagamandala* as a Folk / Fake Morality Play: A Study of the Folk Paradigm in Karnad's play in the Light of the Naga Cult of Kerala". *Girish Karnad's Plays*: *Performance and Critical Perspectives*. Ed. Tutun Mukherjee. New Delhi: Pencraft International, 2008.

Gokak, V.K. "The Concept of Indianness with Reference to Indian Writing in English'. *Indian Writing in English*. Ed. Ramesh Mohan. Madras. Orient Longman, 1978.

Gupta, Sekhar. "The Gathering Storm". *Bouton and Oldenberg*. 25-49.

Gupta, Santosh. "*Naga-Mandala*: A story of Marriage and Love". *The Plays of Girish Karnad*: *Critical Perspectives*. Ed. Jaydipsinh Dodiya. New Delhi: Prestige Books, 1999.

Jacob, Paul. 'Tughlaq' *Enact* (September-October 1975).

Jain, Jasbir. "*Flowers*: *A Dramatic Monologue*: Patriarchal Power and the Nature of Sacrifice". *Girish Karnad's Plays*: *Performance and Critical Perspectives*. Ed. Tutun Mukherjee. New Delhi: Pencraft International, 2008.

Jayalakshmi, P. "Politics of Power: A Study of Gender and Caste in *The Fire and the Rain*" *Girish Karnad's Plays*: *Performance and Critical Perspectives*. Ed. Tutun Mukherjee. New Delhi: Pencraft International, 2008.

Karnad, Girish. "Author's Introduction". *Three Plays*. New Delhi: OUP, 1995.

______________ . "Flowers". *Collected Plays* (Vol. II). New Delhi: OUP, 2005. (All textual references are made to this edition).

Kermode, Frank. *The Sense of an Ending*. New Delhi: OUP, 1975.

Krishnamurthy, H.S. "*Tale-danda*: Text and Performance". *Girish Karnad's Plays*: *Performance and Critical Perspectives*. Ed. Tutun Mukherjee New Delhi: Pencraft International, 2008.

Kurtkoti, Kirtinath. "Introduction" to *Hayavadana*. New Delhi: OUP, 1985.

Lane-Poole, Stanley. *Medieval India Under Mohammedan Rule*. London: Unwin, 1912.

Lukacs. George. "The sociology of Moern Drama". Trans. Lee Baxandall. *Tulane Drama Review* 9:4 (Summer) 1965.

The New Encyclopaedia Britannica (15th Edition) Vol. I. New York: Encyclopaedia Britannica, Inc. 1997.

Pandit, Maya. "The Flickering play of Desire and Memory: Exploring *Driven Show*". Ed. Tutun Mukherjee. New Delhi: Pencraft International, 2008.

Ramanujan, A.K.,ed. *Folktales from India.* New Delhi: Penguin Books, 1994.

Roy, Sumita. "Negotiating Ideological Spaces: Reading *Bali The Sacrifice*". *Girish Karnad's Plays: Performance and Critical Perspectives.* Ed. Tutun Mukherjee. New Delhi: Pencraft International, 2008.

Sudhir, Grace. "On the Wings of his Dreams: Re-viewing the Legend and History of Tipu Sultan". *Girish Karnad's Plays: Performance and Critical Prospectives.* Ed. Tutun Mukherjee. New Delhi: Pencraft International, 2008.

Bibliography

Primary Sources

Karnad, Girish. *Yayati*. Kannada version published by Manohara Grantha Mala, Dharwad, 1961. English version translated from original Kannada by the author and published by Oxford University Press, New Delhi; 2008.

______________ . *Ma Nishada* (1964) Published in *Ekaanka Sangraha*. Ed. Sinduvalli Anantha Murthy. New Delhi: Sahitya Akademi, 1986.

______________ . *Tughlaq*. New Delhi: Oxford University Press, 1964 (All textual references are made from *Three Plays* New Delhi: OUP, 1995).

______________ . *Hayavadana*. New Delhi: Oxford University Press, 1971.(All textual references are made from *Three Plays*. New Delhi: OUP, 1995.

______________ . *Anju Mallige*. Kannada version published by Manohara Grantha Mala, Dharwad, 1977. Its English version as *Driven Snow* by the playwright is yet to be published.

______________ . *Hittina Hunja* (1980) published in English version as *Bali: The Sacrifice* with *The Dreams of Tipu Sultan*. New Delhi: OUP, 2004.

______________ . *Naga-Mandala: A Play with a Cobra*. New Delhi : OUP, 1990. (All textual refernces are made from *Three Plays*. New Delhi: OUP, 1995)

______________ . *Tale-danda*. New Delhi: Ravi Dayal, 1993

______________ . *The Fire and the Rain*. New Delhi: OUP, 1998

______________ . *A Heap of Broken Images (2004)* and *Flowers: A Dramatic Monologue (2005)* published *in Collected Plays (Vol.II) New Delhi: OUP, 2005.*

______________ . *Collected Plays* (Vol.I). New Delhi: OUP, 2005

______________ . *Wedding Album*, New Delhi: OUP, 2009.

Secondary Sources

Abrams, M.H. *A Glossary of Literary Terms*. New Delhi: Cengage Learning India Private Limited, 2005.

Acharekar, Janhavi. "Theatre of Love and Conflict". *The Hindu Magazine.* 130:15 April 15, 2007.

Amur, G.S. "Modern Criticism in Essays". *Modern Kannada Literature.* Bangalore: Kannada Sahitya Akademi, 2001.

Artaud, Antonin. *The Theatre and its Double.* Trans.Mary Caroline Richards. New York: Grove Press, 1958.

Babasaheb Ambedkar: Writings and Speeches. Bombay: Government of Maharashtra, 1987.

Babu, M. Sarat. "A Psycho-Cultural Study of Karnad's Plays". *The Plays of Girish Karnad: Critical Perspectives.* Ed. Jaydipsinh Dodiya. New Delhi: Prestige Books, 1999.

_____________ . *"The Concept of Chastity and Naga-Mandala". The Plays of Girish Karnad*: Critical Perspectives. Ed. Jaydipsinh Dodiya. New Delhi: Prestige Books, 1999.

_____________ . *"Dionysian Ego in Hayavadana". The Plays of Girish Karnad: Critical Perspectives.* Ed. Jaydipsinh Dodiya. New Delhi: Prestige Books, 1999.

Behera, Guru Charan. *Appropriating Folk Culture: A Study of Post-Independence Indian Drama.* New Delhi: Authorspress, 2008.

Benegal, Som. *A Panorama of Theatre in India.* New Delhi: Indian Council for Cultural Relations, 1967.

Bentley, Eric. *In Search of Theatre.* New York. Vintage Books, 1953.

_____________ . *Playwright as a Thinker. New York: Vintage Books, 1967.*

_____________ . *The Life of the Drama.* London: Metheun & Co. Ltd., 1965.

Bhabha, Homi. *The Location of Culture.* London: Routledge, 1994.

Bhatta, S.K. *Indian English: A Critical Study.* New Delhi: Sterling Publishers, 1987.

Bharucha, Rustom. "Notes on the Invertion of Tradition". *The Twentieth Century Performance Reader.* Eds. Michael Huxley and Noel Witts. London and New York: Routledge, 1996.

_____________ . *Theatre and the World.* London and New York: Routledge 1990.

Blame, Christopher. "Indian Drama in English: Transcreation and the Indigenous Performance Tradition". *Postcolonial Stages: Critical and Creative Views on Drama, Theatre and Performance.* Ed. Helen Gilbert. West Yorkshire: Dangaroo: 1999.

_____________ . *Decolonizing the Stage: Theatrical Syncretism and Post-Colonial Drama.* London and New york: OUP, 1999.

Brown, Norman O. "Appollo and Dionysus". *Life Against Death.* London: Routledge and Kegan Paul, 1959.

Borden, Carla,ed. *Contemporary Indian Tradition*. Washington and London: Smithsonian Institution Press, 1989.

Bowers, Falibion. *Theatre in the East*. New York: Thomas Nelson & Sons, 1956.

Brecht, Bertolt. "On Experimental Theatre". *Perspectives on Drama*, Eds, James L. Calderwood and Harold E. Toliver. New York: O.U.P.,1968.

Bree, Germaine. *Camus and Sartre: Crisis and Commitment*. London: Calder and Boyars, 1974.

Brockington, J.L. *The Sacred Thread: A Short History of Hinduism*. Oxford: OUP, 1992.

Bruner, Jerome S. "Myth and Identity". *Myth and Mythmaking*. Ed. A. Henery Murray. New York: George Braziller, 1960.

Budholia, O.P. "Dramatic Art of Girish Karnad", and "Myth as Symbol: An Interpretation of Girish Karnad's *The Fire and the Rain*". *Critical Essays on Indian English Literature*. Jaipur: Book Enclave, 2003.

Cesaire, Aime. *Discourse on Colonialism*. Trans. Joan Pinkham, New York: Monthly Review Press, 1972.

Chari, A. Jaganmohana. "*Hayavadana* and *Nagamandala*: A Study in Postcolonial Dialectics". *The Plays of Girish Karnad: Critical Perspectives*. Ed. Jaydipsinh Dodiya. New Delhi: Prestige Books, 1999.

Chatterjee, Partha. *The Nation and its Fragments*. Princeton: Princeton University Press, 1993.

Chakravartee, Moutushi. "Moutushi Chakravartee talks to Girish Karnad". *Tenor* 7 (September) 1991: 46-50.

Childs, Peter & Roger Fowler., ed. *The Routledge Dictionary of Literary Terms*. London and New York: Routledge, 2006.

Chinmyananda, Swami. "Shri Ganapati-Vinayaka". *Glory of Ganesha*. Bombay: Central Chinmaya Mission Trust, 1987.

Cirlot, J.E. *A Dictionary of Symbols* (1962). Trans. Jack Sage. London and New York: Routledge, 1988.

Coe, Richard N. *The Vision of Jean Genet : A Study of his Poems, Plays and Novels*. New York: Grove Press, 1968.

Crow, Brian and Chris Banfield. "Girish Karnad and an Indian Theater of Roots". *An Introduction to Post-Colonial Theater*. Eds. Brian Crow and Chris Banfield. New York: Cambridge University Press, 1996.

Dass, Veena Noble. "Psychology of Social Development: A Study of *Naga-Mandala* and *Tale-danda*". *The Plays of Girish Karnad: Critical Perspectives*. Ed. Jaydipsinh Dodiya. New Delhi: Prestige Books, 1999.

Devlin, Diana. *From Mask and Scene: An Introduction to a World view of Theatre*. London: Macmillan, 1989.

Dhanavel, P. "The Humanistic Vision of Girish Karnad". *Contemporary Indian Literature in English: A Humanistic Perspective*. Ed. Mithilesh K. Pandey. New Delhi: Kalyani, 1999.

_____________ . "Girish Karnad's *Hayavadana*: A Study in Condensation". *The Quest. 11:2. 1997:13-19.*

_____________ . "The Romance of Influence: A Bloomian Perspective on Girish Karnad's *Hayavadana". Indian Journal of American Studies. 23:1 (Winter) 1993: 118-120.*

_____________ . *The Indian Imagination of Girish Karnad. New Delhi: Prestige Books, 2000.*

_____________ . *"The History and Myth of Girish Karnad's Tale-danda". The Literary Criterion. 35:4, 2004.*

Dharwadker, Aparna, Bhargav. "Introduction" to Girish Karnad's *Collected Plays* (Vol. I). New Delhi : O.U.P. 2005.

_____________ ."Introduction" to Girish Karnad's *Collected Plays* (Vol. II) New Delhi: OUP, *2005.*

_____________ ."Performance, Meaning and Materials of Modorn Indian Theatre : An Interview with Girish Karnad". *New Theatre Querterly.* 11:44 (November) 1995: 355-370.

_____________ ."Historical Fictions and Postcolonial Representation: Reading Girish Karnad's *Tughlaq". PMLA* 110:1,1995:43-58.

_____________ . Diaspora, Nation and the Failure of Home: Two Contemparary Indian Plays." *Theatre Journal.* 50:1, 1998: 71 -94.

_____________ . Playwriting and Criticism: Another Look at Girish Karnad" *Theatre India.* No-1- May 1999.:83 -90.

Dhawan, R.K. "Girish Karnad: The Man and the Writer". *The Plays of Girish Karnad : Critical perspectives.* Ed. Jaydipsinh Dodiya. New Delhi: Prestige Books, 1999.

_____________ . *Flowering of Indian Drama.* New Delhi: Prestige Books, 2004.

Dickinson, Hugh. *Myth on the Modern Stage.* Chicago: University of Isllinois Press, 1969.

Dorairaj, Joseph. *Myth and Literature.* FRRC: Palayankottai, 2003.

Dodiya, Jayadipsinh, ed. *The Plays of Girish Karnad: Critical Perspectives.* New Delhi: Prestige Books, 1999.

Dwivedi, A. N. "Indian English Drama : Past and Present". *Studies in Contemporary Indian English Drama.* Ed. A.N.Dwivedi. New Delhi: Kalyani Publishers, 1999.

Eagleton, Terry. *Literary Theory:An Introduction.* New Delhi: Doaba Publications, 1996.

Edison, Thomas "Back on Stage: *A Heap of Broken Image* and *Odakalu Bimba". Times News Network.* March 21, 2005.

Elphinstone, Mount Stuart. *The History of India*. (Vol. I). London: Murray, 1841.

Fergusson, Francis. *The Idea of Theatre*. Princeton: Princeton University Press, 1949.

Forrest, Denys. *Tiger of Mysore : The Life and Death of Tipu Sultan*. Delhi: Allied Publishers, 1970.

Freud, Sigmund. *Introductory Lectures on Psychoanalysis*. Trans & ed. James Strachey. New York: Liveright, 1960.

Gandhi, Krishna. "*Hayavadana*". *Enact*. (August-September), 1972:68-69.

Gandhi, Leela. *Postocolonial Theory : A Critical Introduction*. New Delhi: Oxford University Press, 1998.

George, Jose. "*Nagamandala* as a Folk / Fake Morality Play: A Study of the Folk Paradigm in Karnad's play in the Light of the Naga Cult of Kerala". *Girish Karnad's Plays: Performance and Critical Perspectives*. Ed. Tutun Mukherjee. New Delhi: Pencraft International, 2008.

Ghosh, Nibir Kanti. "Girish Karnad's *Tughlaq*: History in the Future Tense' *Fifty Years of Indian Writing*. Ed. R.K. Dhawan. New Delhi: Indian Association for English Studies, 1998.

Goel, Savita. "Folk Theatre Strategies in *Hayavadana*". *The Play of Girish Karnad: Critical Perspectives*. Ed. Jaydipsinh Dodiya. New Delhi: Prestige Books, 1999.

______________. *"Girish Karnad's* Naga-Mandala: *Levels of Transformation". Indian Drama in English: An Anthology of Recent Criticism*. Eds. C.L. Khatri and Kumar Chandradeep. Jaipur: Book Enclave, 2007.

Gokak, V.K. "The Concept of Indianness with Reference to Indian Writing in English". *Indian Writing in English*. Ed. Ramesh Mohan. Madras. Orient Longman, 1978.

Gomez, Christine. "Karnad's *Tughlaq* as an Alienated Protagonist." *The Plays of Girish Karnad: Critical perspectives*. Ed. Jaydipsinh Dodiya. New Delhi: Prestige Books, 1999.

Gopalie, S. "Playwright in Perspective". *Enact* 54 (June) 1971: 6-8.

Gopinchand, P. and P.N. Suseela. "Cultural Nuances in Karnad's *Bali: The Sacrifice*". http://www.kritya.in/0301/En/name of poetry, html, 20/5/08,1-8.

Gowda, H.H. Annaiah. "Karnad's *Tughlaq* and Ramanujan's Relation". *The Literary Half-Yearly*. 14:1 (January) 1973.

Goyanka, Jayadayal, ed. *Samkshipta Mahabharata* (Adi Parva). Gorakhpur: Geeta Press, 1986.

Granville-Barker, H. *The Use of Drama*. London: Sidewick and Jackson, 1947.

Gupta, Santosh. "*Naga-Mandala*: A Story of Marriage and Love". *The Plays of Girish Karnad: Critical Perspectives*. Ed. Jaydipsinh Dodiya. New Delhi: Prestige Books, 1999.

Gupta, Sekhar. "The Gathering Storm". *Bouton and Oldenberg*. 25-49.

Gupta, Chandra Bhan. *The Indian Theatre*. Banaras: Motilal Banarasidass, 1954.

Hiriyana, M. *The Essentials of Indian Philosophy*. London: George Allen and Union, 1949.

Iyengar, K.R. Srinivasa. *Indian Writing in English*. New Delhi: Sterling Publishers Ltd., 1987.

Jacob, Paul. 'Tughlaq'. *Enact*. (September-October), 1975.

Jain, Jasbir. "*Flowers: A Dramatic Monologue*: Patriarchal Power and the Nature of Sacrifice". *Girish Karnad's Plays: Performance and Critical Perspectives*. Ed. Tutun Mukherjee. New Delhi. Pencraft International, 2008.

Jain, Nemichandra. *Indian Theatre: Tradition, Continuity and Change*. New Delhi: Vikas Publishing House, 1992.

Jalote, S.R. "Epic Theatre Revisited: A Study of *Naga-Mandala*". *The Plays of Girish Karnad: Critical Perspectives*. Ed. Jaydipsinh Dodiya. New Delhi: Prestige Books, 1999.

Jayalakshmi, P. "Politics of Power: A Study of Gender and Caste in *The Fire and the Rain*" *Girish Karnad's Plays: Performance and Critical Perspectives*. Ed. Tutun Mukherjee. New Delhi: Pencraft International, 2008.

Joshipura, Pranav. "*Hayavadana* and the Interminable Quest for Perfection". *The Plays of Girish Karnad: Critical Perspectives*. Ed. Jaydipsinh Dodiya. New Delhi: Prestige Books, 1999.

______________ . "*Naga-Mandala Reconsidered*". *The Plays of Girish Karnad: Critical Perspectives*. Ed. Jaydipsinh Dodiya. New Delhi: Prestige Books, 1999.

______________ . "*Tale-Danda*: A Problem Play". *Indian English Drama: Critical Perspective*. Ed. Jaydipsinh K. Dodiya and K.V. Surendran. New Delhi: Sarup and Sons, 2000.

Jung, Carl G. "The Collective Unconsciousness and the Archetypes". *The Modern Tradition*. Eds. Ellman and Fiedleson, Jr. New York: OUP, 1968.

______________ . "The Principal Archetypes". *The Modern Tradition*. New York: OUP, 1968.

Karnad, Girish. (Interview) "In his Own Voice: A Conversation with Girish Karnad". *Girish Karnad's Plays: Performances and Critical Perspectives*. Ed. Tutun Mukherjee. New Delhi: Pencraft International, 2008.

______________ . (Interview) *The Hindu Magazine,* June 16, 2002.

______________ . "Performance, Meaning and the Materials of Modern Indian Theatre". (An interview with Aparna Dharwadker). *New Theatre Quarterly.* Vol. XI, No. 44, (November) 1995.

______________ . "Men and Women" *The Times of India.* January 26, 2003.

______________ . "Playwriting and Criticism: Another Look of Girish Karnad". *Theatre India.* No. 1, May, 1999.

______________ . "Telling Tales". Daedalus. *Fall 1989.*

______________ . "Discussion" *Enactment* 54, 1971.

______________ . "The Limits of Human Power. A Comparative Study of *Tughlaq* and *Caligula." Studies in Indian English Literature.* New Delhi: Sterling Publishers, 1987.

______________ . "Author's Introduction" to *Three Plays.* New Delhi: OUP,1994

______________ . "In search of New Theatre". *Contemporary India.* Ed. Carla M. Borden. Delhi: Oxfond University Press, 1989.

______________ . (Interview) "Where is the Tradition". *Frontline.* (September 25) 1992.

______________ . "Theatre in India". *Daedalus.* Fall. 1989.

______________ . "Interview with Kirtinath Kurtkoti". *Contemporary Indian Teatre: Interviews with Playwrights and Directors.* New Delhi: Sangeet Natak Akademi, 1989.

Kermode, Frank. *The Sense of an Ending.* New Delhi : OUP, 1985.

Khandekar, V.S. "Introduction" to his novel *Yayati.* New Delhi: Orient Paperbacks, 2008.

Kierkegaard, Soren. "That Individual". *Existentialism from Dostoevsky to Sartre.* Ed. Walter Kaufman. New York: New American Library 1975.

Kirtkoti, Kirtinath. "Introduction" *Hayavadana.* New Delhi: OUP, 1985.

Krishnamurthy, H.S. "*Tale-danda*: Text and Performance". *Girish Karnad's Plays: Performance and Critical Perspectives.* Ed. Tutun Mukherjee New Delhi: Pencraft International, 2008.

Krishna, N. Anil. "Karnd's *Tughlaq*: A Critical Note." *Indian Scholar.* 11:1(January 1989).

Kumar, Satish. *A Survey of Indian English Drama.* Bareilly: Prakash Book Depot., 1993.

Kumar, Nand. *Indian English Drama: A Study in Myths,* New Delhi: Sarup and Sons, 2003.

Kurtkoti, K.D.,ed. *The Tradition of Kannada Theatre.* Bangalore: IHB, 1986.

Lacan, Jacques. *The Language of the Self: The Function of Language in Psychoanalysis*. Trans. Anthony Wilden. Baltimore: Johns Hopkins University, 1968.

Lal, Anand, ed. *Rasa: The Indian Performing Art in the Last 25 Years*, Vol.II Calcutta: Anamika Kala Sangam, 1995

______________ . *The Oxford Companion to Indian Theatre*. New Delhi: OUP, 2004.

Lane-Poole, Stanley. *Medieval India Under Mohammedan Rule*. London: Unwin, 1912.

Loomba, Ania. *Colonialism / Postcolonialism*. London and New York: Routledge, 1998.

Lukacs. George. "The Sociology of Moern Drama". Trans. Lee Baxandell. *The Theory of the Modern Stage*. Ed. Eric Bentley. Middlesex: Penguin Books Ltd., 1968.

Mahadevan, Anand. *Switching Heads and Cultures: Transformation of an Indian Myth by Thomas Mann and Girish Karnad*. Eugene: University of Oregon, 2002.

Mann, Thomas. *The Transposed Heads*. Trans. Lowe-Porter. London: Martin Secker and Warburg Ltd., 1955.

Maya, D. "Karnad's *The Fire and the Rain*: A Return to Indigenous Tradition". *The Literary Criterion*. Vol. 36, No. 4, 2001.

Mee, Erin B. "Contermporary Indian Theatre: Three Voices." *PAJ: A Jounal of Performance and Art*. 19:1(January)1997:1-5.

______________ . ed. *Drama Contemporary India*. (Reprint) New Delhi: OUP, 2002.

Mohanty, Smita. "Girish Karnad's *Bali: The Sacrifice*: A Study of Existential Dilemma in Mythical Heteroglossia". *Explorations in Indian English Drama*. Eds. T. Sai Chandra Mouli and M. Sarat Babu. New Delhi: Authorspress, 2009.

Mokashi-Punekar. eds. *Perspectives on Indian Drama in English*. Madras: OUP, 1977.

Montrose, Louis Adrian. "The Elizabethan Subject and Spenserian Text." *Literary Theory/Renaissance Text*. Eds. Parker and Quint. Baltimore and London: Johns Hopkins University Press, 1986.

Mukherjee, Tutun. "Of Text and Performance: Girish Karnad's Plays". *Girish Karnad's Plays: Performance and Critical Perspectives*. Ed. Tutun Mukherjee. New Delhi: Pencraft International, 2008.

______________ . "Persistence of Classical Categories in Modern Indian Drama: Girish Karnad's *Hayavadana*". *Literature and Popular Culture*. Eds. R.S. Sharama et. al. Hyderabad: Cauvery, 1990.

_____________ . "The Splintered Self : *A Heap of Broken Images* at Rangashankara". *Girish Karnad's Plays: Performance and Critical Perspectives.* Ed. Tutun Mukherjee. New Delhi: Percraft International, 2008.

_____________ ."Persistence of Classical Categories in Modern Indian Drama: Girish Karnad's *Hayavadana*". *Literature and Popular Culture: A Festschrift for Isaac Sequeira.* Ed. R.S. Sharma et al. Hyderabad: Cauvery Printers, 1987:131-139.

_____________ . ed. "Language as Gesture: A Conversation with Girish Karnad" *Periphery to Centrestage.* New Delhi: Prestige Books, 1998.

_____________ . ed. *Girish Karnad's Plays: Performance and Critical Perspectives.* New Delhi: Pencraft International, 2008.

_____________ . "Introduction" to Girish Karnad's *Tughlaq.* New Delhi: OUP, 1994.

Muller, John P. and William J. Richarson. *Lacan and Language: A Reader's Guide to Ecrits.* New York: International University Press, 1982.

Murthy, U.R. Anantha, Prasanna and Girish Karnad. "Girish Karnad, the playwright: A Discussion". Trans. Sukanya Chandrasekara. *Indian Literature* 38:5 (Sept-October). 1995.

Murthy, U.R. Anantha. "Introudction" to Karnad's *Tughlaq.* New Delhi: OUP, 1977. (All textual references are made to this edition).

_____________ . "A Note on Karnad's *Hayavadana*". *Literary Criterion* 12:2-3, 37-4 3

"The Limits of Human Power : A Comparative Study of *Tughlaq* and *Caligula*". *Studies in Indian English Literature,* New Delhi: Sterling Publishers, 1987.

_____________ . "Girish Karnad, the Playwright : A Discussion" Trans. Sukanya Chandrasekara. *Indian Literature.* 38:5 (September-October) 1995:127-40.

Murty, K. Narasimha. *Modern Kannada Literature.* Bangalore: Pustakalaya Publications, 1992.

Naik, M.K. *A History of Indian English Literature.* New Delhi: Sahitya Akademi, 1982.

_____________ . "Cinderella Still: Recent Indian English Drama". *Littcrit.* 27:1-2 (June-December), 2001.

_____________ . "From the Horse Mouth: A Study of *Hayavadana*". *Girish Karnad's Plays: Performance and Critical Perspectives.* Ed. Tutun Mukherjee. New Delhi : Pencraft International, 2008.

_____________ . *A History of Indian English Literature.* New Delhi: Sahitya Akademi, 1982.

Naik, M.K. and Shyamala A. Narayan. *Indian English Literature 1980-2000: A Critical Survey.* New Delhi: Pencraft International, 2001.

Naikar, Basavaraj. *The Dramatic Imagination*. New Delhi: Sarup Book Publishers Pvt. Ltd., 2009.

Nair, Rama. "Ritual as Self-Discovery in *The Fire and the Rain*". *Girish Karnad's Plays: Performance and Critical Perspectives*. Ed. Tutun Mukherjee. New Delhi: Pencraft International, 2006.

Nandy, A. "Oppression and Human Liberation: Toward a Post-Gandhian Utopia". *Political Thought in Modern India,* Eds. Thomas Pantham & Kenneth L. Deutsch, New Delhi: Sage, 1986.

Nayak, Bhagabat, "Indian English Drama: Tradition and Individual Talents". *The Critical Endeavour*. Vol.XIV (May 2008:134-155.

Nayak, G.H. "Karnad's *Tughlaq*". *Enact*. 193 and 194 (January- February). 1983: 1-5.

Nehru, Jawaharlal. *The Glimpses of World History*. New Delhi: O.U.P., 1982.

______________ . *The New Encyclopaedia Britannica* (15th Edition) Vol. I. New York : Encyclopaedia Britannica, Inc. 1997.

Nicoll, Allardyce. *The Theatre of Dramatic Theatre*. Briston: George G. Harrap & Co. Ltd., 1962.

Pandit, Maya. "The Flickering play of Desire and Memory : Exploring *Driven Snow*". *Girish Karnad's Plays: Performance and Critical Perspectives*. Ed. Tutun Mukherjee. New Delhi: Pencraft International, 2008.

Panikkar, Kavalam Narayana. "Panikkar's Drama Magic". The Times of India. October 21, 2003.

Peyma, Nasser Dash. *Postcolonial Drama*. Jaipur and New Delhi: Rawat Publications, 2009.

Paul, Rajinder. "Girish Karnad Interviewed". *Enact*. No 54,1971

Prasad, G.J.V. "Reality Imagined". *Seminar*. 384.August, 1991.

Priestley, J.B. *The Art of the Dramatist*. London: Heinemann, 1957.

Rajagopalachari, C. *Mahabharata*. Bombay: Bharatiya Vidya Bhawan, 1951.

______________ . "Karnad's Heart of Darkness and Light". in 'Book Mark'. *Sunday Times of India*. November 27, 2005.

Rajgopalchari, M. and N. Anil Krishna. "Karnad's *Tughlaq*: A Critical Note". *Indian Scholar*. II:1 (January) 1989.

Ramamurti, K.S. "Some Aspects of Indian Drama in English with Special Reference to *Tughlaq*." *Littcrit*. 5:1 (1979).

Rajeswaran, Sridhar. "The Words of a Dead man are Modified in the Guts of the Living: Do Touchstones Valorise Girish Karnad's Writing?" *The Journal of Indian Writing in English*. 31:2 (July) 2003.

Rama, P.M. "Once Upon a Time There was an Emperor: A Modern Play by Girish Karnad". *Journal of South Pacific Association for Commonwealth Literature and Language Studies.* No 36, 1993.

Ramachandran, C.N. "Girish Karnad: The Playwright in Search of Metaphors". *The Journal of Indian Writing in English.* 27:2 (July) 1999.

Ramanujan, A.K.,ed. "Introduction "to his *Folktales from India.* New Delhi: Viking,1993.

______________ . "Two Realms of Kannada Folklore". *Another Harmony.* Eds. Stuart H. Blackburn and A.K. Ramanujan. Berkeley: University of California press, 1987.

______________ . "The Prince Who Married His Own Left Half". *Aspects of India.* Eds. Margaret Case and N. Gerald Barrier. New Delhi: Manohar, 1986.

______________ . "Telling Tales". *Daedalus.* Fall, 1989.

Ramamurti, K.S. "Some Aspects of Indian Drama in English with Special Reference to *Tughlaq*". *Littcrit.* 5:1 (June) 1979: 9-22.

Ramanarayan, Gowri. "A New Myth of Sisyphus". *Theatre: The Hindu Folio.* (February 8) 1989: 12-17.

Raykar, Meenakshi. "An Interview with Girish Karnad". *New Quest* (Nov-Dec). 1982.

Raykar, Shubhangi S. "The Development of Girish Karnad as a Dramatist: *Hayavadana*". *The Plays of Girish Karnad: Critical Perspectives.* Ed. Jaydipsinh Dodiya. New Delhi: Prestige Books, 1999.

Rangacharya, Adya. "Classical Indian Drama and Modern Indian Theatre". *Indian Drama.* Ed. H.H. Annaiah Gowda. Mysore: University of Mysore, 1974.

______________ . *The Indian Theatre.* New Delhi: Munshiram Manoharlal Publishers, 1971.

Reddy, Venkat K. and R.K.Dhawan, eds. *Flowering of Indian Drama: Growth and Development.* New Delhi: Prestige Books, 2004.

Roy, Arundhati. "Transposing Realities". *The Hindu Magazine.* April. 14, 2002.

Roy, Sumita. "Negotiating Ideological Spaces: Reading *Bali: The Sacrifice*". *Girish Karnad's Plays: Peformance and Critical Perspectives.* Ed. Tutun Mukherjee, New Delhi: Percraft International, 2008.

Said, Edward W. *Culture and Imperialism.* New York: Vintage Books, 1993.

Sartre, Jean-paul. *Existentialism and Humanism.* Trans. Philip Mairet. London: Methuen, 1970.

Schechner, Richard. *Performance Theory.* London & New York: Routledge, 2004. rpt. (First published in 1997).

Sengupta, Ashis. "Being and Role -Playing :Reading Girish Karnad's *Tughlaq*." *Indian Literatue* (213). New Delhi: Sahitya Akademi, 47:1 (January-February 2003)

Shakespeare, William. *Macbeth*. Ed.D.Wilson. Cambridge: University Press. 1947.

Shankar, A. *Bharat Jyoti*. Sunday 11 March, 1962.

Shukla, A.R. "Caste and Religion in *Tale-danda*". *The Plays of Girish Karnad: Critical Perspectives*. Ed. Jaydipsinh Dodiya. New Delhi: Prestige Books, 1999.

Sharma, P.P. "On Girish Karnad's *Tughlaq*: An Idealist Gone to Pieces". *New Quest* 10 (July-August) 1978: 237-40.

Sharma, R.S. "Karnad's *Hayavadana*." *Literary Criterion*. 13:4. 1978: 69-74.

Shrotri, Sridhar B. and Majan M. Mulla. "Karnad's *Hayavadana* and Thomas Mann's *Transposed Heads*: A Comparison". *Journal of the School of Languages*. (JNU) 3:2 (Winter). 1975-76:78-84.

Singh, Krishna. "Marginal Characters in Girish Karnad's *Naga Mandala* and *Tale-Danda: Explorations in Indian English Drama*. Eds. T. Sai Chandra Mouli and M. Sarat Babu. New Delhi: Authorspress, 2009.

Soni, J.D. "Girish Karnad's *Nagamandala*: An Experiment in Technique". *Indian Writing in English: A Critical Response*. Ed. Syed Mashkoor Ali. New Delhi: Creative Books, 2001.

Srinivasaraju, Sugata. "The Ink is Still Wet". *Outlook*. 45:13, April 14, 2005.

Styan, J.L. *The Elements of Drama*. Cambridge: Cambridge University Press, 1967.

Sudhir, Grace. "On the Wings of his Dreams. Re-viewing the Legend and History of Tipu Sultan". *Girish Karnad's Plays: Performance and Critical Prospectives*. Ed. Tutun Mukherjee. New Delhi: Pencraft International, 2008.

Sundararaman, M.N. "Historical Plays in Indian Drama in English: A Glimpse". *Revaluations*. 1:2. (Summer), 1995.

_______________ . "Tradition and Modernity in Indian English Drama". *The Jounal of Indian Writing in English*. 21:1 (January)1993.

Suneel, Seema. "Karnad's *Yayati* Reconsidered". *The Plays of Girish Karnad: Critical Perspectives*. Ed. Jaydipsinh Dodiya. New Delhi: Prestige Books, 1999.

Suseela, P.N. "Cultural Nuances in Karnad's *Bali*: *The Sacrifice*" http://www.kritya.in/0301/En/name of poetry, html, 20/05/08, 1-4.

Tagore, Rabindranath. *Three Plays*. Madras: Oxford University Press, 1950.

Thompson, Stith. *Motif—Index of Folk Literature*. Bloomington. Indiana: University Press, 1958.

Tillyard, E.M.W. *Myth and the English Mind*. New York: Collier Books, 1961.

Tiwari, Shubha. *Contemporary Indian Dramatists*. New Delhi: Atlantic Publishers and Distributors, 2007.

Tripathi, Vanashree. *Three Plays of Girish Karnad: A Study in Poetics and Culture*. New Delhi: Prestige Books, 2003.

Umachandran, Shalini. "Powerful Plays". *The Hindu*. December 5, 2004.

Varadpande, M.L. *History of Indian Theatre: Loka Ranga*. New Delhi:Abhinav Publications, 1992.

Vatsyayan, Kapila, *Traditional Indian Theatre: Multiple Streams*. New Delhi: National Book Trust of India, 1980.

Virupakshappa, B. "Author's Note". *Basava and His Teachings* (2nd edition) Bangalore: Basava Samiti, 2002.

White Hayden. "The Value of Narrativity in the Representation of Reality." *Modern Literary Theory*, Eds. Philip Rice and Patricia Waugh. New York: Oxford University Press Inc, 2001.

William J. Richardson. *Lacan and Language: A Reader's Guide to Ecrits*. New York: International University Press, 1982.

Yarrow, Ralph. *Indian Theatre: Theatre of Origin, Theatre of Freedom*. London: Curzon, 2001.

Index